The Dead Dad Diaries

Erin Slaughter

Autofocus Books
Easton, Pennsylvania

Published by Autofocus Books
autofocusbooks.com

Memoir/Literature
ISBN: 978-1-957392-40-0

Cover design by Amy Wheaton
Library of Congress Control Number: 2025934445

The Dead Dad Diaries

First delineated by psychiatrist Elizabeth Kübler-Ross in her 1969 book *On Death and Dying*, the Kübler-Ross Model of Grief describes the grieving process, commonly experienced after the death of a loved one, in five stages; the "five stages" have become, as *NPR*'s Krista Tippet notes, our "cultural vocabulary for grief."

I. Denial
II. Anger
III. Bargaining
IV. Depression
V. Acceptance

Later in life, Kübler-Ross expressed her regret that the general public had so widely misunderstood the model; the stages, she explained, should not be assumed as a linear or absolute progression. These stages are not necessarily experienced in order, and do not necessarily lead to "closure."

Some people may experience only one or two of these stages. Some may experience them simultaneously, or as several stages in random order, as a "roller-coaster" effect.

Some people do not experience grief in these terms at all.

Even if a person is able to examine and untangle their reactions to loss, and segment their grief into eras, they may still spend years searching for adequate language to explain them—and need to develop new terms to define them.

Contents

Prologue: The Ghosts That Stories Are....................1

I. Seeing....................3

II. Retracing....................29

III. Hunger....................109

IV. Escape....................167

V. Rendering....................213

The Ghosts That Stories Are

There is a photo. My father and I in the ocean, 2000, the last months of the first year of the new millennium. I'm seven. He is wearing swim shorts, a wool sweater, and sunglasses that look like the nineties. I'm wearing an oversized Chicago Bears sweatshirt, his. His hand on my back, helping me wade through. A wave beginning to swell behind us, asymmetrical landscape. The water clear and green-blue.

The little girl in the picture wears her hair in a ponytail. She doesn't know anything yet and I love her. Her face looks easy—curious, calm, free. I am her and I am not her. Over the course of seven years the human body regenerates its cells so that technically nothing of a person is the same as seven years before. I am her and I am an entirely new person three times over; I know things now and there are things I still don't know, like how taxes really work. Or what were the last words he said? Even scientists still don't know how big the universe is, or how to remove stretch marks.

It has been seven years since the first sentence I wrote about him: *There are some things you never knew about me.* It took me this long to realize I have been talking as much to myself as to him, to whatever slain future we occupy together inside the story.

We all live with dead things inside of us. Some of them are stories.

This is mine:

It has been sixteen years since the man in the picture was murdered and the girl walked upstairs alone and closed her bedroom door and did not cry. I am her and I am not her. The ghost of every cell still lives here.

SEEING

"Youth and death shed a halo through which it is difficult to see a real face."

–Virginia Woolf, *Moments of Being*

Entrance Wound

I'm alone in my lime-green bedroom when JJ finally calls me back. He calls my regular cell phone, the one my parents pay for—not the burner phone he bought me, which I keep under my pillow for when he wants to reach me after my ten o'clock phone curfew. It's still early, even for a school night. He fell asleep and missed my call, he explains. His voice is sleepy, and he's mumbling a little, his words sticky sweet with the baby-talk I've grown to cherish as an indication that he's in a good mood, that he loves me, that everything is alright, at least for now.

When JJ didn't answer the first time, I'd called Kevin. I don't know why I chose him, of everyone I could have called. Kevin has OCD and spent the previous summer in a mental hospital. He's known in school for wearing ten to twenty T-shirts at a time, a manifestation of his mental illness. We've been in theatre together for two years, and once, I let him finger me on the bus ride back from a One Act Play competition. Kevin is a mess. He is the first person I told that my father is dead.

I'm sixteen. I'm graduating early, itching to leave the tiny north Texas town I grew up in, to move away and become an actress, or a writer, or any variation of Somebody. In places like Anna, all it takes to be Somebody is to be gone.

Tomorrow, I begin my senior year of high school.

I tell JJ the news, and his voice loses some of its sleepy edge. "I'm so sorry, baby," he says. "When did it happen?"

"My aunt said around four o'clock this afternoon. She just called and told us. They're donating his eyes," I say, though I'm not sure how I would know that detail yet. "Someone else is going to have his eyes now."

"I'm so sorry, baby," he repeats. "That's horrible."

"Yeah, but I mean, what's going to happen now? School starts tomorrow, but the funeral is in Alabama."

"What do you mean?"

"Like, I have drill team practice. The first football game is next week. I won't even know the dance, I won't be able to perform—and theatre rehearsal, and all my classes...what's going to happen?"

The line goes quiet, and when JJ speaks again, his voice is venomous: "I can't believe that's what you're worried about. Are you serious?"

"Look, I just—I don't know how to handle this. Any of this. I can't just be gone the whole first week of school," I stammer.

"I can't believe you're serious!" he erupts. "Wow, Erin. Wow."

"What?"

"You're not even crying!" he says. "Your dad *died*, and you're not even crying. You're worried about drill team."

"Well, I'm worried about everything," I say. "I don't know."

"I don't think I can be with you anymore," he says.

"Wait, what do you mean?"

"I don't think I can be with someone who is so incredibly selfish."

"No, wait," I begin to panic, "I didn't mean…it's not like I don't care. I'm just trying to be practical."

"I'm sorry," he says, that familiar dramatic edge of resignation in his voice. "I can't be with someone who's so selfish they don't even care that their own dad died. That's not the kind of person I want to date."

"JJ," I say, maybe begging, maybe even beginning to cry for the first time that night. "Please, I'm sorry. Don't break up with me tonight. Not with everything else. I'm sorry, I didn't mean it to come off how it did." But I meant what I said. And when I had expressed the same worries to Kevin earlier, he had been understanding. He had laughed and made dark jokes with me, allowed me to be confused, strange, stoic. But Kevin isn't my boyfriend.

"Goodbye, Erin," JJ says. He sounds like he's reciting lines from a movie. "I'm sorry about your dad."

I hear the receiver click, and I'm alone in my bedroom. I am sixteen, a dead-dad daughter, now and forever.

***

There is a photo. Me in the high school parking lot, wearing my carefully chosen first-day outfit: raspberry lace over a black tank top, and blue jeans. Smudged eyeliner, dark hair curled in ringlets. I'm smiling, posing with my hand on my hip.

The morning after my dad died, my mom and stepdad drove my sister and I to school to un-enroll us; due to some incomprehensible Texas law, if we missed the seven days in a row we planned to be away for the funeral, we'd be considered truants. To avoid being served court papers, the principal advised my mom to take us out of school altogether and re-enroll us when we returned. This severing, however temporary, felt exciting in the nauseating way that standing at the edge of a canyon feels: school was school, but it was the only place I felt fully like myself. I imagined standing in the speckled linoleum halls, untethered, while my classmates rushed by, a synchronized ruckus of backpacks slouching off shoulders, printouts of the new semester's schedule crinkled in sweaty hands. I'd left my copy, printed with blotchy ink on the half-broken printer in my mom's bedroom, at home in the bottom of my jewelry box.

When we arrived at the high school, my sister, Stephanie, stayed in the car. She was thirteen, and closer to our dad than I had been. They had similar temperaments, a similar interest in sports, and similarly, seemed to forget the upsetting things he did and said while drunk. Before he died, she had been trying to convince him to let her move to Alabama to live with him. Now, of course, that would never happen—though it was unlikely to happen in the first place; our mother loved us too fiercely to let us slip away, and our father was a quiet man who liked his space, who got easily overwhelmed inside the messy guts of raising children, even when our parents were married. It had been a long time since then: eight years since their divorce and our move to Texas. Half my age, at that point, and even longer since the bones of their marriage had begun to grind down to marrow. I had witnessed more of that breaking than Stephanie had.

My mom met my stepdad, Mark, while she was gardening in our

front yard three years after the divorce, wearing her trademark "Daisy Duke" jean shorts and a cut-off 80s *Loverboy* T-shirt. Mark, a recovered addict, was living across the street with a friend, but within two weeks he rolled a suitcase over to our house and began to live with us. My mom gave birth to my half-sister, Trinity, and married him two years after, in a small ceremony at a city park.

I don't know where Trin was that morning, which neighbor's house she might've been sent to. Details dissolve beneath the concrete images from that day at the high school:

Mark, a burly, bearded, usually boisterous man, was solemn as he took my mother's hand, tearing up himself as she cried in the principal's office. I loitered in the hallway, and spotted two of my friends, the Berganciano twins, whose house I'd spent all my summers since eighth grade practically living at. Our days lying beside the community swimming pool, nights listening to emo music while we ate boxed mac and cheese and drew song lyrics in non-toxic marker on each other's skin seemed long ago now. They swallowed me in the hardest hug their petite bodies could manage. Somehow, they had already heard. We talked briefly, but soon they joined the sea of students traveling down the one long, gray hallway that was Anna High School, off to their first class period.

My first class was supposed to be Pre-Calculus, which I shared with my close friend, Dylan. He and I had grown more distant, though, in the year and a half I had been dating JJ. JJ disapproved of me having any male friends, and seemed to find some obscure reason why each of them was unacceptable for me to spend time with. In Dylan's case, it had been that I was riding alone with him in the car one night and hadn't answered JJ's phone call. More explosive fights had been set off from less, and when we arrived back at my house, I had to reluctantly leave Dylan downstairs while I went up to my bedroom and did damage control on the phone with JJ. There had been an uncomfortable distance between us since then. I missed Dylan, and ached to think that I wouldn't be able to see him that morning, wouldn't even get to tell him in person what had happened. He was the main person I wanted to talk to, the person I knew would understand, would respond equally dark-humored and sensitive, would accept whatever I was in the wake of my new strange world. Whatever I was I had no words for yet—nothing but the story that had already begun to sound practiced on my lips, on my parents', as they floated red-faced and eerie down the hall toward me.

The next stop would be the DMV, and from there, my grandmother's house in Alabama. Our bags were already packed and waiting in the trunk. In what felt like a small victory, I would still be getting my driver's license that day as originally planned, but only because Mark wasn't joining us on the trip, and I had to be able to help my mom drive the twelve-hour stretch.

I got back in the car with my parents and sister, leaning over to check my makeup in the rearview mirror. The gold glitter on my eyelids was still in place, and I thought, gladly, that at least it wasn't all a waste, that at least if I didn't get to go to school I'd look nice for my driver's license photo. My stomach churned a river of anxiety that in the moment I classified as excitement. Somewhere there's a picture where I am that girl, but it's been lost for a long time now.

***

The week in Alabama is a blur of jutting, beige-tinted impressions; it began with seeing my father's gray Honda parked in my grandmother's driveway. If it was a shock to see his car there, if we flashed for a second with relief that maybe everything had been a misunderstanding, no one mentioned it. Inside the house, my mom, Stephanie and I greeted semi-familiar faces: my Aunt Deb, who I hadn't seen since I was four or five—some vague edge of a snowy memory scraping a car windshield in Illinois—and her grown son, my cousin Mike. Uncertain hugs all around, the soft round fleshiness of kin-bodies. And my grandma, Irma, with a stone face that displayed new lines, saltwater grooves carved before we arrived.

My sister and I put our suitcases in the back bedroom, the room we usually stayed in when we came to visit with our dad, matching twin beds and gold lamps on the nightstands. My mom slept on a cot in the spare room with the treadmill and stacks of VHS home videos. The adults spent a lot of time moving between the scratchy couch and the dining table, sighing.

***

In the days between our arrival and the funeral, my sister and I occupied ourselves with small adventures into town. We drove to the mall and stole hemp bracelets from Earthbound, bumper stickers from gas stations, and snuck halter tops into her purse. We shoplifted and drove around and ate McDonald's in the car. One day, I recklessly sped down a hill in my grandmother's neighborhood and nearly hit a small boy playing in the street, and for the rest of our trip I was paranoid that the parents of the boy had seen our license plate and would track us down; that's what I worried had happened when we returned one afternoon and saw a police cruiser parked in my grandma's driveway.

Inside, a man sat with my mother at my grandmother's kitchen table. He introduced himself as Detective Eric King, the detective in charge of my father's case.

We took turns at the table with his tape recorder, where the detective asked about my father's relationship with his wife, Pam, our stepmother of only two months. My mother went first, and from the other room we could hear pieces: "He called me the day before he went over there… he told me, 'If I meet my demise, this is where I'll be'…he laughed…I told him if he was really scared, he should take someone with…he said it just like that, 'my demise'…he laughed…"

Stephanie and I spent two weeks at Pam's house earlier that summer, where he moved in when they married—though just a week after we flew back to Texas, he moved out. When it was our turn, the detective asked about a fight they'd had while we were in town. Pam is deaf, and one night after they both got drunk at dinner, they stood on the back deck and argued about something—we didn't know what—and during the argument, she lost her hearing aid. We watched through the sliding glass door as my dad crawled around on the ground looking for it.

The detective said he had listened to the voicemails my mom left on my dad's phone the night he died, after she heard the news. He said they broke his heart, and he was so sorry. He gave me his business card.

Later that day, a neighbor brought over a rotisserie chicken, and my sister and I stood at the counter and devoured the entire bird with our hands.

***

The morning of the funeral, I found my grandma in her nightgown and curlers, drinking a glass of Bailey's at the breakfast bar.

"Can I have a little?" I asked, newly sixteen and testing my luck. She consented. I threw a couple of ice cubes in the small glass she poured and took it into the guest bathroom with me while I got ready, feeling dangerous, adult, delighted.

We hadn't had time to shop for funeral dresses, so we made do piecing together what black clothing we already owned. I planned to wear a high-collared lace shirt with dark jeans and combat boots, but Grandma vetoed: "Too goth." I replaced the jeans with a gray skirt, the boots with black ballet flats.

***

Playlist for a Funeral:

1. "Somewhere Over the Rainbow" – Barry Manilow (Chosen by His Mother)
2. "Forever Young" – Rod Stewart (Chosen by His Sister)
3. "Faithfully" – Journey (Chosen by His Ex-Wife)
4. "I Will Follow You Into the Dark" – Death Cab for Cutie (Chosen by His Oldest Daughter)

Directions:

Play on a loop. Sit in the chapel pews. Look straight ahead. *Wake up where the clouds are far behind me*...Do not think about the cousins who hate you because you drove to go shopping and get pizza last night. Do not look at the strangers sitting behind you, who will later want to touch your hand and repeat the same phrases: "better place" "can't believe" "remember talking to him" "he always talked about" "so proud of" "everyone is so." *Forever young*…Do not look at your sister's flushed face or your mother's trembling hands. Let her hold yours, squeeze them even, if only to keep hers still. Allow her this, even though it makes your skin itch. Look straight ahead. *Sleep alone tonight*…Try not to roll your eyes when his coworker, the hairy, kind woman, tells you his soul was saved. Try not to make a gagging gesture like some bratty teenager when she touches your sister's shoulder and says he accepted Jesus into his heart, she was there, she knows. This is supposed to be solace. Look straight ahead. Do not cry, jesusfuckingchrist, do not cry. Maybe let your voice break a little when you stand up to say your speech at the podium. Maybe just a little, so they know. That you are not empty. That you're not going to burn down the building. *Fear is the heart of love.* Do not look beside you. Do not look up. Do not look back. Look ahead. Keep looking ahead.

***

After the funeral, we returned to Grandma Irma's house.

She put her purse down on the counter and said, "Don't think I didn't see you two laughing before the service. Your cousins told me how you girls have been running around town, not seeming sad at all about what's going on."

"We were laughing at a joke they made! They said they were trying to lighten the mood!" I protested.

"You know," my grandma scowled, "I've seen Stephanie cry, but I don't think you miss your dad at all. Now you can have your stepdad walk you down the aisle at your wedding. Isn't that what you've always wanted anyway?" I think I began to cry a little then, or tried to—not out of sadness, but fear. My mom tried to defend us, but it didn't do much good.

My grandma said, "It's been a difficult day. Emotions are high."

My aunt said, "He loved you girls so much. He told everyone how proud he was of you."

"Well," I said, "he didn't tell me."

***

My grandmother was witness to the two ruined Christmases. During the first, he was convulsing on the kitchen floor when she arrived to take us out to dinner. He whispered for Stephanie to come closer so he could tell her he loved her. Last words, like he truly believed he was dying. My sister began to cry. I stood back and watched.

My grandma called the ambulance that took him to the emergency room, where the doctors found four times the legal limit of alcohol in his blood. He called a week after we left to tell us he was sorry, and he was going to quit drinking.

But each time my sister and I visited, another piece of furniture was missing. Of inquiries about the glass coffee table: "It broke," (but the stitches he had to get on the top of his head were from a light fixture that spontaneously fell loose from the ceiling). Of the casts and surgeries to replace the shattered bones in his arm with steel pins: "I slipped in the shower."

He always drank heavily, but it was worse after the divorce. There were multiple drunken voicemails left on our home phone, cursing and calling my mom a whore. When my sister and I visited, he stifled our joy; he couldn't handle us being playful, loud, or energetic, especially not in public. He showed his love with mp3 players and new school clothes that our mom couldn't afford. I'm not sure he ever wanted kids. We were a shock to the system of silence he lived alone in for forty weeks of the year.

On the few occasions my dad left those offensive voicemails on our phone, Mark had been the one to call him up and defend my mother. Otherwise, Mark and my dad mostly remained civil when it came to co-parenting, but they were far too different to ever become buddies;

my dad was a moderate, white-collar man, while Mark's personality was loud and reckless, telling off-color jokes, his cultural identity as a "redneck" a source of pride.

Still, as a teenager when I begged not to visit my dad, it was Mark who insisted, "No matter what he's done, he's your dad. You need to see him." Mark lost custody of his own two children after legal troubles caused by addiction in his twenties, a mistake that still gutted him years later. Although he was sympathetic to my complaints, he said he couldn't allow another man to experience the loss that he had.

My dad spent the second Christmas complaining about a woman he had recently broken up with. He said she was crazy, irrational, obsessed with him. He showed my sister the emails she had written him; I never saw them, so I don't know what they said.

On New Year's Eve, we were getting ready to go to see a play at the local theatre when the woman showed up at his door unexpectedly, a bottle of wine under her coat. When we met up with my grandma in the parking garage and she saw the woman, her eyes went wide.

During the play, the two of them got drunk and talked over the actors. They dropped the empty bottle of wine and it echoed as it rolled through rows of seats. My grandma asked, "Are you ready to leave?" and I nodded, so we left, and they followed us out.

At the house, my sister and I drank sparkling apple juice while the adults had champagne. After the ball dropped on TV, I went into my room to call my mom, and when I came out, the woman was sitting on my dad's lap, sloppily kissing on the couch.

Six months later they were married, and two months after that she killed him with a bullet to the back of the head. I have always wondered what that bullet felt like, if an unfastened skull parts like the Red Sea or opens like French doors to the pale glow of sunlight. If it feels like an entrance wound or an exit.

***

The day after the funeral, we loaded up the car to go home, toting more than we arrived with: my dad's vacuum and microwave ("For your dorm room next year," Grandma insisted), a couple chosen items of his clothing, a box of framed school portraits of us and knick-knacks from his office. My grandma gouged his CDs from the player in his car and handed them to me, taped and wrapped boxy in manila paper.

On the drive back, I sat in the front seat, cradling my cell phone against the window, edged with anxiety while JJ—whom I'd spoken with daily all the funeral week, even as he gave me detailed accounts of the sex he was having with the new girl he was already dating—complained about the background noise in the car, and my mom proceeded to turn up the radio.

I couldn't have known then what kind of year I was falling face-first into with every mile: that none of my teachers were told why I had missed a week of school, as the principal had assured my mom they would be, and were overall annoyed with my sudden, oblivious presence; that I wouldn't perform with my dance team at the next three football games, even as I teared up on the sweaty field at practice, struggling to remember the steps; that I would begin telling anyone who asked and so many people who didn't that my dad was dead, and exactly how, tacking on a manic giggle, an attempt to make the listener more comfortable with my story; the manic giggle I would never shake, even once I realized it had the opposite effect. Stephanie with scars slashing up her wrists, and stealing, and getting dragged out of the woods by police; and the letter my mom would write me from her own term in rehab.

On Senior Night, under the glittering Friday night floodlamps, I would walk across the football field with my mom, Mark, and a framed picture of my dead father. Mark's idea, "So that your dad can be here, too." And me in my sequin-sparkly purple dance uniform, death-sick with embarrassment about the picture Mark held at his side. Eyes focused, shining straight ahead.

Superstition runs in the blood. Even now I fear showering during a thunderstorm, a lingering trace of growing up in the shadow of my father's anxiety. When my sister and I were children, he didn't allow us to bathe if it was raining, regardless of the actual presence of lightning, warning that the stray electricity would climb the metal faucet and fry us in the tub.

These things passed down to us stick, shape reality until pointed out by an impartial party as error or familial quirk—like "uncle" pronounced "onkle" and "neither" pronounced "nee-ther" the way I do; the way my mother does.

I'm fairly certain no one has been struck by lightning in the shower in the last fifty years, since pipes have been grounded against shock (or so it has been explained to me), but the worry sticks. A myth conjured out of fear is stubborn that way, stained bright red until the fear dies, or a new myth is created to take its place.

***

One night, I left a friend's apartment around eight p.m. to find my phone flooded with text messages and tearful voicemails from my mother. With panic in her voice, she said she'd had an intuitive feeling and was worried something bad had happened to me. My mother often reminds me we have a kind of telepathic connection, things like calling the other right as the other is thinking of calling; for whatever reason, that time her "feeling" was off completely. I arrived home safely, a little annoyed, but for days afterward I kept a morsel of dread close, especially cautious of sharp turns and sharp objects, afraid of what I didn't know might be lurking with me in its sights.

My father carried blind anxiety, wild and directionless. He shook with it. His hands held tremors that sometimes grew so strong as to render them temporarily useless—from fear and from the alcoholism, though I'm not sure which came first. From him I inherited an avoidance of heights and a predisposition to wasting a bottle of Jack Daniels over a weekend; from my mother, the understanding that to love is to cleave yourself and then watch your raw heart walk away into the violence-sickened world without you.

My fear manifests most strongly on airplanes: what else but ultimate helplessness is allowing yourself to be suspended inside a metal vessel above the clouds, and what worse way to die than a freefall so sharp and endless? Still, I fly often, and when general statistics or a fistful of Ativan fails to comfort, I remind myself of this: my father, over the course of his life, travelled by plane nearly a thousand times, and he died on solid ground.

***

There's superstition, and then there's precognition. Superstitions are eclectic beliefs that influence behavior, usually in order to avoid something unfortunate: *Step on a crack, break your mother's back. A broken mirror brings seven years of bad luck. Pick up a penny only if it's face-up.* Precognition is the first cousin of superstition, the estranged spouse of religion, and one step beyond déjà vu: a glimpse of the future. A friend in college, an adamant atheist, once told me with certainty that if a person dreams about their teeth falling out, it means someone close to them will die. It happened to him, he said—he woke up the next morning and his aunt had been hit by a car. Studies of both superstition and precognition have been branded pseudoscience, but they permeate our cultural consciousness, forming a small place in the lives of even the most scientifically minded.

Both involve a conscious or unconscious belief in mystical forces. Both rely on the premise that there are no random events, no accidents; the universe is watching, noticing.

***

I almost died before I was born. The doctors told my mother I didn't have a heartbeat, said they lost it, as if it had gotten stuck in someone's jeans pocket and gone through the wash. Now they would have to remove my body from hers, they said. There was nothing else they could do, and all the tests confirmed their stance.

But my mother argued with them. She refused their carefully practiced words and pseudo-sympathetic expressions; she told them they must have gotten something wrong, to double-check the tests. Somehow, she felt the tiny light inside her womb was still glowing, breathing, beating.

So it goes, on a hot August day in the Nevada desert, under a sky glutted with neon, I was born. It was Friday the 13th, a notably unlucky day, though there's no single agreed-upon origin for the cross-cultural fear the date inspires. It's been traced to the Christian belief that Judas was the thirteenth person at the Last Supper, but Hindus branded gatherings of thirteen people unlucky before Christ's time. Norse Vikings attributed thirteen to a myth about the arrival of Loki, the god of mischief, and for Egyptians the number signified bittersweet passage to the afterlife. Regardless, Friday the 13th signifies one common thing for those who maintain it has power: disruption.

Upon my maternal grandfather's first time seeing me, he declared that our Irish blood was strong within my tiny veins, and that my favorite color would undoubtedly be green. He had been born on a Friday the 13th as well, in the springtime some seventy years before. When my mother told the story, she whispered it like a fairytale tinged with prayer. As we celebrated each year at ice-skating rinks, zoos, and amusement parks, her blue eyes followed me.

My favorite color has always been green. I like to think it was my own preference that determined this, and not just a product of being told about my grandfather's prophecy. But it's hard to know if we create myths to make sense of ourselves, or if our myths create us.

***

An article in *Psychology Today* reports that about 50% of the general population claims to have had a precognitive dream. In 1997, Dr. M.S. Stowell interviewed 51 people who claimed to have precognitive dreams, 37 of which came true throughout the course of the study. One report was from a woman who dreamt of a plane crashing on a highway as she was driving under the overpass. Weeks later, a plane crashed on that same highway.

***

It's family legend that our Irish ancestors, the O'Learys, were responsible for starting the Great Chicago Fire. I've told this story at so many parties and on first days of class when reaching for a "fun fact" to share about myself, but the truth is debatable—factually, we descend from the Irish O'Leary family, from whom my grandpa garnered his middle-namesake, and it has been written that the O'Leary's cow knocked over a lantern one fall night in 1871 and began the blaze. Doubt was cast on this narrative after the fortieth anniversary of the event, when a former *Chicago Republican* reporter claimed he and his colleagues had completely fabricated the story. Others have speculated drunkards in the barn; spontaneous combustion; meteor strikes. Still, the original story feels true, has always felt true: my lineage carries with it a history of arsons.

***

I was fourteen, a single weekend separating me from my freshman year of high school, when I first encountered *the number*. It came in the form of a movie at a sleepover, five or six girls huddled around the television on the Berganciano twins' living room floor.

The Number 23 stars Jim Carey in a dramatic role as a man who picks up a random book in a bookstore, written under the pen name "Topsy Kretts," and realizes that it seems to be about him, all the events in his life connected by the number 23. He becomes obsessed with the number 23, sees it everywhere, holes up in a hotel room and goes insane. At one point, in that dingy hotel room, *the number* scribbled over the walls like the claw marks of a massive rodent, he threatens to kill his wife—who is, of course, only trying to save him from his floppy-haired, grim-faced emotional damage. As Jim Carey pins his wife to the scribbled-to-shit wall and brushes those floppy bangs away from that suffering brow, I think I told my friends, "Wow, that's so hot," and met their giggles with sly smile. The film failed miserably at the box office, and deserved to.

That night, after the movie, we all lay in our sleeping bags in the darkness and laughed as we watched the red glow of the digital clock and added up the numbers, waiting for 23 to appear. Craving that current of electricity at the back of our necks when it showed up.

It began to show up everywhere for me, and looking for it became a compulsion. When I entered a room, I would count the objects on the wall to see if they added up to some multiple of the number. I would count the tiles on the floor of my classrooms. I would count the letters in my name, in my friends', and add/subtract/divide the numbers in their birthdates. I looked at the clock and always seemed to catch it right at 2:30, or 3:20, or 1:23. Always right on time.

***

Superstition runs in the blood. The Irish are known for being a superstitious people, and their folktales say that character traits run in families, that "goodness" and "badness" are inescapable, inherent in DNA.

To the ancient Celts, poetry was pulse; *the fe'ith na fili'ochta* ("vein of poetry") resided only in the bodies of writers, snaking up the back of their heads like a thrumming vine. They also believed that poetry, a hereditary gift, would flee the bloodline for seven generations if it appeared in a daughter rather than a son.

***

Apophenia, a term coined by German psychiatrist Klaus Conrad, refers to the human tendency to interpret random occurrences as meaningful patterns. This is where belief in superstition comes from: say you opened an umbrella inside twice, and on both of those days, you slipped and fell in the rain. Say you picked up a penny off the sidewalk, and in the next moment, got a phone call that you had been accepted to medical school.

Because only so many numbers exist, repetitions are inevitable. People remember seeing the number they give meaning to, and forget seeing other numbers.

So much can be attributed to coincidence: if 3 billion people fly every year, and 500 million of those have a dream about a plane crashing, it is likely that over the course of the year, at least one of those people will end up on a plane that crashes (according to *The Guardian*, there are around 80 plane accidents per year, while 36 million flights land safely). Those who dream about plane crashes and land safely will likely never think of it again; for those who don't—and those who survive the ones who don't—the omen of their dream will always linger.

***

The 23 Enigma theorizes that all events are connected to and by the number 23, including life itself: the ovule and sperm contributed from each parent at conception consist of 23 chromosomes.

As I write this, the city bus next to the coffee shop I'm sitting in services route 23.

The 23rd letter of the alphabet, W, has 2 points facing down and 3 facing upwards.

William Shakespeare was born on April 23, 1564, and died April 23, 1616. His first folio appeared in the year 1623. When he was 46 (23 doubled) the first King James Bible was published. In Psalm 46, the 46th word from the beginning of the poem is "shake" and the 46th word back from the end is "spear."

***

In an interview with *TIME Magazine*, former Harvard professor Diane Hennacy Powell said: "One of the things we know is that [precognition] runs in families. If you talk to psychics, they'll tell you there's a family history of it. Though we haven't found it, there's likely a gene for it... Of course, that's not true of all dreams. Some dreams actually are tapping into some other time and place, and there's real information in them. Others are just imagination."

***

When my parents were newly married, my mother had a troubling dream:

She was in the front seat of a car driven by a faceless driver. The car pulled down a long dirt road and drove up to a farm. When they stopped, my mother got out, and the driver opened the back passenger's side door to help an old woman out of the car. The woman wore a burly fur coat, her salt and pepper hair pinned up beside her ears. As the faceless drivers, now multiplied into many, carried the woman across the farm to bury her, my mother screamed and beat them, trying to rescue the woman from burial, as she was still very much alive.

She woke the next morning and told my father her dream, and he immediately called my aunt; apparently, the old woman in the dream was an exact description of their grandmother, who died before my parents met, who refused to sit anywhere in a car but the back passenger's side seat, and whose greatest fear was being buried alive.

***

The Titanic sank the morning of April 15th, 1912. (4 + 1 + 5 + 1 + 9 + 1 + 2 = 23)

The first telegraph message successfully sent was a Bible verse from Numbers 23:23: *What hath God wrought?*

The number 23 represents the goddess Eris, Greek goddess of discord and chaos—her name only one letter off from mine.

My initials, ES, if flipped backwards, or written down and held in front of a mirror, resemble a 2 and 3.

My father was murdered on August 23, 2009.

***

When we spend enough time looking for something, we tend to find it. I don't remember the times the number 23 wasn't in sight, even after counting all the objects in the room, or adding and dividing the numbers that make up the time and date three different ways. I don't remember the dreams that never came true, dreams about tornados and teeth falling out that never resulted in real-life destruction. But I remember the ones that did, and they take root, shaping the story like embankments constructed to keep rivers from running wild—from washing whole towns, whole lives away.

***

On a cold October morning in 1966, a landslide tore through the small village of Aberfan, Wales. Within minutes, a schoolhouse was buried in a flurry of black sludge, the avalanche of rock and wet soil crushing and killing 116 children and 28 adults.

In the aftermath of the disaster, psychiatrist John Barker received almost one hundred letters from people claiming they had precognitive dreams predicting the landslide. A man from north England saw the word ABERFAN spelled out over and over behind his eyes; a woman in Brighton dreamt of a child walking toward her with a black mass looming behind him; another woman's dream featured coal hurtling down a mountain towards a schoolhouse, and a little boy being pulled from the wreckage—a boy she would later recognize on television as a local station aired coverage of the rescue efforts. But the most famous premonition of the Aberfan disaster came in a letter written by the parents of a ten-year-old girl.

The letter claimed their daughter, Eryl Mai, woke one morning, came downstairs, and relayed a dream she had the night before: her schoolhouse had been flattened by "something black." She told her mom she was not afraid to die because she would be with her friends, Peter and June.

The next day, Eryl Mai went to school, where she was killed in the landslide. The girl was buried along with the other victims in a communal grave, laid between her schoolmates, Peter and June.

***

My youngest sister, Trinity, was so named because she is the third child of both my mother and my stepfather (and though they deny it, her name was inspired by the heroine of *The Matrix* trilogy, which they watched nightly during my mom's pregnancy). Her birth acted as a hinge between two families; with two half-siblings on each side, and her own name meaning "three" between them, my sister's life has an ironic symmetry with the number 23. Though my stepbrother and stepsister were raised by their grandparents, our full family consists of 5 siblings—2 in one home, 3 in another. It's a reach, I know. We find these things because we're looking for them. And still a reach, maybe, when my mother pointed out that Trinity graduates from high school in the year 2023.

***

What I'm getting at is this: the summer she turned four, Trinity had a dream she doesn't remember now. If events had unfolded differently—if no one had been in the room when she woke from her nap, if he had died the following year instead of just a few weeks later, had died in some other way—if we were a skeptical people instead of a family willfully embedded in a paradigm of superstition—I wouldn't be telling this story.

My mom was using the computer at the desk next to her bed, and I was on the couch feet away, on the other side of an open door. Trinity stirred and sat up in bed, and began talking about the dream she had.

"Wait, slow down. What happened?" my mom said.

"Mr. Steve sat down in the middle of the circle," she said, matter-of-factly, "and then, behind him, a little bitty—" her fingers made tiny pinches of the air to demonstrate, "and BOOM! Now he's dead."

"That's creepy," my mom said. "It was just a bad dream, though."

"No, for real!" she insisted "BOOM! Mr. Steve's dead."

"Look, I'll call him, you can talk to him yourself and he'll tell you he's fine," she began to dial the phone.

"I don't want to talk to *a ghost*!" she squealed. Everything seems silly when a toddler says it with conviction.

My dad answered the phone, and my mom told him the story. He laughed over the speaker. "Tell Trin I'm just fine."

"See?" my mom said.

Trinity didn't seem sure. A few minutes passed and she lost interest. She left the bed for the kitchen, to climb the counter and reach for the bucket of candy on top of the refrigerator.

And no one thought of it again, until weeks later, when my dad sat down on a couch in the center of a room circularly arranged. And boom.

***

We drove, because my father had died. There would be a funeral, and we would attend it. Somewhere in the twelve hours from Texas to Alabama, Stephanie asleep in the back, I said to my mom, "See, I told you, there is something to this 23 thing."

She knew about my obsession, sparked a couple of years before by that shitty Jim Carey movie. She laughed and shrugged it off, "Yeah, whatever."

At that exact moment, an eighteen-wheeler merged in front of us. Painted on the back of the trailer: a huge, red, number 23.

***

Remember: I'm not telling you the truth. I'm telling you what I saw.

***

Superstitions are stories about how to survive. They flicker in the space between faith and delusion, blurring the borders until they are indistinguishable, until we no longer have a clear sense of the truth. Superstition is the belief that there *is* a truth, that fate is a red string you can tug at to guide you through the dark forest of your life.

Kevin Foster, an evolutionary biologist at Harvard, says that we will always choose the warm nest of this belief "as long as the cost of believing a superstition is less than the cost of missing a real association."

What is the cost of believing the universe has a blueprint with your name on it, that every cell in the atmosphere is rooting for you, pulsing in delight? If you walk into traffic, entranced in the most gorgeous dream, what is the cost of waking to the pain of impact?

To attach meaning to the events of our lives is to armor ourselves in the hope that we can control how the stories of our lives are told. Truth is nothing but glint of silver in the bottom of a pocket if, instead, we can choose to be stories.

***

A 1978 Gallup poll found that 37% of Americans believed in precognition. In 2007, a similar poll found that women were more prone to superstitious beliefs than men. A 2013 study discovered that people who had experienced trauma, or generally felt less in control of their lives, were far more likely to believe in precognition and superstition, possibly as a psychological coping mechanism.

Even without my father's death, and my mother's superstitious sensibilities, I fall into all of these categories. I am American, a woman, and very, very afraid.

Viewing

The viewing room was all dark wood and floral chairs. Dim yellow light shone on his coffin. When we got there, we saw that his hair was styled all wrong, in a way he never wore it. My grandmother took a fine-toothed black comb from her purse, spit on it, and combed back the dark strands.

My mother held his cold hand and kissed his face and cried. She told us we should touch him, too, that it was our last opportunity; he was going to be cremated. She said, *It's still your father. The last time you'll see him.*

My sister and I stood back, not wanting to come too close to the dead body. We asked everyone to leave the room, so we could be alone with him. It's the kind of high-maintenance request that we never would have gotten away with if we hadn't been, on that day, Princesses of Grief, the young, bereaved daughters of the beloved. Family and strangers alike closed the heavy oak doors behind them, closing us in.

My sister and I looked at each other, smiling the way children smile when they know it's inappropriate. We dared each other to step toward the casket, into the yellow light. Tried to shove and then jumped back, until together we walked forward.

What was lying there didn't seem like our dad, but a wax mold of him, a shell. Though the grotesque inanimateness startled us, so did the sense that he could begin moving at any second, zombie-like. His body looked like it could just as easily have been shucked-off empty as rise up out of the coffin and begin to scold us.

My sister poked his hand and giggled, squeamish.

Cold, she said.

I said, *He's wearing eyeliner.*

We looked at the place his head rested on the white silk pillow.

I wonder if they stitched it up, one of us said or didn't say.

I peeked behind the pillow, where the bullet made contact, and I saw red.

RETRACING

"The whole tragic history of our family comes down to this: none of us knew how to save ourselves."

–Heather Young, *The Lost Girls*

The Grief Archive

There is a folder. It lives at the bottom of my desk drawer, laid flush to the splintering wood. An inconspicuous manilla file stuffed with notes, cards and clippings, and a stack of photos in an orange envelope with a typewritten label that reads *Mary's Savings Account Info.*

This is where I keep all the evidence I have, scraped together to divine from these fragments what is left unexplained: how my father's murder was foreshadowed by the history of damage that led to it, and how it became the catalyst for the damage that occurred in its wake.

I have become the archivist of this grief, an investigator sifting through the evidence, piecing together narratives of character, motive, cause and effect. Curating a vision of who my family is and who my father was; a purgatorial decade spent sketching, erasing, and revising toward some final rendering.

My experience of owning this folder is much like my experience of grief itself: I am tender to its significance and resentful it exists. Diligent in collecting materials privately, then quickly exiling it to the furthest corner of my life to escape it. In the face of an abstraction like grief, like history, we grasp for tangible proof, searching for answers in the ashes that death leaves behind.

[Exhibit I]
Victim Impact Statement

Because Pam plead guilty to my father's murder, there wasn't a trial, but two years later there was a sentencing. I flew from my Texas college to Alabama, stayed at my grandmother's house, like the week of the funeral. On Monday morning we rose for the judge, and Stephanie and I saw Pam for the first time since that long-ago summer. She was dressed in jail stripes, wiry hair and no makeup to hide the puddle of her face as she took the stand and said her piece. About how she wasn't a bad person. How she felt her soul drain out like a bucket of cold water when she reached for the gun.

After Pam spoke, we were each required to read an "Impact Statement." The one printed here is the original one I read in court that day, with the bracketed edits added in January 2016, four years after the sentencing:

I was 16 years old on August 23, 2009. *[I thought I was so miserably old, and then—]* It was the night before the start of my senior year in high school, when a phone call caused my entire life and the lives of my family to be decimated beyond recognition. *[Who even uses the word 'decimated'? It was more like a mouth full of sores than a wrecking ball.]* Nothing you could ever see on TV or read in the newspaper prepares you for the shock and sense of surrealism at having something like that happen to you, in your life. *[Mark said this for a year afterwards, watching crime shows on TV in the garage.]* On a night my sister and I should have been picking our outfits for the first day of school, instead I was witnessing my sister collapse in tears on the stairs as my mother told us what had happened; that my dad had been senselessly murdered by his wife, Pamela, someone he had loved and trusted. *[I didn't know if he had really loved her, trusted her. How could anyone, even him, truly know?]*

Consequently, the first week of my senior year was spent in Alabama attending my father's funeral and dealing with the details of his death. *[Sitting on the twin bed in the back room of my grandma's house, whisper-singing Taylor Swift songs to JJ on the phone, because he said if I wasn't going to be useful to him he might as well call the new girl he was dating.]* It was like a sick, twisted dream, to see your dad, the man you spent childhood memories with, who talked to you and hugged you and supported you, now an empty shell in a casket who would never be able to do any of those things again. *[We saw him in the casket and we laughed because there was nothing else to do.]*

My mother couldn't speak a few sentences without bursting into tears, and it was impossible to be at home without being constantly reminded that everything we knew was in shambles. *[The week we got back, I got a part-time job at the movie theater so I had an excuse to be with people who didn't know me.]* My sister, Stephanie, who was thirteen at the time, began to make some bad decisions that I felt I had to cover up from my mom, as neither of them could handle it. *[The Adderall nights, the cutting and puking, stumbling home into the dim glow of our kitchen, as if dragged through mud.]* I was preparing to graduate high school at sixteen years old, working a part-time job, involved in extracurriculars and trying to figure out my future, all while feeling as if I was the one responsible for holding my family together, since no one else was able. *[You do what you have to and you keep moving. No one else was able.]*

In January, my sister went into rehabilitation for drug and alcohol use after being brought home by the police twice. *[What I found most troubling was that I never would have gotten away with the things she did, but my parents were too tired to fight her. I resented that freedom, and her, for allowing herself to take and take and take.]* In June, my mother went into rehabilitation herself, after turning to alcohol to cope with the sudden loss of my dad, her friend and partner in raising us. *[He called my mother to tell her he was going to break things off with Pam and joked that he should give her the address so we'd know where to find his body.]* Neither of these major events, occurring within six months of each other, would have happened without the loss of my dad. *[An avalanche lived inside all of us, just waiting for a reason to press through our skin.]*

As for me, I didn't turn to drugs or alcohol *[yet]*, or break down, incapable of continuing daily life. *[I told everyone I knew about what happened. I told strangers.]* Instead, I was forced to sacrifice the last morsel of my childhood that I had left. *[That was the only sentence I teared up while reading; selfish even then.]* I had to be strong for everyone else and I didn't get an adequate chance to grieve, something I am still dealing with now. *[When I passed Stephanie on the witness stand, after she read her statement, I hugged her and told her I loved her for the first time in two years and the last time since.]* I graduated and moved out of my parents' house two months before my seventeenth birthday. *[My dad paid for the summer classes that got me out of high school a year early.]* I ended up spending a year at community college, which never would have happened if my dad had been around to look at colleges with me, something he was so excited about doing. *[I felt like a failure, but it had nothing to do with him.]*

There are some days that I still think, "Hey, I haven't talked to my dad in a while, I want to call him," before remembering that I can't. *[In the O'Hare airport, in the aquarium, at my desk at work.]* When I want to tell him about my travels and plans for the future, I can't. *[In a hotel room in New Mexico, on a plane to London, on the first day of grad school.]* On my wedding day, he won't be there, just as he wasn't there at my high school graduation and won't be for my college graduation. *[And please don't make me carry his picture down the aisle or stitch it into my gown.]* When I see a man who looks like him, I stare and follow them around to try and get a glimpse of my dad. *[I still do.]* I am severely damaged and that is something that contaminates almost all aspects of my life, no matter how much I try to hide it. *[I am severely damaged and I am very good at hiding it.]*

The worst part in all of this is knowing that my dad was brutally murdered at the hands of someone he loved and trusted, his own wife, Pamela. *[Years later, a friend would remark: "Of course you don't know how to have a healthy relationship!"]* Because of her actions she has irreparably inflicted pain upon our family as well as her own. *[She said the reason she didn't kill herself after killing him was because she thought of her kids.]* While everyone deserves forgiveness, everyone also deserves justice, and I hope that for the sake of everyone affected that she is sentenced accordingly for selfishly ripping the life from someone whom she once promised to love and protect. *[My aunt joked at the sentencing, underneath her sweater, she'd be wearing a shirt that read:* Hang the Bitch.*]*

[Exhibit II]
Photographs Entered Into Evidence

1. My father behind me and the sea behind him, a green-blue ombre that melts toward the sand. There is no sky in frame, so the ocean ripples onward forever. I am seven and he is alive. We are looking in different directions, avoiding or unaware of the camera's gaze, but we know that we are in the water together.

2. *April 1962.* The monochrome polaroid shows a child on the front steps of a brick house. He is dressed like a little gentleman, his hair combed cleanly to the side. Moments before taking the picture, his mother has run a plastic comb through water to make the part, just as she will do forty-six years later as he lies prone in a coffin, hours before he vanishes to ash. The little boy stands up straight and smiles.

3. My parents on their wedding day stand together by a tree, their features young and softened, a glowing tint to the scene. They clasp hands and look at the camera. Stuck to the back of the photo, a label for *Portraits of Distinction, 1988,* and a phone number with a Dallas area code. My father's hair is brown and boyish in strands that fall onto his forehead. My mother's small body is drowned in ruffled layers of white satin and lace, the long wispy train of her veil swept behind her, but she looks like she is meant to be there. It's difficult to imagine what happens when she breaks the pose, steps out of this moment, releases my father's hand, hikes up her skirt and walks back to the church, goes to live a life composed of small normalcies. And maybe she can't imagine what comes after this, either.

4. My father's 40th birthday party in our dining room, stripes of beige

and olive green wallpaper. Black balloons and a multicolored "*40!*" from Party City taped on the wall. My father is holding an open card, looking away and smiling at someone out of frame, while I stand beside him, age six, balancing on my tiptoes to read what is written inside.

5. My father stands on a rooftop wearing a T-shirt, jeans, and blocky white Nikes, crossing his arms and smiling proudly. Next to him are two women, one whose face is obscured by a windswept veil of brown hair, her hand reaching to brush it away just as the camera snaps. I don't know who these people are or what they're doing on a roof, but I imagine they worked with my father, and have just accomplished something of importance. On the back, the only clue is blue ink spelling out *Brussels.*

6. My mother's handwriting explains: *Erin & Steve – Girl Scout Father-Daughter Dance – 1/30/99.* In front of the green and black faux-marble fireplace, my father is in a suit and I am wearing the burgundy velvet dress with white pearls I called "my Belle dress," after the princess I most enthusiastically identified with: brunette, bookish Belle from Disney's *Beauty and the Beast.* My long, sun-blonded hair cascades from a big white bow. We are both looking down, almost reverently, as my father bends to tie a corsage to my wrist. White velvet ribbon, blood-red roses.

7. *Panama City, 1999,* my father and mother both wear blue swimsuits and dark sunglasses, lounging on slatted pool chairs. My mother's head is turned to him, smiling brightly, but my father's expression is blank, staring straight ahead.

8. My grandpa in large wire-rimmed glasses smiles and stands straighter than he was ever able to do in my lifetime. My mother's arm is clinging to his, her other hand lost under a huge bouquet of white lilies, a string pearls draped over her sharp clavicles. Her face is partially hidden by the white veil drawn over it, but her eyes are round and blue-lined, and though she stares directly at the camera, she is not smiling.

9. I am a curly-haired toddler burritoed in a yellow blanket. My dad sits on the floor behind me and wraps his arms around me. His face is hidden in my shoulder, but mine is cheesing for the camera, giggly and gleeful. *Erin & Steve, 7/1/95.*

10. My father, mother, and Grandma Bea stand in the beige sandstone doorway of our Las Vegas house. I am a newborn in my mother's arms, wearing a baby-blue dress and white socks—tiny and wrinkled, like a kitten who hasn't yet opened its eyes. This is the day they brought me home from the hospital. These are the people who brought me into the world: proudly presenting me on the threshold of the first home I was given, the only home I will forget. Twenty-eight years after this day I will revisit the same spot, walk up for only a few seconds to stand where they stood. Someone will quickly snap a picture of me in front of the sun-bleached house and the door that's now locked behind an iron gate. But in *August 1993*, mouths slightly parted, we are all squinting in the sun.

11. The same father-daughter dance, the same red ruffled dress, a polaroid of my father and I perched on the back seat of a blue 1960's convertible. The space around us is decorated in colorful cut-outs, peace signs and flower power. It drips with kitschy vintage, but in some way we look regal, like Jackie O and JFK riding through Dallas.

12. Also in the folder: pictures of my mom, Mark, and Trinity a few Thanksgivings ago, cell-phone photoshoots in the gray Tennessee woods. Not pictures that belong to this particular grief, but where else could I put them without surrounding myself in the guilt their kindly stares inspire? The Grief Archive is for these pieces too heavy with discomfort to keep, and too important not to protect.

13. My dad, Stephanie, and I are sitting in the wagon of the pumpkin patch that spreads out behind us. My dad is wearing sunglasses and smiling wide, his dimples showing (I didn't realize he had dimples), and my sister's cherubic toddler face is alight in the sun, smiling with an uncer-

tain squint. I'm sitting next to my dad, his arm around me, and the black shadow his body casts blots me out, nearly erases me from the picture. But if you look close enough to make out my face in the shadowed dark, I'm turning away from the camera, from my family. I'm smiling softly at whatever's out there, yet unseen, across the expansive field.

[Exhibit III]
Objects Entered Into Evidence

[a]: The Effects of the Dead

- Gray stainless-steel watch. Behind the glass face, three small circles each with their own tiny silver hands, black and grooved like the topography of vinyl records. The back says the brand is *George* and it was made in Japan. It lists features that make it fancy, likely expensive, but I don't know what they mean, and it doesn't matter. The ticking stopped years ago.

- Burgundy baseball cap embroidered with *HARVARD 1636*, the felt rich and unblemished.

- Gray T-shirt with *HARVARD* in red letters across the front, size XL. It fits me but can be at times a little too tight to wear comfortably, depending on how my weight and acceptance of the past fluctuates.

- CDs wrapped and taped in a folded sheet of thick yellow paper. Written on the front in black pen: *Stephanie and Erin – these are the CDs I found in your Dad's CD player in his car. Love, Grandma.* The collection includes Pink Floyd's *The Wall*, and the plastic case for *Dark Side of the Moon* with a Stone Temple Pilots CD inside. Then, three unmarked silver burned CDs—I swapped these in and out of the radio in my truck during my senior year and listened to them while I drove to school. I wasn't going to tell you this envelope includes a Nickelback CD, not even torrented and burned, but bought for money at the store—I was going to allow my dad to retain his dignity in musical taste, at least, but fuck it. My dad liked Nickelback.

• A brown box made of plasticky fake bamboo. He could've bought it anywhere. He could've used it for anything.

• A framed portrait of me wearing my dance team uniform, sparkly purple sleeves and a tasseled skirt, white cowboy hat with a rim of purple sequins, and white cowboy boots. Freshman year of high school, my hair long and bleach-blonde with dark roots, my eyes thick with eyeliner, bordered by silver and purple pom-poms where I pose on the gym floor. I was told he kept this picture on his desk at work.

• A bronze chalice, the rim warped and the metal oxidized black. Around the stem, a lace ribbon that seems to have once been white. A faint engraving: *Steve & Mary, November 21, 1987.*

[b]: Photocopied documents labeled MOTION FOR PRE-SENTENCE REPORT

IN THE CIRCUIT COURT OF
LIMESTONE COUNTY, ALABAMA
STATE OF ALABAMA *vs.* PAMELA TERRY

On July 6, 2011, some motion is granted, scribbled with the signatures of attorneys whose names I don't recall, who I likely never spoke to. On the flip-side of this page is The PLEA AGREEMENT announcing Pam WILL ENTER A PLEA OF GUILTY to the charge of MURDER (136A-6-2) with FIREARM ENHANCEMENT [13A-5-6(a)(4)].

[c]: Photocopied documents labeled WAIVER AND CONSENT TO FINAL SETTLEMENT

IN THE MATTER OF
THE ESTATE OF

STEVEN C. SLAUGHTER
Deceased.

My mother's signature, the sweeping "M" that I learned to expertly forge on permission slips in middle school, stamped over with a seal for the State of Texas notary and dated July 26, 2012. All these summer notes and notices, days spent tying up the details of a life. All these papers and I don't know what they mean, what other people signed or signed away on my behalf. In the archive is not only the settlement waiver with my name on it, but a version with my sister's name, and my mother's, and my grandmother's—I don't know how I ended up with these, either, but I've always had them; from the very beginning, I was designated to catalog the grief of an entire family.

[d]: A Note

A square piece of white paper, 3x3, slipped between boxes of baby pictures, and later stolen to be preserved here. In red lettering, the header reads:

a memo from
MARY & STEVE

My mother—memory-gatherer, archivist in her own way—dated the top right corner *7/14/94*. A month before my first birthday. All these summer notes.

Steve—

Some pictures so you don't forget us. HA HA. We love you and miss you terribly! Be careful and hopefully we will be together very soon.

Love forever,

Mary

[e]: Birthday Card #1

There was nothing special about the last birthday card my dad sent me, except that I would keep it.

On the faded pink envelope, his all-caps handwriting reads, in quotes: *"Sweet Sixteen!!"* Two exclamation marks. A blue butterfly. Green polka dots. A generic birthday card slogan:

Happiness is the best gift anyone could have.

It was a day or two after my sixteenth birthday. I'd spent it with my mom and stepdad, and JJ had driven two hours to be there. There was ice cream cake.

I called my dad to thank him for the card. An obligation. I was sitting in bed, the blankets pulled up over my legs.

It was never quiet in our house, but it felt quiet. When I remember, it felt very quiet.

Inside the card he had written, in the same structured script: *Happy 16th Erin! Love, Dad.*

He had underlined *Dad.*

I think he must have been in rehab then, when I called. Either in it or just recently out of it. Not that it meant much to me. Not that I thought it would change anything.

It was the last call I made to him while he was alive, and it went to voicemail.

I don't remember what I said, but it was with burning eyes and a hitch in my voice. This was not normal, not for me, not when it came to him. The disarming sting in my throat washed over me rapidly.

May it be yours on your birthday and always.

I don't remember what I said, but I said, "Thank you so much for the card."

Before I hung up the phone, I said, "I love you, Daddy."

[f]: Birthday Card #2

GRANDDAUGHTER, the card reads in sparkly letters, purple, blue, and metallic green. What glitter hasn't trickled down the front now smudges white stars into my fingertips.

I follow the scrolling text of Hallmark birthday platitudes to the inner-left fold, where Grandma Irma has underlined a passage about how *your achievements make your family proud!!* Two exclamation marks.

Written in her tight black cursive at the bottom-right: *I hope KY will be as pleasant for you as Washington was.* My twenty-second birthday. The card likely arrived a few days late; I'd moved into my new apartment in Kentucky a week before, and probably procrastinated on telling her the new address.

Inside, something falls loose—not a check or gift card, but a large white index card filled-in tidily by hand:

Office of the Attorney General
State of Alabama
████ Washington Ave
PO Box ████
Montgomery, AL 36130-0152

Director of Victim Services
(███ was our server)
Office: (334) 353-████
Fax: (334) 353-████
Toll Free: 1-800-626-████

Love, Grandma

[Exhibit IV]
Annotated News Article

Ardmore woman gets 30 years in prison for killing husband of two months

blog.al.com | By Shelly Haskins | September 19, 2011 at 3:05 PM

ATHENS, Alabama -- A Limestone County woman was sentenced to 30 years in prison today for killing her husband just two months after their 2009 wedding.[1]

Pamela B. Terry, also known as Pamela Terry Slaughter, 50,[2] pleaded guilty July 6 to the Aug. 23, 2009 murder of Steven

---

[1] "...she's at home taking a nap...that's what five orgasms does to a woman..." –My dad, overheard talking to my grandma in her kitchen while my sister and I sat in the living room. We'd planned to go to the beach, but Dad and Pam had a fight the morning we were supposed to leave. It was about Pam's twelve-year-old daughter, how she'd started following Stephanie and I on our walks around the neighborhood, asking us questions about sex. I don't remember what we could have possibly told her. Maybe to ask her mom—maybe something about condoms? We spent our last four days in town at Grandma Irma's. My dad went to smooth things over with Pam, but we never went back to that house.

[2] "She was his midlife crisis. He didn't want to turn 50 alone. He should have waited." –My grandma, or my mom. Or both.

Charles Slaughter, according to a release from Attorney General Luther Strange.

Strange said after Slaughter and Pamela Terry decided to separate after two months of marriage, he was writing her a check to reimburse her for wedding expenses when she shot him in the back of the head at her home in Ardmore.[3]

She then called the Limestone County Sheriff's Office and confessed and waited for deputies to come and arrest her [4]

Post comment as...

buckelew Oct 19, 2011
Welcome to Ardmore.[5]

14Liberty Sep 20, 2011

---

[3] "Execution style." –An attorney at the sentencing.

[4] "She called me and said what she'd done and I told her you have to call the police I kept her on the line until I called them and they were on their way to her house I asked her where she'd done it she said the living room I said no where like where on his body..." –Pam's sister at the sentencing.

[5] "It's still Madison, basically, but the address is in Harvest." –My dad, explaining where he lived now, as he drove us from the airport to Pam's house. I don't know how Ardmore is in Harvest, or how Harvest is in Madison, or why everyone who lives anywhere seems to think their town is especially wild. There were no other murders in Ardmore that year. Not even my dad's, according to the crime rate statistics, which lists the number of murders at 0. The number of rapes is also 0. The number of burglaries and thefts is 13. You could argue it's all the same, burglarizing bodies, stealing another 30 years or so worth of breath.

30 years? Why not LIFE? Oh, yeah, double standards.

And NO, 30 years in her case is NOT the same as life because she'll be out in just a few years.[6]

Jerome Stcharles Sep 20, 2011
now us taxpayers have to support her for the rest of her life..very pitiful.
she needs to be shot in the back of her head.[7]

Elliott Sep 20, 2011
This is one strange story.[8] [9]

---

[6] "You have the Alabama Attorney General's Information, right? Every time you move, make sure to call and let them know your new address, so they can notify you when she's up for parole. So you can go down there and make sure she stays in jail. They say the family's statements are the most persuasive." –My grandma, approximately every six months.

[7] LOL

[8] I never noticed that the Attorney General's name was Strange. LOL.

[9] "What an incredibly strange thing to have happen." –A friend, when first told her The Story. Is it strange? I suppose the answer is: of course. But every time I tell someone The Story and they react this way, it catches me off guard. I mean, people kill each other all the time. The only strange thing is that it happened in my life, but I was quickly ready to accept it as just the way things were, the way life worked. I had accepted it, I think, before I walked back up the stairs to my bedroom that night. Processing it was a different matter.

12chimes Sep 19, 2011
killed him..called the police..confessed..waited for them to show up to arrest her..sounds like she watched "slingblade" one too many times.[10]

User Friendly Sep 19, 2011
2 months? geez. 30, 1/3 of the sentence she'll be eligable for parole (10 years), then every 3 years from then on she'll be up for parole hearing. ugh keep her in [11]

jarhaid Sep 19, 2011
Gee whiz. I hope she waited until he at least signed the check. [12] [13]

tcarl Sep 19, 2011
I never heard of a woman who did not take the money first, cash

---

[10] "I've never seen *Slingblade.* People say it's good, or whatever. I don't know. I'm not really into action movies." –Me, in some conversation long before I found this article and read the comments. I've still never seen *Slingblade.* I wonder if Pam had. I wonder if they have movie nights in prison, like they do on *Orange is the New Black.*

[11] "Who knows where I'll even live when she's up for parole? What if I have a job I can't take time off from to travel to Alabama? What if I don't care if she stays in jail or not? What if I just don't want to deal with it?" –Comments I do not make.

[12] LOL

[13] Did he sign it, though? I don't know.

the check, then do whatever. [14]

Creole Chavez Sep 19, 2011
RIP. Slaughter is her married name. That's ironic.[15] [16] [17]

[14] "You're only afraid of guns because of your dad, though. And because you're a woman." –A male acquaintance in grad school. Neither of those are the reasons I don't want to own a gun, or be near one. It's because I don't want to be in the same room with anything whose only purpose is to harm.

[15] "Based on your name, I definitely thought this was going to be some kind of horror story. I was pleasantly surprised." –A journal editor, after reading an essay I wrote about my father's murder and its connection to my inability to trust romantic partners.

[16] "Slaughter. You know, like the murdering." –Me, restating my last name to one of my students on the first day of the semester.

[17] It is ironic. It truly is. LOL.

[Exhibit V]

Redacted Newspaper

The News Courier: Tuesday, September 20, 2011

WOMAN GETS KILLING

Judge: Pam 'not a danger ' despite shooting husband of 53 days

her estranged husband, was sitting on the floor writing her a wedding . He enraged her so she went numb, got a handgun and shot him in the back of the head. and Slaughter had worked together at a military contractor and had dated before they married. She was planning an end only… (See Killing, page 4)

[white woman frowning in prison stripes]

[white man smiling in suit and striped tie]

LEGISLATURE TO DECIDE

Is home protected?

This damage in . The violent spring and now an all-time high of wondering: can they count on anything safe from staggering loss? (See Insurance, page 3)

National Weather Forecast

TODAY	WED.	THURS.	FRI.	SAT.
Highs	and	lows	are	likely

Death toll for

Today in History

Today is the 2 3rd day this day a century ago collided with a vessel dam- aged by its own power. In 1519, an explorer set out to find Islands and was killed but eventually circled the world.) In 1870, mourners took control And panic swept in the wake of fai- lures. 1958 was seriously wounded when stabbed in the chest. Ten years ago: a nation shaken learned war begins but it does not end . It will not end ever .

KILLING

(Continued from 1)

53 days. to serve 30 years She was given credit for Her guilt to Slaughter's mother, Irma "She deserved agony The attorney said she was still angry at the victim and summed her motive as "Hell hath no fury like a woman

destroyed because of jealousy . It was an execution." After the murder affected them, Pam requested Slaughter had lived However, Slaughter's

mother said that Pam would not allow
her son to be
a person. On the day of the shooting,
Slaughter
on the floor between the coffee table and
the couch, believed
in his life. She testified, "I said
it was a mistake and he didn't
living
in a daze, she shot twice
and
called her sister. She apologized to the person
who shot him the person she is.
Before a sentence,
family members accused.
the late hus-
band will now sell away
the life his mother finds
comfort in and has left the image
of her house in a body bag the coroner calling
his eyes the final impression
Stephanie was 13 when her father
fell apart scars a girl
should seek treatment for Erin
who was 16 at the time had to hold
her father's death. She said she lost the last remnant of
help . She grieves the
day he won't be there to
remark on
who looks like him, to glimpse
The defendant's victims She
tried to offer

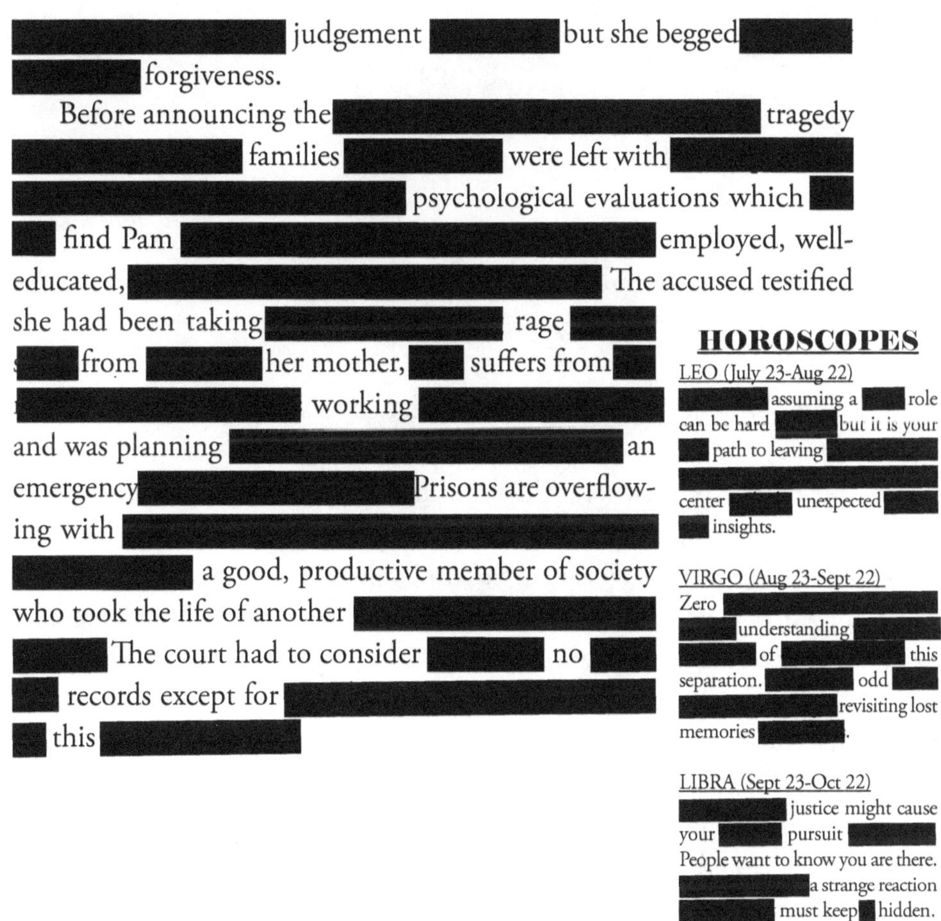

judgement but she begged
forgiveness.
Before announcing the tragedy
families were left with
psychological evaluations which
find Pam employed, well-
educated, The accused testified
she had been taking rage
from her mother, suffers from
working
and was planning an
emergency Prisons are overflowing with
a good, productive member of society
who took the life of another
The court had to consider no
records except for
this

HOROSCOPES

LEO (July 23-Aug 22)
assuming a role
can be hard but it is your
path to leaving
center unexpected
insights.

VIRGO (Aug 23-Sept 22)
Zero
understanding
of this
separation. odd
revisiting lost
memories .

LIBRA (Sept 23-Oct 22)
justice might cause
your pursuit
People want to know you are there.
a strange reaction
must keep hidden.

[Exhibit VI]
Witness Testimony #1

Let the record show this account was written by RW (the closest friend of ES at the time of her father's death) and reads as follows:

I don't remember the exact words she used to say it, but I do remember the way she said it. With nonchalance akin to a housewife reading off a grocery list: Bread, check. Chicken, check. My dad's dead. Carrots, check.

Some people wear their hearts on their sleeve; Erin keeps hers in a safety deposit box upstate. I was probably taken aback at the time, but in retrospect, this episode of compartmentalizing seems apt. I remember that she said, maybe even with a misplaced giggle, "You know, Trinity saw it in a dream." She seemed overwhelmed by her situation and so her attention turned to her younger sister and the supposed premonition of her father's passing. Unlike myself, Erin has always attached a certain weight to her subconscious and intuition, a trait that made her a captive audience for such an idea. Especially one that distracted from the larger issue.

There was a pretty abrupt shift in the conversation: She talked about getting her driver's license, her new car, school. Suddenly life and all its mundanities took precedence over this large, traumatic event she had just experienced.

But that's understandable, for her. That's Erin.

Witness Testimony #2

Let the record show the names of the accusers have been scorched from the record. This is an act of tenderness.

ES uses tragedy as a carnival. ES profits from the spectacle of death. ES is insensitive. ES is selfish. ES is guilty of not feeling guilty enough. ES is unfazed by injustice, indifferent to the untimely loss of loved ones. ES is ungrateful. ES is immoral. ES is secretive and deflects with humor. ES tries too hard to distance herself from herself. ES is quick to normalize. ES claims hardship as identity when it suits her, but does not suffer accordingly. ES is frivolous. ES is masochistic. ES tells secrets that do not belong to her. ES tells stories that are not hers alone to tell. ES offends the memory of the deceased. ES is neglectful of the obligation to live solemnly. Or at least appear to. ES is disrespectful to the importance of appearances. ES is inappropriately composed. ES does not confide in her bloodkin. ES does not cry in public, does not react like others. ES does not care that her father has been murdered. She is not to be trusted, even by herself.

[Exhibit VII]
An Interview with Emptiness

Conducted in the back room of an unfurnished apartment in Bowling Green, Kentucky, August 23, 2015.

How did it start?

It started with condensation on the windows, with time rolled out like a velvet carpet.

You didn't know what to do with it.

I slept a lot. Drove. Filled it with cheap sweaters and buttered bread.

Filled.

Yes.

How did it start?

It started with I was starving for nothing and burning burning burning wanted everything wanted anyone couldn't stop, every single moment of pain longing so eloquent so sharp and gorgeous like raindrops suspended in glass, like astronomy and the mountains and all that light and heat you can't touch, all that emptiness.

There were places.

There was concrete. There was water. There were bookstores, fingers ghosting over the worlds of the long-dead, the spaces I wasn't.

What did you do there?

I waited.

Waited for what?

A sign, a sigil, a fucking earthquake.

You wanted someone to see you. To reach out. To mean it.

I wanted what anybody wants.

Why did you not go outside?

I was terrified. The grass. All those foreign bodies.

What about now?

Most days still. But it's not the same.

What about the snow?

I cried about the snow because it was impossible and delicate. I cried about the snow when I thought it might be the last I ever saw.

Why the last?

Because my body is suspended in a constant state of helpless frightened grief. Smoke rising up from the fields. The lilac sky and the abandoned road. I thought I had died and wandered into some parallel eternity.

Do you believe in God?

I believe we mostly get what we deserve.

You think you deserve this.

I dream about poisoning him with animal crackers. I dream he was alive the whole time but he won't come in this room and he won't tell me if he likes the words he's bald he's lying naked on the wooden floor not saying anything he's on the computer he's looking at pictures from last year but he won't talk he won't tell me.

It wasn't your fault. You didn't kill anything.

I killed years. I filled weeks with smoke and haze and lard. I bulldozed my flesh into numbness.

Was it the casket? Or what came after?

It's never been about that. If anything, it was before. The knives in the walls. Or sleeping on the floor next to the radio.

Tell me about the barn.

A therapist once asked me to envision my hunger. It was the shape of a barn, and it was outlined in blue and yellow. It came from my guts, from the pit of my stomach and it hovered there and filled me up and demanded filling.

There's that word again. Fill.

Yes.

What did you fill it with?

Everything. Nothing. Seawater, on my best days.

Tell me about the sea.

I wanted to submerge my entire being, to open up and fill every orifice with dark violent insatiable water, to drown. I wanted to be consumed.

Was it like prayer?

It was like burial. Which is the same thing.

Why didn't you let it take you?

The ceiling fan. The little girl on the beach. The seals and rocks and sunlight.

You still had more left to say.

That depends on who is listening.

What about forgiveness?

Forgiveness is a charcoal sketch and I prefer painting. I like to give the colors a chance to escape.

What do you paint?

Hands in the mouth, hands erupting from the mouth, my body as a series of slashes and spheres.

Do you ever wish for someone to share them with?

There is no honest way to answer that.

It's why you go to museums and graveyards.

I go to remember those who no one else remembers.

What about prayer?

What about memorizing the veins of leaves. What about closing your eyes as a voice reads poetry and breath touches your face. What about a car set on fire on the side of the highway, and driving past, wondering if anyone is inside.

What about guilt?

Exactly.

You thought you knew the antidote.

I thought that I was someone else.

Someone who could do this alone.

Is there a choice? There is a reason we go to work and the supermarket. There is a reason we tell ourselves these stories.

What are you afraid of?

My dad has been dead four years when I find myself living in the same city where my parents met and fell in love. Everywhere I go is like stepping on a grave. Here are the apartments he lived in, just two streets over from mine. Here is the library he liked to study in, his hands moving over the dark wooden surfaces for hours.

The summer before I moved to Denton, my mother told me that when she was in college, she used to have a recurring nightmare about being shot in front the campus library building. I was in my subleased apartment in Waco, cleaning paint off the kitchen countertop, the phone lying in the crook of my neck as she spoke two hundred miles away.

He was my age when he lived here and now his life is over, and my mother has a new husband. At night she sits and smokes cigarettes in a broken chair in the garage and watches preachers on television.

She is worried about me and tells me never to go to the library.

"Just be careful," she says. "It didn't come true for me while I was there, so it might come true for you. Maybe it was a warning."

"You can't be serious," I laugh into the receiver. I tell her I don't believe her premonition, but I avoid the library, just in case.

***

The University of North Texas was the last place I ever wanted to end up. Three generations of my family's footsteps silently line the walkways of this campus: My great-grandmother, Helen, who married at fourteen and had two children before she learned how to boil water on the stove, the stories say—she earned her GED in 1975, the year her husband died, and went on get her business degree; my grandmother, Bea, who rented a room in a boarding house on Fry Street after the second World

War—she studied business, too, for only a year before she left in 1950 to work as a typist and met my grandfather, a veteran who "wanted to be a photographer, but they handed him a rifle." And my mother, Mary, who majored in real estate in the 80s, who met my father at a Halloween party in Clark Hall, who was maybe the reason I had avoided UNT like the plague.

I wanted to create my own history, be more adventurous (a word that in my teens was synonymous with "better,"—*better* than the people I grew up with whose big move away from home was only to the next town over with the Wal-Mart, *better* than the women I'd grown up surrounded by, who shucked off the passions of their youth for a husband and children, and only got to become themselves again once the years left them hollow). I wanted an escape from the life I felt closing in, one identical to my mother's: being married at twenty-one, and returning fifteen years later, divorced, in a Honda Odyssey stuffed with suitcases, two children and various animals in tow. But after failed attempts at finding some sense of belonging at two separate universities, I turned to what seemed like the last viable option. Standing on the campus I had so strenuously avoided, I couldn't help feeling lost to stories of other people's pasts, wondering what I was supposed to make of the time still ahead.

***

A boy in my statistics class asks me on a date. He is tall and has brown hair that falls in his eyes when he leans down to write his number across the top of my lecture notes. We meet two nights later, at a coffee shop I vaguely remember going to in high school, after I drove to Denton with a friend who wanted to sneak into a bar. The walls are overflowing with wooden knickknacks and local art, and we sit at a booth table where the cushion foam spills out from the lining of my seat. Over the speakers, a pop-punk song I loved years ago plays, and he knows all the words. We talk about music with nostalgia in our voices, and he tells me that his first concert was to see the same band I had a poster of above my bed when I was fourteen.

We talk about statistics, but not in the way I want to. I want to ask, *What is the probability that you will marry me, divorce me, and die before the age of fifty?* and *Can we ever really know if we're headed for exponential growth or for decay?* Instead, I don't say much at all. I sit in the warmth of the broken booth seat and let him tell me about the trees where he grew up, about his mother and father who backpacked across Scotland for their honeymoon and ended up staying until he was born a year later. He tells me about his sister, four years younger, who found a dying rabbit underneath their porch, how she nursed it back to life and named it Roger. I let him talk because I like the passionate waning and waxing of his voice, like the rise and fall of waves pulling sand from the shore. I don't want to acknowledge the thought that's been looming over me since the start of the semester: that any boy I meet here will end up like my father, as dust in a jar on someone's cabinet shelf.

***

"How did you know?" I ask my mother over the phone. It was that same night she told me to avoid the library, that same long summer characterized by indecision and the eternal scrubbing of paint from surfaces.

"How did I know your dad was right for me? I just knew. It was a feeling, the song that played when he asked me to dance: Journey's 'Faithfully.' It was the start of the semester. I had just turned eighteen, and your dad was a senior. He asked me to dance, and everything felt perfect in that moment—"

Stephanie picks up a phone somewhere else in the house and comes on the line, "Mom and Dad slept together on the first night they met!"

"Eeewww…" I say, obligatorily.

"I know, right?" My sister laughs.

"Come on," she says, "You weren't there. You don't know what it was like, the air between us. It was electric."

***

There is a photo. My sister and I, sleepy in pajamas and hoodies, messy preteen hair. It's Christmas, and we are beside the tree, tearing paper from boxes with careless ferocity. My mother spent long nights up late for those gifts—after ten-hour days working at the daycare, and dinner, and dishes, scrubbing the counters with a wet rag, waiting for us to go to bed so she could lock herself in the lamplight of her bedroom and make sure the creases of the paper were folded and taped just right, the ribbons majestically scissor-curled.

My mother's not in this picture, but behind it; like her aspiring-photographer father who was never caught without his black Canon hanging from his neck, she is the taker of so many boxes full of pictures, the diligent recorder of memories. We found her impulse annoying, groaning whenever she forced us to pause the surge of our lives to smile and pose. Now, I find myself annoying my friends with the same habit, the same itching need to create a record of the moment. Something that captures, proves, preserves. Something to retrace when everything but the memory has fled.

My mother tells stories of a different time, when she and my father would bring a real pine home, before they invested in the wire tree I've always known. Though it never lived in a forest, nothing about this tree feels fake to me; the rainbow assortment of lights casts an ambrosia glow that radiates in me as some distilled essence of childhood. The ornaments are collages of time: my great-grandmother's glass antiques, my grandmother's cloth angels, the popsicle stick and glitter-glue projects of our childhoods, and Disney characters, and plastic snowmen, and porcelain baby shoes with our names hung high at the crown. On top is our angel: blonde-ringleted, harp-holding, beautiful in gold-embroidered silk, and the spitting image of my mother—holding her likeness still for the camera as the years slide out of her behind it.

***

Of the myths that run riverlike through my mother's side of the family, the stories about my great-grandmother, Helen, carved the deepest furrow. A notebook entry from second grade reminds me that I used to pray to her. A framed picture of her gazed down from the top of our computer desk, with her wire glasses and toothy smile, her liver-speckled skin. But I always imagined her as beautiful.

After her husband died, she began to travel the world, voracious for all she'd spent her life not seeing. And she painted, though no one ever spoke of her as an artist. I discovered it on my own, the month before moving to Kentucky for graduate school, searching through the moth-ridden cosmos of my grandmother's basement in Tennessee for chairs to furnish my apartment. I found stacks of oil paintings lying under tarps, behind dressers, stored under the pool table and in the storm closet. I found my great-grandmother's art, the record of her life that one no one tells, collecting dust in the basement.

***

My great-grandmother, Helen: the traveler. My grandmother, Bea: the historian. My mother, Mary: the teacher. Three women before me, and three alongside me, including my sisters and myself—though often, I barely feel comfortable calling myself a woman. A "woman" has a partner, children or the possibility of them, a certain perfume sparkle to her. A woman is held stationary by love, her place in the world cemented. A woman has something that passes for a rooted life.

Stephanie has a daughter of her own, and Trinity is still young enough to be satisfied with being someone else's daughter. I am a daughter, but I am many other things a daughter doesn't have the luxury of being. I am still trying to work out how to inhabit these roles: a woman, a daughter, and—somehow, between the two—free.

***

I once asked my mother, "Did you ever date anyone besides Dad when you were in college?"

"Oh yes," she said. "In my senior year, your father and I broke up, and he moved to Boston for a job. I came back to find all my stuff in garbage bags on the front step. It was really upsetting. A few months later, I dated this man in his forties—I was probably twenty at the time. He took me to nice restaurants, and he never tried to get me to meet his kids, which I was glad about. But he always wanted me to wear hats. We would be at the mall or window shopping somewhere, and he would pick up a hat and say, 'Try it on!' and have me model it for him. I tried to tell him I don't look good in hats, but he would always say, 'Oh no, you look beautiful. I'm going to buy it for you.' I've never been a hat person.

Then, on my last day of college, your dad showed up at my door out of nowhere. I hadn't spoken to him in months, and he said, 'Will you go somewhere with me, please?' and that day he proposed to me."

"I can't believe you said yes!" I said. "You broke up, and all the sudden he randomly showed up and asked you to marry him?"

"Well," she said, "I never felt anything for anyone else like I did for your father. Also, he never asked me to wear a hat."

***

On a Tuesday afternoon, my roommate and I skip class and take a road trip two hours north, to a park in Oklahoma called Turner Falls. It's early November, which in Texas feels like a dim echo of summer fading into fall. We make a point of stopping at the *Welcome to Oklahoma* sign to take pictures, even though we live only an hour from the state line. Back on the road, I snap pictures of everything through my sunglasses, pretending this is more than just a day trip, that we're charting our escape across the country.

As we approach Turner Falls, we follow a winding road into the mountains, where magenta wildflowers grow off to the sides. Inside the park, the stone ruins of a castle are perched on a hill, the remains of a doctor's summer house built in the 1930s. We climb the steps, lamenting our unfortunate choice of footwear, and walk through the abandoned castle. I wander from room to room, running my fingers over the names carved in the wooden doors and painted in graffiti over the fireplace.

We venture further near the woods, where a waterfall fills into a swimming pond. We've been in the park all day and haven't seen any other visitors, so we decide to strip off our clothes and leave them on the sandy shore as, giggling and apprehensive, we glide our bodies into the water. It's a sunny day, but the water is clear and cold, and even as my skin raises with chills it's a total freedom I've never felt before; being naked and swimming underneath a waterfall in public in the middle of the day.

On the drive home my mom calls, and I tell her about our adventure.

"You're lucky you didn't get arrested," my mother says, but I can hear her smiling through the receiver. "Where was this at?"

"It's this place in Oklahoma called Turner Falls. They have these amazing castle ruins, and caves out in the woods…"

"I know where Turner Falls is," she says. "Didn't I ever tell you? That's where your dad proposed to me. I think it was beside a waterfall…."

***

Three women before me, three among me, and a history of cancer. Helen died of breast cancer when I was a peach-fuzzed toddler at her hospice bedside. Bea and Mary had double-mastectomies within two years of each other. Between myself and my two sisters, statistics suggest at least one of the three of us will develop breast cancer, too.

If I had the choice, I'd choose to take that burden. Stephanie has a family, and I would never want Trinity to experience the panic and pain that comes with your body turning against you, consuming in its multiplication. Maybe my theoretical sacrifice has nothing to do with them, with martyrdom, or even a secret death-wish; the women in my family are all petite, ever-shrinking with age as their husbands' ghosts grow and swell and flood, while my body has always taken up too much space.

My great-grandmother did not call herself a painter and my mother does not call herself a writer, but before the surgeon took her breasts, she stayed up all night writing a poem. She printed copies on the marbled paper she used for job resumes and sealed them in plain yellow envelopes. In the morning, before we left for the hospital, she handed the envelopes to each of us: words to remember her by, words to keep the record.

***

In my second year of grad school, I'm at a cabin getaway with friends when I begin puking my guts out. I find myself pinned to a bed for five hours, sweating and shaking as bony tree limbs loom through the windows and a ribbon of searing pain constricts around my ribs.

Two months later, the morning of the surgery to remove my gallbladder, winter storm Stella is barreling up the East coast. As they wheel me down the hallway into surgery, I'm so frightened that I hyperfixate on the light fixtures on the walls: angular and green, an eerie art-deco I appreciate, should they turn out to be the last thing I ever see. My mother is there, and I don't want to cry in front of anyone, especially her, so I focus on the news as I wait for the anesthesiologist to slip behind the curtain and calm me with his steady-handed potions.

I'd never met the anesthesiologist, only the surgeon, who'd also done my best friend Lena's gallbladder surgery the year before. He was a jolly man with a bright Kentucky accent, and his name—I swear—was Dr. George W. Bush: a piece of information I will joke about at every opportunity for years afterward, reciting how "George W. Bush took something out of me I can never get back."

I don't remember the face of the anesthesiologist who walks in and sits at my side, but I remember his hands; red and cracked, bulging slightly around a plain gold wedding band. They look like my dad's hands. When he slides latex gloves the color of deep-freeze over them, tears fall, and I apologize. He reassures me in some good-natured way and pumps me with valium.

After surgery, I wake howling; uninhibited, throat-raw gasping, sobbing, a blur of half-drowned white fog. From some distance, an infant begins to cry. A nurse says, "Wow, calm down…that's a little much…" and spurts something into my IV.

When I surface again, I'm upstairs in the room with my mom. I watch the news from my hospital bed as I drift in and out of nauseous consciousness, anesthesia and morphine wearing off in shifts. She sits in a chair grading her third-grade class's papers, a project to keep her occupied while she sleeps on my living room futon to care for me that week. Outside the hospital window, a speckling of snowflakes blankets the parking lot.

My mom tells me a story of who she was at 23, the age I am then. She was a wife, my father's, and they lived in an old Victorian house near Boston. She says she can remember the upstairs window she stood at once when she was the sickest she'd ever been, vomiting up food poison while wearing a bikini, because there was no air-conditioning in the old house. She can vividly remember looking down from that window at the front yard, at all the green grass.

While my dad was at work, she made the house her project. She spent her free time peeling a century's worth of paint-coats from the walls, pulling up linoleum, restoring the original wood doors. They only lived there a year before they moved again for my dad's job.

She searches the address and pulls up a picture of the house on her phone. It's blue with a rounded doorway, a flag hanging over the entry, a large yard. It looks satirically all-American. A section has been added on in the years since, she says, but otherwise it's the same as when she lived there. I realize that as we stare at the picture, the house is being pounded with feet of snow, Boston icing over as we speak. She says she can remember it so clearly, what it was like to walk up the front steps and unlock the door, what it was like to be that person, the 23-year-old person who lived there. Just one of so many of her lives buried under layers of paint and past.

***

Before my mom's freshman year at UNT began, she visited the boarding house on Fry Street where my grandma lived in college. She walked up onto the creaking porch and met the lady who owned it, the same one from all those years ago. The lady pulled out a dusty ledger-book filled with decades of boarders' names, and my mom flipped through the pages until she saw her own mother's name written in faded cursive. We are all retracing someone's footsteps, unable to escape or embrace what bore us through the years to that spot. We can only search for the faint seam where time and place overlap, only reach out to touch the letters left on the page.

Literary scholars Cixous and Clement write: "…the repressed past survives in woman; woman, more than anyone else, is dedicated to reminiscence…[her] body is transformed into a theatre for forgotten scenes." And what is a writer but someone who transforms their body into a theatre and expels those scenes into the world? What is the root of memoir, of keeping the joys and sorrows of a life on the record, if not, "…festivals of remembrance…for each of the private catastrophes that have affected her"?

The lady who owned the house on Fry Street no longer rented rooms. She'd converted the garage into an apartment, but some guy was already living there.

I never went back to see her, my mom ends the text message, punctuated with an emoji that turns its eyes down in regret.

***

When I finally tell the boy from statistics The Story we are sitting in his apartment. His roommate has just finished cooking, and the room smells of cinnamon. I tell him:

> "When I was sixteen, the night before my senior year of high school // I went downstairs and my sister was crying and my mom told me // my dad's new wife of two months had killed him because he asked her for a divorce. // He sat down on the couch to write her a check as severance // and she shot him in the back of the head with a revolver."

As it falls out of my mouth I wonder if he can tell that it's been rehearsed, that the timing of each word made a place for itself in the thousand times I've had to tell this story in the four years since it happened. I wonder if he could possibly know that when you tell it over and over, it starts to sound like lines from a play, like something that happened to someone else a very long time ago. That it becomes a recitation rather than a memory.

I don't tell him about the greasy rivers of mascara that ran down my mother's face as she and my sister sobbed together on the stairs, and I stepped over them to walk quietly to my room. I don't tell him that later, when we went through his belongings, my mother put on an old pair of his socks and didn't take them off for weeks—she said they reminded her of when they were married, all the times she had washed and folded them.

My father was cremated, and the night before we left town, I woke up and saw my mother in the next room, sleeping on the floor in the room that would soon hold his ashes.

The night that I tell him, after he falls asleep, I run my fingers across his body and wonder which parts I'll miss the most in twenty years. Which ones I'd cross the country to sleep next to.

***

Grandma Bea is a slight, pale woman, with white hair the texture of stuffed animals' insides, and a snail-curve spine. She has piercing blue eyes and a thin smile lined in hot-pink. As I speak to her on the phone, her backwoods landline eating blips of sound, I imagine her standing in her vast, log-built house, every surface in knotted chestnut.

I ask her about the house on Fry Street, and she describes a white wooden house with a porch. She claims she can still see her roommate's face clearly, though she can't remember her name. There was a boys' boarding house next door to theirs, and she and her roommate could watch the boys come and go from their bedroom window.

"We had a lot of fun there," she offers, almost suggestively.

"Oh yeah? What did you do?"

"Studied, of course!"

Her voice is rounded with Texan vowels from growing up in San Antonio, hidden under a thicker Tennessee twang from her thirty-plus years living in Crossville, in the log house my grandfather built on an acre of forest and field, at the end of a gravel path off Old Peavine Road.

In her second semester of college, she convinced her parents to give her cash to buy her own meals, and saved enough money to buy material for two dresses, which she remembers staying up late to sew in the laundry room of that house. On weekends, her friends would take the bus downtown to the movies; once, she went to see a show with a boy who lived in the house next door, but when she came back, her roommate made it clear she didn't want Bea to see him again. The roommate ended up marrying him.

She goes on to tell the story of her life after, of my mom's infancy "in a little crackerbox house" in Dallas' Highland Park, of meeting my grandpa, who'd been wounded in France during the war and lied bleeding in a snowy valley for hours until a French solider carried him to a nearby home.

"Actually," she says, "your grandpa is the reason I started the binders."

I can visualize the binders in their slots on the second-floor bookshelf, staring down through the wooden staircase bars. All of them with plastic, navy blue covers and typewritten dates on the spines, bulging with antique photos in their page-protector tenements. My sisters and I skimmed them over the years while visiting, seeing my mom's and uncles' baby pictures alongside the sepia-tinted scowls of ancestors we'd never heard of.

"It was when we retired and moved up here that I started getting into genealogy, because your grandpa had this old Bible from his great-grandfather, who'd been a horseback preacher..."

I don't know many details about my grandfather's early life, but I've gotten the sense that his childhood was a dislocated one. Grandma Bea tells me after she started collecting family trees and photos in the binders, she planned trips to pin down my grandfather's history; they veered a day away from their visit to see my parents in Illinois to track down his still-living aunts in Wisconsin. A year before he died, she drove him around East Dallas to revisit the houses and schoolyards of his childhood, retracing her husband's life for him.

Before ending the call, I ask if she remembers when my mom first introduced her to my dad. She said it must've been in Denton, at my mom's graduation, the same trip my dad asked for my mother's hand in marriage.

"What did you think of him?"

She pauses for a beat, as she often does, muscle-memory from a lifetime of being cautious with her words. "I had mixed emotions," she says, "I didn't know him very well. But I didn't say any of that, I just let your grandpa talk it over with him." Then she mentions, as an afterthought, the true reason for her apprehension: she'd heard my dad had lived with another woman before my mom, a ballerina.

"All Mary told me is that his girlfriend had been a ballerina, and your dad hated ballet after that. I suppose that's why he never would go with you girls to see *The Nutcracker* on your school trips."

I consider not correcting her, but then I decide to go for it anyway: "Well, um…I don't want to get Mom in trouble or anything, but I think she might have sugarcoated it for you. The story I always heard is that dad's ex was an 'exotic dancer,'" I grapple for terminology that won't embarrass her, adding, "at a gentleman's club."

My grandma laughs nervously.

"Well," she says, "That's the past. There's no use bothering with the past."

***

I set foot inside the UNT campus library building exactly once: to read an early version of this essay, at an event celebrating the undergraduate literary journal where my essay was published. I was twenty, a semester away from graduation, and it was my first-ever invited reading. In my excitement, I charged a new dress and shoes to my credit card, researched DIY updos for my hair, and rubbed orangey home-tanner all over my body. My mom and Mark dressed up, too: Mark in his Sunday church outfit of black jeans, a pale yellow button-up, and black cowboy hat, and my mom in a sparkly top. They drove down to Denton and met me in front of the fountain at the library entrance, and my high school best friend, Rachel, walked from her on-campus apartment, wearing a turquoise dress with extensions clipped into her hair.

When we approached the room next to the computer lab where the reading was being held, I shriveled with embarrassment. Only a handful of people were there, almost entirely students wearing jean shorts and tank tops—most of them, I assumed, the student editors of the journal. Even the stray couple of moms who were there to see their kids read were wearing T-shirts and slacks. I had—as I'd accidentally done many times before, and would inevitably continue doing for the rest of my life—arrived enormously overdressed. I tried to plaster on a confident smile, feeling monstrous in my two-inch wedges.

When I stood to read my essay, though, the shame faded away. I felt a flame spindle through me as I measured my story out to the audience, speaking with a power that felt like staring the universe in its lolling eye and demanding: *Look at me. This is who I am.*

I read, "The University of North Texas is the last place I ever wanted to end up," and paused, fate holding me steady to the floor. My mom sat with her second husband in the building she once dreamed she'd die in, the seam of time and place overlapping in her smile.

***

They almost didn't come.

A week before, we'd gotten into a drag-out fight on the phone, my mom muddling her words with tears and Mark interrupting to steal the phone out of her hand and scream at me through the receiver. The issue was one line in the essay, in which I described my mom "sitting in a broken chair in the garage, smoking cigarettes and watching preachers on television." When I wrote it, I thought it was innocent enough—I'd meant it as a descriptive detail rather than any kind of judgement. The image of her sitting in in front of the fuzzy, cracked flat-screen, the tin bucket full to brim with Marlboro ashes at her side, the menagerie of brown beer bottles resting on the dirt-streaked patch of carpet—they were as clear to me as anything from my youth, a fondness ingrained in the familiar. Most of all, it was the truth.

It didn't matter. Mark yelled through the phone, accusing me of "trying to gain recognition" for myself by exposing the "dirty secrets of their lives." My mom whined, "Why do you only write about the bad, depressing things, instead of all the good things we've done?"

My gut stretched around a boulder of terror and self-hatred. I thought I'd written something good, and maybe people were finally noticing. I thought I deserved to be excited about the reading, but any excitement I'd felt curdled in my throat, choked like sour curd.

Once Mark stomped off to another room, my mom reclaimed the phone. "Honey, I'm just saying I've changed. If people change, they shouldn't have to be portrayed as they were in the past. It's not fair." As if moving forward through the river of time demands the past be washed from the record, like it never left a mark at all.

***

A week after I graduate from UNT, two days after Christmas, I wake my mother at three a.m., shaking her shoulder and calling her *Mama* like I hadn't since I was a child. The tree is still plugged-in, casting its orange glow across the dining room. She packs me a tin of homemade chocolate-covered peanut butter balls, and Trinity sneaks one or two into her mouth with a smirk, her hair ratty from sleep.

I spent the previous day loading boxes into my used Kia, everything I owned but my twelve-year-old mattress and a bookshelf. I'm driving across the desert and up the coast to Seattle, where I've landed a publishing internship that begins after New Year's.

My mom says, "Hold on, I have something I planned to give to you," before shuffling to her bedroom. When she comes back, she's holding a small, blue velvet box.

"Grandma Helen brought this back from her travels," she says. "I must have been ten or eleven? Just a little older than Trin. And I kept it all these years. Even my grandmother's handwriting is still there."

Inside the box is a delicate silver ring, the thin band worn, like it could have once been gold. Crowning it, a silver flower, and a Star of David at its mouth, embellished with one tiny diamond. The note inside reads, in blue pen on faded blue paper: *Haifa Israel, 1976.*

"This is so beautiful," I say, hugging her. "Thank you."

"Well, I always said Grandma was my guardian angel, and now you'll have her keeping you safe on your trip."

A few minutes later, I sling my sunflower-printed duffle bag into the passenger's seat and feel a lump in my throat as I start the car, watching my mom and nine-year-old sister shrink as I pull away. I know, as I exit onto the highway, that when I come back, Texas won't be home any longer, just another place with some of the people I love inside it.

I try to slide the ring onto my finger, but the band is only wide enough to reach the knuckle. On my pinky, it's too loose, in danger of flying off with one eccentric hand gesture, so I jam it down over the meat of the thicker finger. I make it fit.

***

It took years after my father's death to realize how little I knew him. I learned that more than ever living in the city he lived in at my age, walking around and seeing the ghost of his youth in everything.

Here is the bar where he spent his weekends, sitting at the table in the corner with my mother and a group of friends. Here is Earl's Liquor on the outskirts of town, where he worked; it remained the same for all these years, until one day I drove past and it had become a 7-Eleven.

I was trying to excavate pieces of my dad, to learn who he'd been in that place and to predict what might become of me when Denton was another ghost in my rearview. In retracing his and my mother's steps, I was inadvertently examining their love story for some glaring catalyst—a foreshadow of their divorce, which led to his remarriage, which resulted in his murder. If I could map a clear line through to his fate, maybe I could avoid the same fate; and if I could avoid love's slow decay and sudden destruction, maybe I could live long enough to come to understand him.

After he came home from work, my father liked to spread out a bath towel and sit on the floor while he cracked peanuts between his teeth and watched the racecars on TV wind themselves around the asphalt track. One of my first truly clear memories is sitting in his lap as we watched the cars drive on an endless loop. He'd say, "If you were a racecar, you'd be the number one, because you were my first born. My number one."

These days, I sit on the floor in my living room, peeling sunflower seeds and watching reruns of *The Office*. This detail has given me more insight into who he was than any other echo of him I've tried to run from or chase down—different rituals, meaning the same thing: *I am an island.*

***

A year after I leave Texas for Seattle, I move across the country a second time, toward the opposite coast. There, in Kentucky, one of my great-grandmother's paintings hangs in my apartment: a seascape in lavender and blue that reminds me of wandering the stony beach, when I was lonely and afraid and alive, the Puget Sound a seething friend at my bedroom window.

My last day on that beach was gray and still as I parked by the sand. My car was stacked with the same boxes I had arrived with, a hoard of new books bulging from them. I stared in the direction of the lighthouse for a long time, trying to carve its silhouette inside my skull. During the summer, they open it for tours, allow people to climb inside and look out over the glistening cove. But I wouldn't be there to see summer.

In the glass jar that sits under my great-grandmother's painting, I collected shells and sea glass, souvenirs of a life I'd once belonged to. It's there under the painting the year I turn 23 and finish the first draft of a book about my father's murder; it's there when my life cracks open painfully gorgeous, when I fall in love with a place and a group of people, stumble into a makeshift home I've been aching, scraping for my entire life; it's there as I let grief flood in and wrack me until I become myself.

Years after that, the painting will follow me to Florida, where the jar of sea-glass sits on a windowsill overlooking legions of mystic, mossy trees, and later to a pink townhouse on the coast of South Carolina. I will still remember that gray day clearly, but it will seem a very long time ago.

A Thing That Should Be Beautiful

"There is a temptation to eulogize that which I do not understand and to think of a sister as a thing that should be beautiful. A thing that does not bleed at night. Whose horrors are lesser than or equal to my own. As if I could know my own."

—Alicia Jo Rabins, "Sister"

I was named for roots and nostalgia, a country whose tongue is knife and earth. My sister's name is bread broken and given, first my father's and then my mother's. Body and blood.

//

Our mother taught us songs to spell our names. They sounded suspiciously like jingles from cereal commercials.

//

She called me *Sissy*. I called her *Bissy*. We caught frogs in Grandma's backyard and named them after each other.

//

You were small and loud and bright, like a city filtered through a keyhole.

//

On the afternoon of my sister's wedding, we are drinking mimosas from paper cups in a stranger's kitchen. In an hour, she will get married in a stranger's living room. The doors and shutters are closed, and bodies are rustling outside. She is wearing white. My dress is black lace.

//

When you went to rehab, we found your toy box filled with cans of Budweiser and Four Loco, your backpack stuffed with aluminum and glass. Behind your dresser: eyeshadows stolen from Sephora, and a $1200 camera stolen from our mother.

//

I was sitting in my car in the Wendy's parking lot when she called and told me she was pregnant. She was freshly eighteen and dating her boyfriend for three months. I said: Holy shit, Jesus Christ. She said: I'm going to keep it. We hung up the phone and I cried.

//

Remember when we played house and dolls were children? When the rooster crowed we'd sit up from the carpet, wipe the fake sleep from the corners of our eyelids? And the rooster sounded like a villain in the basement of a haunted mansion?

//

When she came back from rehab, her hair was short and her face was the kind of gnarled swamp I've only seen in the eyes of evangelicals. She painted her walls blue and my mom bought her brand-new furniture. I locked my bedroom door at night.

//

Items at your wedding: Three Christmas trees. Two strings of pearls our mother wore at her wedding. A picture of our dead father on the fireplace mantle.

//

In a dirty Dollar General, my sister tells me the baby's name will be Gracelyn, and for days afterwards, my heart echoes: *Gracie.*

//

When we were young I promised you that once older and able, I would buy you a kitten. Now I have a cat, and you have two bloodhounds. You have a daughter, and I have only these stories.

//

When she was pregnant, I met her for lunch to convince her that she shouldn't disown our mother. She said our mom was weak, she didn't trust her with her child, didn't care. In the restaurant bathroom, she lifted her shirt and said: Feel, the baby's kicking.

//

Our dad called you the son he always wanted.

//

When my niece was born, my mom only saw her granddaughter through pictures on my phone. The neighbor's wife had a baby girl and my mother cried every day.

//

You were always the beautiful one.

//

The story goes: when she was a toddler, she bit me so hard she caused welts, drew blood. Our mom took us to the doctor, and the doctor said she would only learn to stop if I bit her back. I began to cry and said: But I could never hurt my little sister.

//

The story goes: I told you that you would fly if you jumped from the top of the swing-set, but you fell and broke your arm. When I saw the cast, glorious purple and waterproof, I practiced jumping from the fence every day.

//

You were always the beautiful one and you knew it.

//

Stephanie is a shame that lives in my blood, like my father; the shame of family members awful and loved and not loved well enough. The difference is in breath, in pulse. The difference is that she's alive, and there is no eulogy for the living.

//

In childhood we took our pets in twos, building an ark of animals Mom couldn't manage to say no to. After his death, we took a watch and a T-shirt each from the pile of what was left. How we mirror one another in items and absences, even now, across the continent. How one year, we forgot to feed our mice and they cannibalized each other, their cage silent on the desk in your bedroom.

//

My sister is an item on a to-do list, a trip to the post office, a story still moving, dancing, shifting like smoke.

//

I call you to ask what we called the sticks we used to beat our father with when he screamed at our mother, and you were too young, you don't remember, but I know it's not your fault.

My first car was a 1981 Chevy pickup truck. Mark came to my room and shook me awake, and as I shrugged off blankets and rubbed sleep from my eyes, I followed him downstairs, through the carpeted garage, into the front yard. Hazy and half-asleep, I didn't realize what I was doing when I felt the prickle of warm night air on my skin and the sandpaper burn of concrete on the soles of my feet. Standing in the driveway in my pajamas, I barely registered what was in front of me: the truck, its metallic blue shell glistening under the streetlights, next to my parents' wide, conspiring smiles. It was May, four months before my sixteenth birthday.

We took it for a test drive around the neighborhood. I sat in the passenger's seat, barefoot, childishly amazed at every blaring vrrroom and groan of the engine. The truck's asthmatic breath stuttered through my body as Mark explained:

"There are some things on it that need fixin' up. I've got a buddy who knows about cars and he said he'd help us do it. Are you gonna help?"

I nodded yes. Of course.

"I figured it would be something we could do together this summer," he said. "Do you like the truck?"

I didn't know how to possibly voice the extent of the YES that rang out inside of me, so I just said, "It's perfect." And it was.

When we got back to the house, I didn't slam the heavy door hard enough while getting out. He said, "Here, I'll show you how to do it. You've got to bump it closed, like this—" and rammed the side of his hip against the passenger's side door. There was a popping noise, like the sheets of aluminum used backstage during plays to create sounds of thunder, and my mother gasped in horror at the large dent his body had made.

I laughed. "It gives it character!" Mark agreed. After a mispronunciation of the central swashbuckler from *The Three Musketeers,* I named the truck *Dartanian.*

***

That first summer we propped Dartanian's metal hood open, took the whole engine apart and rebuilt it, inside out. Mark's friend Brad wore a slate-colored mechanic's uniform with his name sewn in cursive over the breast, like in the movies. We parked the truck in the side yard of his double-wide white-paneled trailer, alongside a picnic table, a rusted yellow tractor, and some portion of what seemed to have once been a go-cart. Plastic toys were strewn in the grass like buoys, though if he had any children, I never saw them.

We painted and sawed down rusted parts I still don't know the name of, replacing crumbling black fixtures with shiny new chrome. In our down time, we rode in Brad's air-conditioned Tahoe the three miles to the nearest AutoZone to pick up valves and sprockets, clean belts and filters that would replace Dartanian's decaying innards and bring renewed life to the thirty-year-old truck. Brad rarely spoke except to ask if we'd like sweet tea, or to correct my stepdad's amateur mechanical knowledge, and when he did speak it was always softly. He didn't seem to mind that there was a teenage girl and an ocean of bad spark plugs littering his yard for two months straight. When our work was finished, grease stains splattering our calloused hands and sunburnt faces, I revved the engine and it roared back, the rumble of victory reverberating off the trees, the grass, the gravel underfoot.

***

Dartanian was my liberation, my salvation, my time machine. A metal ship with the name of an explorer, he and I split open that small Texas town, the rubber petal pressed to the floorboard with a blazing restlessness. All the world belonged to me, as long as it had a paved road running through it. Those were the days when, after school let out, we sped past glossy suburban streets, out into the winding back roads, the windows cranked down by hand, the autumn wind a cyclone through my hair as I drove Rachel home, taking the long way. The engine bellowed, cranking out generous speed with labored breath. We turned the radio up over the blaring pound of the wheels, thunderous joyful music echoing like a swirling baptism of sound, and lo, for the first time in our short and frustrating lives we were well and truly free.

***

By the second summer, it seemed something was always breaking. Numerous times Rachel and I stopped at the gas station for a soda, only to find that the engine wouldn't start again, left stranded with no choice but to push Dartanian up the street, and wait inside until Mark or a tow-truck came to our rescue. It had no air conditioning, and I couldn't drive it long distances without getting a sunburn across the top of my thighs.

One month, the water pump broke and the engine overheated, leaving me in the middle of the street at two a.m. with smoke billowing up from under the hood. The next month it was the starter, and after that, the fly belt. (An old man at the gas station with overalls and a Santa beard fixed that one for me, with a crowbar he happened to have handy.) The fuel line got jammed, and I was cursing and pressing sharply on the pedal the whole drive, feeling out every subtle vibration of the engine like an art, praying and finagling and beating the hell out of the dashboard, hoping it wouldn't leave me stranded on the highway.

My mom, exasperated by the constant mechanical problems, offered, "You know, they're still doing that 'Cash for Clonkers' thing for another week. Maybe it's time to just trade it in and get what you can for it?"

"It's the only thing I've never given up on," I told her. "I've been through so much with it already, to sell it would be a waste."

Those were my excuses. Mark had his own for each time something broke:

"Well, I guess that's the *one* thing we didn't get around to replacing, and now you'll never have to bother with it again. Every part on that truck should be new now."

And the next month it was, "Every part on that truck should be new *now*."

***

I hung a poster on my dorm room wall that read: *There's still time to change the road you're on.* I stared at it as I sat paralyzed with anxiety in my twin bed, longing for the courage to make it true. I'd hoped, after a year at the community college fifteen minutes from where I grew up, that transferring to Baylor would solve me; I'd have friends, meet my soulmate, find my voice, fall into the drumbeat rhythm of the "college experience" at last.

I hated it. Other than my roommate, a football-loving Christian girl named Shelby who spent most weekends at her boyfriend's apartment in Temple, and her own friends she'd introduced me to, I had no friends to speak of. There were no clubs to join except for Greek Life, and the thirty pounds I'd gained from stuffing to-go boxes full with pizza from the campus dining hall made me feel too awkward and ashamed to try to meet people, itching with fear every time I spoke that they were looking at me and not seeing me at all, but some bumbling expanse of flesh, a morose shackle to their carefree lives of football games and frat parties. I was majoring in Neuroscience, but instead of studying the names of synapses, I spent nights sitting in the blue armchair in the corner of our living room, typing fragments of stories and poems on my laptop while Shelby watched detective shows on the ancient television.

During my visit home for Christmas break, I drove with Mark to the grocery store. He told me to drive us in Dartanian, wanting to see how the truck was holding up.

He said, "So, you're going to be a psychologist, huh?"

"Yeah, that's the plan."

"Do you like it?"

"Yeah, I guess. I'm learning a lot."

A pause.

"Is that what you're passionate about?"

"No," I answered honestly. "But I'll get a good job."

"What *are* you passionate about?" He asked.

"I don't know."

"What if you could do anything?"

"I would move to England and be a writer," I said, meaning it. "If I wasn't afraid of being homeless."

***

There is a photo. In it, Mark and I are hugging, him smiling proudly, my long, dark hair flowing down my back, my face smooshed into his shoulder. In my billowing purple robe, I have just graduated high school. Ten months since my dad died.

In those ten months, Mark's looming anger softened briefly, wore down like an old cotton T-shirt. My sister in rehab and back. My mother, too, would be going soon. Was he simply tired, or answerless? How to be gentle while watching your wife mourn another love, a different, deified piece of her past? Somehow he managed, between the twelve-hour night-shifts as a manufacturing mechanic and clanking of pans and TV noise and bodies shuffling through our home, to find a patient strength.

In the photo, it was seven years since I first met Mark, standing with my mother in our dim garage at night. He said my mom told him I write poems, that he writes poems too, and could he read mine? When he looked up at me, ten years old, over my purple spiral notebook and asked, "Do you really feel these things?" he was the only person who had ever asked.

***

I called in the morning, two days before they were expecting me home for spring break. My mom picked up the phone.

"Hey," I said. "I just wanted to let you know I'm going to drive home today instead of Friday. Maybe surprise Mark and Trin, since Mark was giving me a hard time about not coming up there until the weekend."

"I should tell you, something happened…" she sighed. "Mark's in jail."

The static on the line fell still.

"Are you still there?"

"Yeah, I need to call you back," I said, my voice strange and heavy.

I hung up the phone. I cried in the shower. I debated whether or not to even go back and see my family. My impulse was to drive four hours in the opposite direction, to end at the gulf and spend the week sleeping in my truck and not answering anyone's calls.

I drove home.

The story was different according to each person, but the general summary seemed to be this: While Stephanie was getting ready for school upstairs, she got into a screaming fight with my mom, and shouted down something snarky and malicious at Mark as he came in from the garage. He lunged up the stairs and confronted her—he said he "got in her face"; my mom said "attacked"; Stephanie said "strangled." Either way, the police were called. I suppose it must have been my mom who called them. When they arrived, they handcuffed Mark on the front lawn, in only his socks and underwear. Trinity hid in her bedroom closet.

***

I drove Trinity to visit Mark where he was staying, at his friend's house in the next town over, because she and I were the only ones exempt from the restraining order.

The air was stained with grief and guilt as soon as I pulled into the gravel drive. Trin hopped out of the truck, and although he smiled as if everything was normal, Mark hugged her for far too long. Dark circles rimmed his eyes, and everything about his presence seemed to be sliding downward. He began to cry. I stared at the seam of his shirtsleeve, feeling as though this was not something I should be allowed to witness.

I drove us to lunch in Dartanian, the whole ride Mark talking to Trin in a voice that curved upwards at the end, trying to convey enthusiasm. When he thought she wasn't paying attention, he kept muttering to me, "I just can't believe this. This is such a mess."

At Outback Steakhouse, the waiter sat us at a small table with tall chairs. He told Trin she could order anything on the menu; overcompensating the way divorced parents do, the way my dad used to when Stephanie and I visited him.

Over the Awesome Blossom, he asked, "No matter what happens, you'll still consider me your dad, right? You'll still keep in touch, and come see me?"

"Of course," I assured him.

Mark didn't cry again until Trin got back in the truck and I hugged him goodbye. As I drove down his street, Trinity tucked herself underneath my arm.

"I really don't want Daddy to live somewhere else," she said.

"It'll be okay," I kissed the top of her head, her sweaty hair, wishing I could do more. "How about we get some ice cream. Would ice cream make you feel better?"

She sniffled and wiped her eyes. "Yes," she said, sounding unsure.

***

When I got back to Baylor, I made the decision to transfer schools. I wanted to run and run far—not just from my family, but from my quiet desperation, from the conservative university where I could never make friends or a place for myself. I wanted to blow up my life, destroy it irreparably and reconstruct it into something I could live with. I decided to move to England. I changed my major to Creative Writing. I got the wrist tattoo I'd always wanted, the one my parents told me would prevent me from getting a job as a psychologist. In the angst of those weeks, I found a nihilistic freedom.

When I started sending applications to universities in the U.K., I began to have reoccurring nightmares about selling Dartanian. In my sleep, people took him away, trashed him, set him on fire. Each night I was at a car dealership, or trying to drive him across an ocean.

I loved that Dartanian was stubborn; he was falling apart piece by piece but for so long he'd fought being completely obliterated, and I was stubbornly fighting to keep him "alive." As much as I craved escape, I wondered if I could embark on a new life if it meant parting with something that had become an extension of my own existence.

***

There were talks that summer. Talks with my mom about whether she would ask for a divorce. Talks with Stephanie, brief and uncomfortable, about how she resented my mom for even considering taking him back, for "putting her in that position."

Once the restraining order ran out, my mom began to visit Mark at his friend's house on her lunch breaks. It was close to her work, and easier than driving the twenty minutes home, she said. Stephanie lashed out, feeling that my mom had chosen him over her.

I avoided talking to Stephanie. Maybe I shouldn't have. But her anger was so blinding and venom-drenched it was repellent to me. I'd spent my adolescence stuffing down my own despair, developing an emotional echolocation that could anticipate the smallest rise of pressure in our home, in order to de-escalate or flee before an eruption; the way she blew a hole in the atmosphere to claim space for her own feelings struck me, at the time, as disgustingly selfish.

I wished I could have been there for Trinity, to protect her— but I was far away, and busy planning ways to be farther.

***

At the end of that summer, I met my parents at the house where Mark lived. The sun filtered through the white kitchen. There were two brown glass bottles on the table, and Mark held my mom's hand. She was wearing her blue work polo and khakis, her hair pinned back in the familiar gold clip she'd worn my whole life.

She pulled x-rays out of a large envelope. "I have breast cancer," she said. It was her 46th birthday.

After that, the applications to England stopped, and so did the nightmares.

***

When Stephanie and I were young, my mother made an effort to be *open* with us. She said she didn't want to be like her own mother, who was prudish and closed-off, never let her children see her as human. This mostly manifested in her walking around the house naked, until Mark jokingly hollered out, "Put some clothes on, woman!" and the lot of us laughed like child actors in an off-center sitcom.

Trinity is eight, and when she puts on my mom's bra and walks around the house, laughing and pretending she has "big boobies," Mark gets angry. He doesn't approve of her fascination with when or how or why she will grow breasts.

Trinity has learned a lot about breasts after watching my mom lose hers to cancer. Through some unspoken congress, my family has decided that of two undesirable conversations, it is more appropriate to talk about breasts than about death. I listen silently as my mother explains the tubes that drain fluid from her sides, and how the doctor will cut off a section of her earlobe to form a new nipple during reconstruction. Mark is at her bedside, emptying her fluid-and-pus-filled bags, bringing her water, and sleeping on the couch while she recovers.

These are the things she talks about because these are the questions we ask. She says the reconstruction is the most painful part, and we don't ask why she chose to do it, when she is in her late forties and has a husband and can no longer have children.

A few days after the diagnosis, I drove her to work. She said, "You know what's weird? When I found out, the first thing I thought of was how much I hate all that pink ribbon stuff. I think it's stupid."

"You don't have to start liking it just because you have breast cancer now. You're allowed to hate it, if you want to. I mean, you're still the same person," I said.

She sighed, "Yeah, I know."

A few months later, our house is covered in pink ribbons and things that say *Survivor* on them. My mom drinks tap water from a pink mug while she is on bed rest, recovering from her surgery. My mother is alive, and she is alive because she gave up a part of her body. But looking at those pink ribbons, I feel an ambiguous sense of loss.

***

I finally sold Dartanian after my mother's cancer diagnosis, after I moved closer to home and transferred to UNT, when it got broken into and trashed in my apartment's parking lot; its old locks had never worked, and someone finally noticed.

A year or two later, I reminisced with Rachel over everything we'd done together because of Dartanian, how the freedom of our youth lived and died in that cab, when grass and gravel were the only gravity we knew. "What I remember most about riding in your truck was always feeling like I was going to die," she said, sitting on my apartment floor with a glass of whiskey and coke in her hand. "But, like, in a good way."

It can be hard to decipher the difference between giving up and moving on. When I'm sitting in my air-conditioned Kia, driving quietly down the highway, I'm aware that I've sold out a piece of myself. I don't know if we can trust ourselves to know when it's time to let go or to dig the claws of our loyalty in deeper. I know my life is certainly more comfortable now, but I don't know if an interesting and meaningful life can be made out of comfortable experiences.

What I do know is this: sometimes as I'm driving I'll see a truly wrecked antique car, pumping out fumes and stuttering with every exhausted revolution of the tires, rumbling a shockwave that spreads like bathwater over the asphalt, and I'll feel a sudden, warm longing as it passes me and disappears around the corner.

Wingless Requiem

They hung from a string, one after the other like rungs of a ladder, each separated by two faded green beads. Wrapped in red, black, and yellow cloth, different patterns adorning each, sequins sewn into the sides—something you might see hanging from a flea market stand to remind touristy Americans of an East Asian country they've never been to, or in a bohemian loft with a beaded chandelier and a mattress on the floor.

It may be hard to tell that they're birds from far away. The wingless torsos could easily be croissants, or little boats. At the bottom of the string hangs a small metal cowbell, painted rustic gold. When the birds sway, the bell rattles softly, like one isolated note of a wind chime.

They were simple birds and I liked them. I must have liked them, to have picked them out from my father's things on my grandmother's dining room floor the week of his funeral. I don't remember thinking about it—I'd be moving away from home and into an apartment soon, I probably figured, and liked them for their aesthetic value. It's not impossible that I was considering the décor of my future apartment even at that moment, with the black garbage bags spilling over our laps and the plush white carpet. Stephanie and I each took one of his watches and a T-shirt. I took some other things, practical things, and the birds. I didn't think about them again for a long time.

***

My father hated the birds. When the package arrived, my sister and I were visiting his house for winter break, so I was there to witness the confusion and slight revulsion that contorted his face as he walked into the living room holding a cardboard box.

"Look at this," he said, pulling them up out of the box to show us.

"What kind of present is this supposed to be?" The package was from his father, my Grandpa Chuck, who lived in a trailer outside of Las Vegas. There was no card, just a folded slip of paper that read: *Happy Birthday!* My dad's birthday had been three months before.

"I think my dad is losing it," he said, holding the string with pinched fingers like a dirty washrag.

"What is it?" my sister asked.

"Some hippie crap," he said. "The tag says you're supposed to hang them by your front door and the bell will ring to warn you of evil spirits coming into your house."

"That's kind of cool," I said, perking up at the superstitious backstory. But although my father was well-acquainted with fear, he had no patience for entertaining the idea of ghouls.

"I mean, what kind of gift is that?" he said. "I really think your grandpa is losing it."

That night, he closed the box and stored it away in the coat closet, but the next summer when we came to visit, the birds were hanging by his front door.

***

Though in her nineties, Grandma Irma, my paternal grandmother, is hawk-sharp and undeniably full of life, her large brown eyes twinkling in her wrinkled olive skin. She's round and sturdy in a way that makes you think she could arm-wrestle somebody and still have a fighting chance, but too elegant to bother, dressed in finely pressed khakis, watching a Chicago Bulls game on the small plasma TV in her condo, surrounded by mirrored shelves that display her prized porcelain Lladros. Grandma Irma speaks with frankness in her Illinois accent, her consonants stretching high and steely as skyscrapers.

I call and explain the birds to her, ask if she ever noticed them; when my dad was alive, they lived just a few minutes from each other, and she was in his house often.

"I have no idea what you're talking about, I never saw any birds at his door," she says. "But when Chuck moved out to Vegas, he used to do some very strange shopping."

She tells me that my dad and aunt made a sport of comparing the wild gifts their dad sent them: used children's toys from garage sales, disco balls with black gap-teeth, bulky aquariums for magnetic fish—and one Christmas, gingerbread houses, the plastic covered in a thick layer of dust, the cookie inside so crusty that Aunt Deb yelled at my cousin for trying to unwrap it, convinced if he bit down it would break his teeth.

"Why do you think it started when he moved to Vegas?"

"Well, Chuck would go to these weird resale shops with Ray, because Ray never had money to buy anything new. When they came to visit, Ray made me take him to a resale shop just to buy socks and underwear."

"So you think Ray influenced him to buy these things?"

"I think Ray influenced him," she says, "plus, the alcohol fried his brain."

***

I don't know much about my dad's relationship with his own father, in part because I didn't know my grandfather very well. When I was seven or eight we traveled to Las Vegas on vacation, and I have a memory of Grandpa Chuck on a dock, newly wheelchair-bound from the diabetes that took his foot, holding me over the water by my ankles while I attempted to catch a catfish with my bare hands. That night, we went to a barbeque restaurant and ate ribs with him and Ray, his roommate of twenty years (who everyone insists was *only* a roommate).

We didn't visit Grandpa Chuck again, and when I was eleven, he died. I didn't go to the funeral. It was as if a stranger had died, and I remember my response surprising me. I didn't know, until then, that I was capable of seemingly inappropriate apathy.

***

Ray and Chuck met while my grandparents were still married, working for the same printing company in downtown Chicago. After the divorce, my grandfather bought a three-floor apartment building in the city, and Ray became his tenant: Ray lived on the bottom floor, Chuck lived on top, and a young white couple lived on the middle floor between them. Chuck liked that Ray was a good cook, so Ray would take the elevator up to Chuck's apartment to cook him dinner a few nights a week, and soon they struck a deal: Ray would move into Chuck's apartment and do all the cooking and housework, and Chuck would take care of the cars and manage the building repairs. It was the same agreement they kept when Chuck retired and Ray moved with him to Las Vegas.

My grandmother insists Chuck never had a drinking problem until after their divorce; before, he'd had a demanding job, and she speculates that once he was no longer required to hold himself to its standards, he crashed. Grandma Irma describes his Vegas years as one long, debauched party, two old men pressing each other to the brink to see who would break the cycle first. Neither of them gave, and the days rolled away from them.

"When the kids were growing up, Chuck would take your dad to Cub Scouts, he was involved in the church and would do activities with him there," she says. "I mean, we were a perfectly happy, close-knit family. There's no getting around it. We were really very happy."

***

This is what I knew about Grandpa Chuck: he grew up very poor, and walked to school through the snow without shoes, the stories say. When they were newlyweds, my grandma worked to pay his way through college, and sacrificed finishing her own degree. They had two children: my dad and his older sister, Deborah. When my dad was in his twenties, my grandparents amicably divorced.

This is what I knew about Ray: A few years after my grandpa died, he discovered he was HIV positive, and shot himself inside of that trailer in the desert. By the time his body was discovered, it had been sweltering in the heat for days. Because the trailer was registered in my grandpa's name, my dad went to Nevada to empty and sell it. The stories say that they found VHS tapes with child pornography in Ray's closet.

My dad said he cried out there in the desert—not for his father, whom he resented for willing his life and everything in it over to Ray; not for Ray, whom he loathed—but because the world smelled of death and waste and he wanted so badly to go home and forget.

***

"There was never any child pornography," my grandma corrects me. "Your dad and I flew to Nevada to clean up the trailer together. I looked through every bit of that house and I never saw any pornography." She pauses for a minute and adds, "There *were* girly magazines."

She tries to summon up the name of a "popular rag" Chuck and Ray kept copies of in the house. I guess *Playboy*, but she says no.

"*National Enquirer*," she remembers. "You know, with the aliens and political figures who are lizard people and that nonsense. Chuck liked those gossip magazines."

Chuck left the trailer in my dad's name, and after the hazmat crew had come and gone with Ray's remains, he and my grandma got to work cleaning it up to sell. A week of long days hauling trash through the desert barely made a dent in the hoarders' palace Ray had turned it into. My grandmother recalls wax splatters caked like waterfalls on the walls, where Ray burned candles down to their nubs.

"Yes, Deb told me he had AIDS, but he didn't kill himself because of that; he killed himself because he had no money and no way to get it."

It was no secret Grandpa Chuck had been supporting Ray for years, and when my grandfather died and left only a small checking account, Ray was nearing his seventies with a ten-year gap in his resume and no retirement fund. He'd filed for disability and used those funds towards their bar and gambling debts, but a few months before Chuck died, he got a letter in the mail informing him that he was being sued by the government for falsely claiming to be injured, and would need to pay back thousands of dollars he didn't have.

When Chuck told Irma—long divorced but still friendly—that he was going to pay off Ray's debt, she hollered at him to think about what he was throwing away.

"If I don't bail him out, where's he going to get the money?" Chuck argued. "Where else on this earth is he going to go?"

***

Grandpa Chuck was raised in Shinnston, West Virginia: a sawmill, coalmine, oilwell town, host to the deadliest tornado in West Virginia history on June 23, 1944, when my grandpa was thirteen, which killed over a hundred people and lifted the West Fork River from its bed.

Chuck's father was an alcoholic, a "mean son of a bitch who beat his wife and drank his paycheck rather than feed his kids," as my grandma tells it. A rough coal miner, a "nasty man." His mother was a "sweet woman" who ran away to marry her decade-older husband at age thirteen. When he began to abuse her, she escaped to her family's house, only to be turned away because they were so angry about the elopement. She was their oldest daughter, and it had been her responsibility to marry respectably so they'd be taken care of in their old age. She was ruined; she was stuck with him.

Unsurprisingly, my great-grandfather abused his kids, too, tossing them into walls and tables like a blockbuster monster batting away pedestrians as it stomps through the city.

"Chuck's dad only really beat him up once," Grandma Irma says, "and then said he'd never do it again. He said Chuck was too scrawny, and he knew that if he went in on him, he wouldn't be able to help himself—he would end up killing him."

***

The first gash in the felled tree of my grandparents' marriage was when Chuck came to Irma, unprompted, and declared they would be retiring in West Virginia. She told him in blunt terms that there was no way she'd be doing that. He retorted, mired in midcentury machismo: "You're my wife and you'll go wherever I tell you to go."

Grandma Irma pushed back, and they got into an argument that ended with Chuck throwing a couple clean shirts in his car and taking off to West Virginia for a week, threatening as he pulled out of the driveway that he might just check out the real estate in Shinnston, he might just buy a piece of land while he was there.

I guess Grandpa Chuck considered this the beginning of the end, too, because Ray brought it up to my grandmother years later. "I don't know what the big deal is," he'd said, "I'd have been more than happy to go out to West Virginia with him."

As she tells me the story, she can't help but laugh. "Can you imagine? I mean, Tennessee is bad enough." She'd moved to a suburb of Nashville against her will four years ago, when my aunt decided to retire there, and she never gained her sea-legs for Appalachia.

"I told Ray if he liked it so much, he could go and move there. Can you imagine," she laughs, "me with those *hillpeople*?"

"Is that what led to the divorce?"

There is a weighty silence before she answers.

"Your grandfather didn't like the fact that I gained a backbone." She pauses. "Do you want to hear about that?"

***

Grandma Irma's first and greatest love has always been numbers, but she gave up the chance at a degree in accounting so that Grandpa Chuck could get his college degree instead. "We were newlyweds, and we were in love; it didn't bother me at the time. It was just what people did," she says.

The years went on, Chuck got a job, and Irma worked in his office. Throughout their marriage, she handed over her paycheck to him, and he took care of the bills. It was what people did. But when she began moving up in the company, gaining admiration at work, Chuck became resentful. She was asked to join the company bowling league, who played after work one night a week. But Chuck forbade it.

"You're not doing that," he said, "because you've got to fix me dinner." Being a practical woman, she came up with a plan: she'd make dinner the night before and leave it in the fridge so it would be there waiting for him when he got home.

But he refused: "When I get done with work, you're supposed to be there to pick me up at the train station and then be here, in my house, cooking me a meal."

"Too late," she told him. "I already signed up. I'll be home before eight."

On the nights she went bowling, Chuck went out to get drunk with Ray and the guys from work, stumbling home angry and reeking. She started running the numbers—putting her preferred language down on paper, the numerals like ants she could marionette into neat columns at her will—to see if she'd be able to make it on her own. When the numbers assured her she could, she went to her husband and asked for a divorce, telling him she didn't want child support or alimony, only a promise he would pay for their children's education, as she had done for him.

She says she's always regretted not going back to finish her degree, still dreams of the opportunities that would've opened to her if she had.

"There's still time," I tell her. "Why don't you? Even if you don't have the degree, you still have years of experience. You could do part-time bookkeeping online."

She sighs, "You have to realize, my age works against me. People don't think a ninety-two-year-old woman knows what she's doing."

"Still," she says, a familiar pang of hunger in her voice, "I'd just love to get my hands on a set of books that are out of balance. I'd do it for free. I'd just love to get my hands on a set of books and make the numbers work."

***

It was a story I'd heard before: when she finished high school, she worked out a plan for college—she would live at home for free, calculated commute times and train fare, and portioned her savings to pay for books. All she needed was her parents' help with tuition, but her stepfather refused to pay it because she was a woman.

"Spend all that money and all you'll do at the end is get married, it's a waste," he told her. I've heard the story before, but it doesn't make me ache for her any less now.

Then, the tone in her voice shifts, and she says, "My stepdad was the best thing that ever happened to me. I'd still be back in Tacoma washing dishes if not for him."

My grandmother was born in Washington state and spent her childhood being passed between her aunt and her paternal grandmother (her namesake). Great-great-grandma Irma made sure her son stayed out of her granddaughter's life. "I got the sense he was a bad man," she says about her father. "I never had even a glimmer of a relationship with him, although I knew who he was, what he looked like. When he came over to the house, my grandmother would give me money and tell me to go to the movies."

Her mother, Anne, was a "flapper" who spent her days and nights trailing through bars. One night, when the younger Irma was six weeks old, Anne came home drunk and nursed her, and she turned blue. After poisoning her child, the doctor told Anne she couldn't both drink and feed the baby, so that decided it: Anne abandoned her daughter.

When my grandma was nine, her aunt called to say she'd taken a night-shift job while her husband was deployed at war, and she needed Irma to come live with her to babysit her infant son. After she got home from school, her aunt would make her a snack and then head off to work, and Irma would care for the baby alone until two a.m., when her aunt returned. "That baby still calls me!" my grandma laughs, eighty years distant from that awful time.

Her aunt was the closest thing she had to a mother, but her uncle was an abusive drunkard, and found entertainment in torturing Irma. My grandmother was left-handed, which her uncle deemed "unnatural," and refused to let her eat unless she used her right hand for everything. With her non-dominant hand, her handwriting would stumble out unintelligible, and wasn't coordinated enough to use a fork, so she often went to bed starving. During one of his drunken rages, he hit her with a piece of plywood that left a scar she still carries. Her aunt's pleas and attempts to protect my grandmother only seemed to make him lash out more.

By the end of the war, Anne had remarried. It was Anne's new husband, her stepfather, who insisted Irma rejoin their family. She describes him as a kind, mustachioed man, shaped by his time in the Navy, when he found himself stranded in the Atlantic for twelve hours, listening to screams ricochet across the water as sharks picked off the men around him.

When she was twelve, my grandmother moved with them to Chicago, and was miserable; she missed the friends she'd grown up with, hated the slicing-cold wind, and was homesick for her aunt. She remembers her first Christmas in Chicago, when her aunt sent her a sweater and skirt, and she wore the outfit nearly every day to remind her of the one person who loved her.

Her stepdad worked as an accountant, and would gladly sit with her at the table for hours to help her with her math homework. It was he who planted her passion for numbers, and he who took her dream away. I ask her if she ever confronted him about it in the years after.

"Oh, sure, I'd dig at him a little," she says. "He'd just laugh and say I was probably right." Her tone is light, but I can hear the frustration in her voice. "I always told him, if he'd only sent me to college, there'd have been no stopping me."

***

Even now there are missing pieces in her story, things she wishes she'd asked her mother: why she gave her away, why she had her in the first place, when she began abandoning herself to the bottle. All Anne told her is that she'd tried to have her aborted: she borrowed money from her boss at the coffee shop for the procedure, but Irma's father found out and threatened to turn the doctor in to the police, so the doctor refused to do it.

Anne babysat her grandchildren only once: she accidentally zippered

Deb's skin into a snowsuit, and later, Irma and Chuck found a bottle of whiskey tucked in the diaper bag.

Grandma Irma tells me, "I confessed to the parish priest and asked, 'Is it more important to honor thy mother and father, or to protect your children from harm?' She was never allowed alone with the kids again when she was drinking, but I don't believe she reached a day in her life when she wasn't drinking."

These stories confirm what I have always known in theory: I am spawned from generations upon generations of people who abandoned themselves to the desperate need within them, and abandoned everything else in their life to surrender to that need. Aside from my grandmother, who only sips an occasional glass of rosé, addiction is in every drop of the blood that begat me. I can feel it there, transubstantiated in my center, as I come home from the bar, groping for the light, and knock against the birds hung next to my door—the bell trilling at the arrival of a ghost who is always only me.

I have not harmed a spouse, or given away a child, but there is a wide, deep rot in me that craves absolute abandonment to anything that glitters like salvation. My bloodline is *half in love with easeful death*, as the Keats poem goes—a lineage of faces peering into the stained-glass hallway of a bottle for the glimpse of an intoxicating flutter: darkling, swallow.

***

After Grandpa Chuck died, as my grandmother tells it, Ray began to harass the family.

"It was like he assumed we were his new family, like when Chuck died, he got to inherit all his children and grandchildren. He called your mom over and over, too—I remember Mary getting very upset about it, and your dad had to take over and have words with Ray."

She believes Ray thought if he stayed close to Chuck's family, they would continue to support him financially, the way Chuck had. "It got to the point where I had to get on the phone with him and threaten him. I told him, 'You are to have no contact with this family whatsoever.' I told him, 'We are not your family.'"

I ask, "Why did everyone hate Ray so much? Was it just because of the money, because you saw him as mooching off Grandpa Chuck?"

She takes a moment to think, and I wonder for the first time if this is difficult for her, to remember her ex-husband and what became of him in his last years.

"Yes, the money, but there was more to it than that," she finally says. "Ray didn't care for your grandfather the way he should have. When all was said and done, he was only out for himself. He was...a predatory person."

She explains that in the last years of Chuck's life, Ray had power of attorney over his healthcare—it was a matter of convenience more than anything, Chuck assured them. They lived together, spent every day together, and if something were to happen, Ray would be right there. But when Chuck's diabetes escalated, and the doctor said he shouldn't drink, Ray enabled him to keep going. If Chuck no longer drank it meant Ray would have to stop, too; it meant their endless desert party would be over.

When Chuck's foot went gangrenous and had to be amputated, Ray packed him in the car with his wheelchair and drove to the Vegas strip, where they'd sit drinking and playing slots in a mid-day fog of pinging lights and stale smoke.

I finally ask the question I know she's braced for: "I know you don't like to talk about this—and Dad especially got angry if we asked—but what do you think was going on between Grandpa and Ray? Do you think they were more than friends?"

"I don't know," my grandma says, and repeats the line she has always answered this question with: "All I know is he wasn't gay when he was married to me."

I don't bother trying to explain the Kinsey scale, and continue, "Well, sure, but do you think there was, like, a romantic relationship there, even if it wasn't sexual? Twenty years is a long time to live with someone who's just a friend."

"Well, Ray was gay, of course. We all knew that."

In the obituary I pull up online later, Ray is listed as my grandfather's "companion." The memorial I didn't go to, back when I was eleven, was held in their trailer, and donations were asked to be given, simply, "to charity."

"Do you think Ray was in love with Chuck?" I ask.

"Yes," she says, so quickly it surprises me. "But your grandfather, I don't know. He wasn't gay when we were married, but I can't say what he did in the years after. I saw how they were together, and it didn't seem like Chuck returned his feelings. I think he was lonely, and liked having someone to drink with. And then he got sick, and his life depended on Ray."

"But I don't know," she says. "In the end, no one knows what they really were to each other."

***

I call my mother, who is stripping off galoshes after cleaning the chicken coop. I ask her about Ray.

"Yeah, I remember Ray calling after Chuck died," she says. "I think it was after your grandmother had words with him. He said, 'You and me are the outsiders. I thought you'd understand.' But I told him I didn't understand him. Honestly, I couldn't stand the man."

"Why did you dislike him so much? Other than him taking advantage of Grandpa Chuck—which it sounds like he did, to some degree."

"When you were a baby and we lived in Las Vegas, he and Chuck came over for dinner a couple times, but he made me really uncomfortable. He would always comment on how you had 'the cutest little butt'—he said the same things about Deb's boys, too. He was so over the top with it, like he was infatuated."

"Are you sure it didn't just bother you that he was gay?"

"No—I mean, him being over the top like he was, maybe that was a gay thing, I don't know," my mom says, "but it seemed out of the ordinary. He gave me the feeling like…oh, what's that word—when adults are attracted to kids?"

"Pedophile?"

"Yeah, he gave me the feeling he was a pedophile."

I ask her about the story I'd heard somewhere long ago, the one my grandma had denied, and she confirms: "Yes, there was child pornography in Ray's closet. Your father told me he found it there after Ray died. Photos, I think."

"Dad told you that?"

She sighs, "Yeah, but at the same time, your dad wasn't all *there*. It was during that time after the divorce when I'd heard from people in Alabama that he lied and told everyone I was living with you girls in a trailer in Oklahoma, and that I was pregnant and didn't know who the father was, all this crazy stuff. And then he totally went off on Quato."

Quato was a family friend during my childhood in Alabama: a tall, handsome Black man who worked with my dad, whose wife was short, blonde, and white, like my mother. I remember having my palm read on Halloween at his house, and playing Neopets with his teenage daughter on the computer upstairs while the adults held a cocktail party below. When we moved, our family lost touch with Quato's, and after the divorce, my dad called him up and accused him of sleeping with my mom during my dad's 40th birthday party.

"The only thing that happened at that party is your dad got so drunk he passed out with his head in the toilet bowl, and Quato had to help me carry him to bed," she says.

I tell her, briefly, what I've learned from Grandma Irma about Chuck's family and about Anne, the long lineage of addiction and abuse. "Did Dad ever mention Grandpa Chuck's alcoholism influencing his own? Did he ever talk with you about his family history?"

"Your dad always felt he had something wrong with him," she answers.

"Wrong with him how?"

"Wrong with his mind. He always felt there was something…not right within him. He called his drinking problem a '*hereditary defect.*'"

***

Once, when my father was visiting his father in Las Vegas, my grandfather fell ill. My dad sat with him by the false fireplace in the trailer's central room, as Chuck shivered in his wheelchair, and a wild party raged around them.

My dad was trying to speak over the noise, but Chuck seemed lost in a feverish daze, his hands trembling as they gripped the arms of the chair.

"Dad, are you cold? Do you need me to go find you a blanket?" he might have asked.

Grandpa Chuck nodded, and my dad went searching for something to cover him up with. He found Ray in the kitchen and told him his dad was obviously sick, that Ray needed to call off the party and get rid of all the people so Chuck could rest.

Ray told him to mind his own business—screamed at my dad that it was his house and nobody but him got a say in what went on there, then headed to the bathroom to snort a line of something powdered.

It is not because my grandmother tells me this story, but because my father never got the chance to, that I hang up the phone and cry.

***

My dad's relationship with his own father may have been complicated, especially in those last years—the bird-giving, forgotten birthday years—but still, the birds hung by his front door. They remained there until he sold his house and moved in with Pam, where their home was already furnished with her things.

When I hung the birds in the first place I lived on my own, a bedroom in a shared house with a gun enthusiast and his pottery-making girlfriend, it was because I liked how they looked. I wasn't hanging them for my dad. I already had a box of his things in the closet that I was unsure how to feel about: my Awkward Daddy Shrine of postmortem belongings hidden behind a framed picture of him smiling from a helicopter.

Despite their origin, despite the guilt and confusion that came with inheriting them, the birds have hung in every place I've lived; that first house that smelled of raspberries, a dorm room, multiple apartments, a cramped bedroom in a seaside town, the spare room where I wrote in Kentucky, beside the door of my crumbling Florida bungalow, and here.

Even now, they're still here: lined up front to back, dangling eyeless larks—warning of what spirits thrash their wings against the door.

HUNGER

"...as if keening on your knees were somehow obscene...as if there were a control so marvelous you could teach it to eat pain."

–Maggie Nelson, *Jane: A Murder*

Holes

When I was in third grade, I began wearing my mom's black cardigan, borrowed out of the dark recesses of our coat closet, the one we'd stumble into hastily to huddle under the stairs during a tornado warning. I chewed up the sleeve of that cardigan, laced the black thread through my molars, sucked my own saliva from the cotton like a feverish waif on her deathbed. In a matter of days, it hung from my arm in two jagged halves, like a split flank of raw meat.

When my mom found it stuffed behind my laundry hamper, she was shocked; specifically, she said it looked like it had been eaten through by a family of mice. Or maybe I thought that myself—imagined an army of long-bodied rodents slipping into my bedroom, summoned psychically through the walls and floorboards to lend me their fangs. Now, the texture of wet yarn makes me gag.

I chewed holes into everything as a child; I decimated bendy straws, the edges of plastic cups, fingernails, hoodie laces, shirt collars—anything in proximity to my mouth I took into it, gnawed at it, left it mangled. I wonder now if this was about hunger, a simple oral fixation, or the insatiable desire to leave some trace of myself on everything I touched. Proof that it had crossed my path and I had changed it, that I had been somewhere and it had mattered.

Carving myself into existence by leaving panicked bitemarks on the pieces of my world.

Stephanie was in sixth grade and I was in ninth when she brought home the fainting game. A girl who lived three streets over told Stephanie about it on the bus one day. "People play it at sleepovers," she said. We retreated into Trinity's disused nursery which had become, mostly, a space where junk collected, marshmallow purple with a Winnie the Pooh border.

"So you squat down against, like, the wall or something, and you take deep breaths, really fast, ten of them," she demonstrated. "Then you stand up fast and hold your breath and someone pushes hard on your chest or the top of your stomach and then you faint."

"You really faint?" I asked.

"Yeah, for a second."

"How do you know it works?"

"I've done it." It was like she'd told me she had done cocaine.

"You do me first," she said, and squatted down, hyperventilated her breath, stood quickly, and I pinned her against the closet door, my hands pressing into her chest like I was performing CPR. Her eyes rolled and fluttered closed, then her body went slack and floated to the ground. Seconds later, she stirred from unconsciousness, as if waking up from a nap.

"My turn," I said.

***

This was perhaps the most innocent, the most like fun, of the ways I performed my adolescent longing for hurt. I had not known much else in the parts of my short life I could remember, except for occasional periods of numbness. Most people would probably describe it as feeling normal, content. I would have described it as gray-tinted complacency.

Luckily, there was plenty of gleaming red drama and bottomless blue emptiness to fill out my life, and if I began to find myself feeling content, I knew that some deep and impossible pain was on its way. In sixth grade, I manifested my identity as a misunderstood-miserable-damaged-girl by rubbing pen caps across my wrist until they bore pink stripes that burned if I placed a finger over them. I hid the wounds under plastic bracelets; a dangerous secret about my body that only I knew. The newfound autonomy delighted me.

Until my parents found the scars, and threatened to send me away.

"You're going to stop this," Mark boomed, "or we'll take you somewhere and they'll sort you out. If we ever find out you're doing this again."

"Do you want to be wearing these bracelets at your graduation?!" my mother cried, approaching hysterical.

"I don't know," I said, and apologized. I threw away the bracelets, secretly treasured my shameful scars, though I wasn't sure why I had created them in the first place.

***

When I woke from my first faint, I almost didn't believe it had happened. The last thing I remembered was my sister standing in front of me, pressing down on my heart, backlit by sunbeams, and then my face was on the scratchy beige carpet and I was gasping for breath and giggling. It was amazing to know what my body was capable of, like unlocking some forbidden secret. Like this was a long-held conspiracy we had stumbled upon, the fact that no one had told us we could do this to ourselves, induce a swoon, make a child's game of our physical state. I liked the sore, heady feeling that came after, the secret blush of rug burns on my legs.

"Don't tell Mom and Mark," Stephanie said.

"Duh."

***

When I recall being a teenager, I think only of helplessness. And yes, there was love in our home, too; Mark making breakfast burritos for my friends and I the morning after a sleepover, dancing goofy and snapping our legs with a dish towel to make us squeal. There were our three boxers romping in the backyard, chasing a soccer ball, and my mother pulling weeds with pink floral gloves.

But the walls were heavy with tension and uncertainty. Mark would often boom in after work, covered in grease, shaking the whole house. Our bedrooms were above the staircase, and Stephanie and I knew immediately who was coming up and how afraid we should be based on the cadence of the footsteps. If they were heavy and slow, he was probably just coming up to tell us dinner was ready, or to check if our rooms were clean. If we heard the door to the garage slam, and it was followed by a stampede, there was hell to pay; all we had on our side were those three seconds to anticipate the verbal battering, think of every wrong we could have possibly done, and brace for what came next: A door ripped open. A voice like a bomb gouging you from your bed. Spittle flying from his beard. Confiscating your phone, your makeup, your privacy, your tiny, fragile freedoms.

In these instances and others, when I fell so deep into the sinkhole of despair that I couldn't stand to be inside of my own life, I did strange things to cope. I would sleep backwards in my bed, my head where my feet usually went. I'd turn on my stereo and lie with my face close to the speakers—so close that I could hear the intimate, tiny inhale of breath the singer took before belting out the next line—and play the same CD on repeat. Or I would pull my blankets off my bed and sleep on the floor, sometimes draw crosses or hearts or song lyrics on pieces of paper and lay them next to me, making an altar for my impenetrable sadness.

When I was fifteen, I wrote in my journal: I *think the problem is that I can get so stressed out and don't cry that I overload and have freak attacks…* and listed some of these strange behaviors I was prone to, these "freak attacks":

Biting my hands raw when I'm crying really hard, scratching myself, eventually made a pallet of blankets on the floor next to the boom-box, slept next to a piece of paper I made that said "I love Jesus" or "I love God" or something like that. Turned on music, went into my closet, pacing and doing high-knees with my legs, couldn't stop moving, cut myself on my right hip, rocking back and forth, ended up in the fetal position on the closet floor afraid to come out. Spelling out words over and over obsessively in my hand.

***

After school, my friend Dylan came over and we showed him the fainting game.

"You do it first," he said, "then maybe I'll try it."

Stephanie went down fast and hard, as usual. After my turn, I came to on my back, hallucinating squirrels and birdsong. I saw Stephanie and Dylan laughing in the doorway. Had I fallen asleep there? I didn't remember laying down, but it almost made sense. I faintly heard my mom call out from downstairs, "What did I just hear fall up there?"

We replied, in unison, "Nothing!"

I noticed my head was moving, bobbling up and down involuntarily.

"Yeah, that happens sometimes," my younger sister said, knowingly.

***

In seventh grade, I made out with a boy and thereafter was so disgusted by him that if he was in the room with me, I could barely sit still. I rubbed my palms raw, rolling the skin from them with hot friction, spelling out words over and over in my head and scratching their letters into my cupped hand to distract myself.

In seventh grade, I kissed Ryan in the woods behind the undeveloped part of our subdivision—the first time another person's tongue had touched my tongue—and a wasp stung me on the soft white flesh of my stomach, and he sunk down on his knees, kneeling in the wet leaves and twigs, and removed the stinger with his teeth.

After, I rode my bike home and said goodbye to him in the driveway, messy Maybelline eyes fluttering with want. My stepdad stomped my wobbly new joy when I walked up into the garage, where he sat on the old futon, a cigarette in his mouth, and growled out in his southern drawl with three-fourths hate and one-fourth amusement, “That boy’s a faggot.” And I told him *no* but spent the night heavy with dread, and by the end of the week, I was sitting on the metal slide at the neighborhood playground and Ryan was telling me he was gay—the first of many beautiful gay boys I would fall in one-sided love with over the next ten years, boys with kind eyes, artful hands and bright, gushing hearts, boys who would go to prom with me, or take me to their church, or write me songs, or get high enough to fuck me on their bedroom floor. Boys that smelled like cinnamon or sea salt or Christmas trees, who filled me wild with panicked longing until they came out, or turned to Jesus, or fell mysteriously out of my life.

When Ryan told me, his red hair flaming against the malnourished Texas grass, I realized Mark had been right. I felt sick. It wasn’t just because I knew that he wanted to kiss boys, and I had been told that in itself was wrong, unforgivable. I thought of the woods, his tongue magenta in my mouth, how I held his sweaty hand. No, it wasn’t his attraction to boys that destroyed me—it was that no part of him had ever wanted to do those things with *me*, and he still had, and until then I hadn’t known it was possible for someone to fake desire when the other person was not faking it, and I felt horribly abused by the universe for waiting until I had already given myself over before it came around to revealing that this was how it worked.

***

And more and more and more: when my eighth-grade boyfriend, a funny, snaggle-toothed boy a head shorter than me dumped me, I ran the shower for noise, shoved the back end of a toothbrush down my throat, and vomited up alfredo. I continued the ritual every night after dinner for close to a week, until Stephanie heard my retching and told my mom, who pulled me out of the bathroom, sobbing, scolding me in between tearful questions about how she had failed me as a mother, what she could have done to help. I hated her then, for making my pain about her—as if there was anything a mother could possibly do about the social ramifications of middle school heartbreak—but I hated her even more for taking my vice away from me, leaving me with no way to purge my body of its smoke-like, swirling anguish.

In high school, after an embarrassing hallway rejection from the guy who I'd used to rid myself of my virginity, I boiled with self-hate and attempted to soothe it by covering my platinum blonde highlights with dark brown box dye at a neighbor's house. When I came home and Mark saw what I had done without his permission, he threw a steak knife at the wall.

After my father's death, while Stephanie blazed angry, stealing, wrecking, screaming, I retreated inward. Destruction sizzled sweet and sharp and needy inside of me, but I destroyed only myself, in secret ways, so as not to inconvenience anyone. So as not to make myself unlovable. So as not to claim any space with my grief.

If my body—my life—was something I owned, I was never encouraged to believe it was.

***

So one night, when another attempt at a traditional family dinner ended in argument, Mark flipping the dining room table, tumbling plates and silverware, and Stephanie ran to her bedroom, and my parents went to the garage, where Mark would howl through the bones of our home, my mother silently crying until she broke and he laughed meanly at her futility—I retreated to the nursery, the purple walls and soft pastel light. I pressed my own body against the closet door, tackled my own heart in my hands, and felt myself falling to my knees, hallucinating orange and pink carousel lights, the music of carnivals, and woke on the floor smiling, nearly smiling, breathless.

When you are a girl and you grow up fat, there is nothing in your world, glossy with hormones and multicolored hair barrettes, to make you believe even a little bit that some boy is going to want to put his hands on any part of you.

When I was young enough to have only a vague idea sex involved kissing and maybe a bed, I rationalized that God must have made me fat to keep me from overindulging in the bodies of others. Like the biblical Paul with his deformity, I believed my body's unruliness was a necessary curse—because I knew, if I weren't self-conscious about my baby-fat boobs and the way my stomach hung over my elastic leggings, if boys could relent a crumb of their desire to some creature like that, I would never want to do anything else but touch them. If I was allowed access to such easily won intimacy, such validation, I knew I could never be stopped.

***

The first boy I tried to love had full, plush lips and an unshapely nose. He said most women either found him devastatingly handsome or repulsive. Resting, his face did look a bit like he was smelling something sour, but when he smiled he lit up childlike, sparkling like a Christmas village full of innocent joy.

I fell into feelings for him at fourteen, in the middle of my freshman year, when he was only a disembodied man-voice over the phone—and when he happened to be the long-distance boyfriend of my friend, Sara. He was two grades ahead of Sara and me, but they'd grown up in the same small East Texas town before Sara's family moved two hours northwest, to mine. As soon as we stepped off the school bus at her house, she'd call him immediately. He'd often just be *there* on speaker phone, a rustle in the background as we sat on her bed and did homework or gossiped about drill team. Sometimes she'd leave the room to do chores or talk to one of her siblings and hand the phone off to me, to keep him company while she was busy. He was friendly, sometimes a little flirty, and once, as I stood in Sara's kitchen with her flip-phone to my ear while she unloaded dishes from the dishwasher, he told me he loved me and called me *babe*.

It took me by surprise. I began to whir with that sickly, elated feeling of being offered something I wanted and wanted to run screaming from. I was conflicted, but after we hung up the phone, I nervously told Sara what he'd said.

"Oh yeah, JJ already told me he's getting a crush on you. He falls in love so easily," she replied nonchalantly.

"He told you that?" I was flattered, amazed, even, but wary. JJ and I had spoken on the phone maybe four times, never without Sara being the impetus for it.

"Yeah, he's just like that, though," she said. "JJ gets crushes all the time, but it doesn't mean anything. We're already planning on being together forever. So it's fine."

***

When I was in fifth grade, passing through the hallway after lunch—I'd probably pretended to forget mine at home, rather than succumb to the crippling embarrassment of eating in public—a mature, sixth-grade boy with the round, brown face of a cherub shouted something unintelligible at me as I walked by. When my mom picked me up from school that afternoon, I lied and told her the older boy had hollered out, in front of so many witnesses, that he wanted to take me on a date. Not just any date: an *ice cream date*.

More than likely, the boy was making fun of me; I was an easy target with my middle-school-principal haircut, held back by the green plastic hairband I'd chewed to jagged smithereens and wouldn't leave the house without, and the stretchy velvet dresses that accommodated my roundness as jeans wouldn't.

I know why I dreamed up the lie, but I don't know why I said it out loud—except that maybe I thought roping another person into my fantasy might make it true. If I was afraid of getting a bad grade, or afraid I'd get in trouble for running up the bill on our cordless phone, I'd go to school and tell everyone I encountered about my specific fear, and then I noticed it usually wouldn't happen. It was one of many ways I began, from the earliest years of my life, to rely on superstition to shape the narrative of my life into something survivable. Of course I'd try to apply the same improbable beliefs to love.

Even deep into my twenties, I wholeheartedly believed (as women are taught to believe) that some person (usually a man, any man) deciding to love me someday in the future would be the universe's reward for all the sorrow I'd survived. I was okay with the parts of my life that burned with unfulfillment, because I assumed them to be plot points that hadn't materialized to their conclusion yet. I was okay with mystery, because I took it to mean "everything you've ever wanted, but only when you least expect it."

And because I believed life was a long, dazzling story of trials and triumphs conducted by a universe that ultimately roots for our happiness, I clung to superstitions that swirled around every interaction with a prospective love interest, scouring the memory for reasons we were destined to be together, just as I used to count objects and divide clock notches until I found the number 23. In my loneliness I often felt delusional, ashamed of my relentless hope that persevered despite the many rejections that seemed to prove the contrary. To have hope is vulnerable, and I did not want to hope; I wanted cosmic assurance that the thing I most hoped for would come true eventually, erasing the need for hope.

***

I admit that I've already lied: JJ wasn't the first person I tried to love.

He wasn't even close; I had been trying to love men and boys, individually and collectively as a species, since before I had memory or language for it. Since the second-grade boy who pushed me down the slide in Kindergarten and the fourth-grader who popped my bra strap on the jungle-gym. Since my third-grade boyfriend of ten minutes, who pressured me to kiss him behind a picture book during group circle and when I wouldn't, for fear of being seen by the teacher, promptly broke up with me. Since too many Disney movies: my first memory of what I recognize now as arousal came at four, replaying the scene in *Beauty and the Beast* when Belle refuses Gaston and he flings the door to her house wide open anyway, pinning her against the wall with a torso the size of a mattress and a formidable smirk.

In real life, though, I told my mom about the various assaults of those boys on the playground, and when she called the school to report them, I smoldered darkly with a secret fondness for the perpetrators, even as I rallied for justice. Something in me sparked early at the idea of desire-driven violence, but it would quickly arrive of its own accord, real and harsh and plentiful. The only thing I'd wanted enough to create on my own, when it proved seemingly impossible, was the promise of being someone's choice: that fantastical wish of an ice-cream date.

***

JJ and I began texting and talking on the phone, separate from those instances with Sara. I told myself I considered him a friend, but the conversations grew increasingly flirty. Often he called in the middle of the night, crying about a fight he had with Sara or with his mom. Sometimes he just wanted a person breathing on the other side of the phone so he could fall asleep and not feel alone.

At the end of our freshman year, I took a trip with Sara's family to visit her aunt in the town where JJ lived. An hour or so after we arrived, he drove over to her aunt's house, knowing I'd be there with her, and we'd finally meet. When he walked through the door, my body tingled with discomfort—he wasn't at all like I'd expected. I'd seen pictures of him, of course, but his presence in real life was startlingly different. He was quieter, reserved, lanky and awkward. Even when he laughed, it was strange to hear the voice I knew coming from this crow-like stranger's face. His dark brown eyes seemed bottomless, and when he looked directly at me, I couldn't hold his gaze for long, shying away from the intensity.

At some point that first day, Sara went to the bathroom, leaving JJ and I alone in her aunt's office. The moment Sara closed the bathroom door, he pushed me up against the wood-paneled wall and kissed me, his unfamiliar tongue working its way hot and woozy into my mouth. He grabbed my breast through my padded bra and squeezed. When Sara returned to the room, he was already back on the other side of it.

I would like, in retrospect, to say that I felt disgusted. That I was wracked with guilt for betraying my friend. I can say I wouldn't have initiated anything boundary-crossing, physical or otherwise, with JJ by my own choice. But I was indoctrinated—by all those fragments of culture I ravenously hoovered up and called a self—to understand that saying no was not an option, especially when it came to boys and their hungers. To refuse male desire directed at me was unthinkable, like refusing a winning lottery ticket while starving in the gutter. Whether or not I desired them barely crossed my mind, and seemed an air-thin consideration in comparison to the panting animal of their lust—without which I would be alone, cast into the void of irrelevance. I was not skinny or hot enough to be picky, so I took what I was given and freely gave whatever of me they wanted, feeling lucky they wanted anything from me at all.

Later that day or week, JJ, Sara, and I sat at a picnic table in her aunt's yard, the pine trees muggy with spring. Sara lay in his lap, facing away, one of his hands holding hers. His other hand rested sweaty inside my bra.

***

In middle school and beyond, I continued to search for new solutions to occupy my mouth. After school one day, when Mark was napping and my mom was still at work, I watched *Bridget Jones' Diary* on cable and learned that if you smoke a lot of cigarettes and/or have a lot of sex, you can prevent yourself from eating, maybe even from caring about food at all. The concept of food becoming so completely incidental to one's existence was alien and gorgeous to me. For months after, I coveted the pack of disgusting-smelling Marlboro reds my parents kept in the freezer in the garage, believing it to be the answer to my problems—all of which amounted to the body I lived in. When I couldn't take up smoking, I fantasized about being older, living in an apartment alone where I could schedule a cavalcade of boys to come over for hours-long blocks throughout each day, letting them solve my body by occupying it.

As early as second grade, I remember walking through the school halls trying to sway my hips like the popular girls on *Lizzie McGuire*, and inspiring confusion in my classmates by spending recess under the slide fluttering my lashes in a compact mirror, lacquering my mouth in wet glittery gloss à la *Irresistible*-era Jessica Simpson.

Seemingly as soon as I was conscious of myself as an individual, I was ingrained with the notion that it was my most pressing purpose to be desired romantically. Without understanding or questioning why, I was, from early childhood, desperate to gain the prize of someone's brief attention. By the time I realized "someone" was supposed to mean "boys," I figured that even if my hopeless body meant no boy would be capable of loving me, maybe I could use the allure of sex to convince them—despite my body—to give me attention: the closest substitute for love.

***

You can admit it: the phrase DADDY ISSUES is flashing through your mind in blinding neon. It's telling that in the cultural consciousness, we see only fathers as impactful enough to leave a wound that takes a lifetime (and predictably, the love of some other man) to solve. That the disinterest of the first man who was supposed to care for her and failed to is what makes a girl "broken," doomed to ruin every future relationship and, ultimately, herself. Even a click-bait article titled "8 Signs You Have Daddy Issues" aptly recognizes, "[the] term 'daddy issues' gets thrown around a lot—usually in a derogatory way towards women, as if they are the ones who have done something wrong." It's one of a thousand labels applied to women who have the nerve to be hurt, and verbalize that hurt, when a partner treats her badly.

The theory supposes, then, that growing up with an attentive father is the only way to prevent a girl from shaping her life around desperation for men's' approval, but I would posit that our real "daddy issues" stem from patriarchy itself—the rules of which are most often learned from and policed by mothers and female friends. Sure, some fathers are vanished, or addicts, or emotionally inaccessible, and that affects a child's psyche, but to blame all emptiness on absent fathers adheres to the premise that women's damage is always, at its core, caused by lack of a man, and that gaining a new, better man can fix her. The idea assumes that only men are powerful enough to hurt or heal, and women are only impressionable by-products of the men who have acted upon her.

For a father-figure to truly free us from this system, he would have to reject patriarchal values himself, and encourage his daughters to decide the value of their own thoughts, desires, and goals. Yet, few people of privilege—even once that privilege is realized—can bring themselves to reject a system they benefit from, whose ugliness is not always visible to their lived experience, and whose tenets are tied up with their own emotional wounds.

It is not the presence or absence of a Daddy, but a darker, stealthier myth that leads young women to throw ourselves at the dicks of strangers: the story that to be desired sexually is the only way to earn love, and to be loved will save us from our self-hatred, our childhood trauma, our social isolation, our career dissatisfaction, and the spiritual emptiness of our very being. The people who most zealously perpetuate this myth are other women striving for the same impossible cure—or women who have succeeded in securing a man's affections only to realize they have not been cured, but can't bear to admit it to themselves or anyone else, because then what has their whole life been for?

In all honesty, most women don't want to reject the patriarchy at all; they want to be its star pupil.

***

I am sixteen, and my mom tries to set me up with a boy who works at the pizza parlor. She goes earlier that day to pick up a pizza, thinks he's cute and funny, and tells him, in the words of all mothers who fear their homely children will die alone: "You should meet my daughter!" Unbeknownst to me, she tells this pizza-wielding stranger I will be there to pick him up from work later that day.

When she comes home and informs me, my stomach quickly begins to fill with nervous excitement. A purportedly cute boy wants to meet me. Maybe this could be "my person." Maybe it can be that easy, I think, the great love of my life living in the same time and space as me all this time, in boring, simple Anna, Texas, discovered through a random encounter with my mom at a take-out pizza restaurant. I get dressed in the most flattering outfit I own, do my makeup meticulously, and anxiously drive to the pizza parlor.

The boy who eventually gets in my car is older, pimply, unkept, and does not, for all my excitement about the possibility of such, smell at all like the hot, gooey glory of pizza. He smells like the garbage in the back of the restaurant where a fine young pizza, formerly full of so much potential, goes when it's ready to give up on its dreams and rot in the dirt. The first thing he says to me before we pull out of the parking lot is, "I asked those guys I work with about you, and they all warned me you were fat, but you're not really *that* fat."

***

I am sixteen, and have reoccurring nightmares about being caught at school with no makeup on, or crawling into bed with a boy only to discover in horror that my legs aren't shaved. In one of the dreams, I sneak away to the bathroom to shave in the sink before he notices, but I keep cutting myself accidentally, covering the cuts with tape so he doesn't see the blood. After some time of this, I no longer have skin left. I am raw everywhere.

I walk back into the room, and he sees me, and says:

You've never been so beautiful.

***

So, yes, when a boy who begins as someone else's boyfriend wants to remove my sweater, when he presses his lips against my forehead, when he holds my hand, when he licks sugar off my wrist, when he says he wants to share the same air, when he listens to my music though he doesn't understand it, when he writes me letters ending *love forever* though he never signs his name, when he hides from my parents in my bedroom closet, because he *did* drive two hours both ways to see me though it was unannounced, when he tells me he needs me, when he tells me to promise to die for him because dying is what it feels like to need me, when he cries suicide on the phone to scare me into staying, when he swallows a bottle of cough syrup and lies about it, when he doesn't swallow antifreeze but lies about it, when he swallows someone else's heart and lies about it, when he keeps me up all night before a college interview demanding phone sex, when I begin to disintegrate beneath his touch, when he traps me in the hell we've built together with my locked door and his voice, when he wants to own me, when he hands me a bottle of pills, when he tells me he loves me, yes, I say *yes*, and I believe him.

***

There is a photo. In it, I am fifteen, JJ is eighteen, and it is the night before his high school graduation. His mother took the picture in their kitchen, the flash too bright, making both of us look vaguely greasy. In a T-shirt and ponytail, my bangs stringy and eyes hazy, our heads are pressed together like two animals trying to merge; birds of prey before consumption. There are many pictures of JJ and I—Myspace-era kissing selfies, or cellphone photoshoots before a friend's quinceañera, where we stare lovingly into each other's eyes, him wearing a dress shirt the color of the sky and me in a long white dress, my jawline as sharp as I hoped it would be on my wedding day—but this is the one where we look most human.

The summer after my trip to East Texas with Sara, she and JJ broke up, and he and I began to date. That meant weeks of constant phone conversations, punctuated by a day-or-two-long visit he'd make every couple of months. Perhaps nothing born from deceit can end well, but the middle was muddy too; all anxious longing and tear-your-hair-out pain with brief periods of rest and glow, of what I came to believe was love. And who would go through what I endured for him, if not out of love?

After we'd been dating about a year, his family invited mine to come downstate and stay with them so I could attend his graduation. Trinity and my mom slept in the pop-out camper in their yard, and I slept on the living room couch.

JJ told me he hated his mom. He said she was the reason he didn't trust white women, and therefore, could never trust me; when he was a kid, his mom had cheated on his dad, a quiet, self-made immigrant from Mexico who JJ idolized. When I met his mom, she reminded me of my own. She was sweet, a little loud, made lame jokes, scrambled to be hospitable. We all have reasons, tangled wires sparking the love and damage we bring into the world. I try to remember that now, even when it comes to JJ. No one can walk away from a life blameless.

***

One night in my early twenties, I was talking with a friend about our shared history of seeking out romantic partners who we believed would save us, when he added, "And of course, that's ridiculous and it never works."

I agreed, "Oh, yeah. Of course."

But the young and hopeful part of me did still believe, down to the cobwebbed corners of my psyche, that finding the person I decided to build a life with, a mutual love so bone-deep it could penetrate the distance of a continent or a casket wall, would solve me. Or at least, would hand me the tools of self-worth that allowed me to solve myself. That I thought self-worth was bestowed on a person through the grace of their beholder was one of many issues I would spend the next decade unraveling.

Intellectually I know better, but I still have trouble shaking all that Disney-esque programming: to know someone regards being with you as the best of all possible options, and to be able to reciprocate it fearlessly, without self-censoring, is the greatest freedom I could imagine. But I'd like to revise what I told him that night: what I've been searching since childhood for, like a flicker of lamplight at the end of a dark hallway, is not just love, but to *belong*. To create a separate, private world with another human being. A belonging that ripples through ordinary experiences and connects us to whatever is beyond us; life-defining, whether it lasts eighty years or eighty minutes.

The truth is, I used to hate even my name until I heard a person I loved say it, the full thing, like a ribbon with beads dangling on its edge. Like it was something definite. We expose so much about our own holes when we identify the ways that others fill us.

***

This is a story I never tell: after the divorce, my mom dated a man she met down the street from our house. It was a new house, and the deed was in my mother's name. She was proud of that. She worked hard to keep our tiny world afloat, and she was beautiful, really beautiful. She said it felt like being in high school all over again.

Bill was visiting our neighbors. He stuck around for a week or two, enough for my sister and I to notice him hanging out in the garage during the day, and sleeping over some nights. There was no money then, but my mom tried hard not to let us know. Even her work uniform came out of her sparse paycheck, and then there were our Goodwill/Wal-Mart school clothes, and the WIC-bought cans of ranch-style beans. My mom loaned Bill two hundred dollars, no one can remember what for, and he ghosted out of town soon after.

On Mother's Day almost six months later, he called to let her know he was coming back to town and wanted to see her. She was in her bathrobe, frantically applying mascara and brushing her hair, when she sliced her retina on one of the bristles of the round-brush. A neighbor drove her to the hospital, and took us to the mall to buy her a Mother's Day gift while she waited to see the doctor. The money never showed up, and neither did Bill.

***

The summer I am twenty-six, I travel with John, a man I'd been dating for three months, to Wisconsin, where we've both taken jobs at a children's summer camp. While I'm sweating in my repurposed dorm room, chewing my way through a package of watermelon-flavored Double Bubble I found in the office desk, my mom texts me:

Steve died. I just found out. Cancer.

The ellipsis bubble hovers on my phone screen, and then: *He was my first...you know what I mean?*

The day my parents divorced and my mom drove us over the Texas state line, we stopped for lunch at Jack-in-the-Box. There, a man was waiting for us: Steve, my mom's high school boyfriend, a milk-skinned man with the same name as my father, who she'd been in contact with for months as the divorce papers were drawn up and we prepared to move away. That night, when we arrived at our new apartment, he slept downstairs with my mom as Stephanie and I lay in sleeping bags on the floor of our shared bedroom. Months later, when the divorce was finalized, the four of us went to the apartment's community pool, he and my mom passed a bottle of champagne back and forth in the water.

Steve, who had lived with us a little over a year more than a decade ago, was dead. Rather than the last words he left her with, a slimy-drunken voicemail on our home phone threatening to kill himself, the fact that she lost her virginity to him in high school wins out in my mother's memory. That he was someone she loved, before she didn't.

The two Steves in my life, both lost now, she writes.

***

In an Airbnb in Arkansas where we'd traveled for an academic conference, I told my best friend, Lena, about the only time I remember my mom lifting a punishment: I was grounded from going to the seventh-grade school dance, but tearfully told her that my boyfriend would break up with me if I wasn't there. My mom took back all her staunch attempts at discipline, immediately told me to go get dressed, and drove me to the dance. Lena pointed out the many problems with what this teaches a daughter about relationships, the main one being: when a boy threatens absence, you come running, no matter what the cost.

When I consider my mother's relationship to men—my father, Steve, Mark, and a small handful of others—I believe her to be the victim of a kind of violence, though she would never describe it that way. I remember how she worked twelve hours a day and came home tiptoeing over nails to wash my stepdad's oil-stained jeans, cook some kind of dinner he would eat, and usually ended up out in the garage getting yelled at anyway. I remember how Mark dented our front door, just over my mother's shoulder, when he threw a baby bottle in the direction of her head as she stood holding my infant sister. Now that I see these things from my current vantage point, I feel sorry for my mother; I have spent much of my adult life trying to become the opposite of her, to evade reliance on relationships rather than be endangered or stifled in them, but no matter where you live or what job or degrees you hold or whether or not you choose to have children, to be any kind of woman is to be violence-adjacent.

***

A few months after we return from Wisconsin, I'm lying in bed with John and I tell him tentatively, politely, that I would prefer he not choke me during sex anymore. It's something I'd asked for when we first started dating, and something he had grown to enjoy, so I feel guilty about taking it away. Guilty about asking for anything to be different than it is. He's fine with it, of course, but wants to understand why. I think about it, and the only word that feels right, even though it doesn't feel like mine to use, is *triggered.* I qualify my answer, telling him, "It feels silly to say it that way, though. I mean, nothing has ever *happened* to me."

I am one of the only women I know who has never been raped. In a grotesque way, I add a silent *yet* to that sentence, always braced for rape to show up like some horrible marker of womanhood, just as I once waited patiently for my turn as my friends descended one by one into the secret cult of menstruation. This struck me for the first time during the Brett Kavanagh hearings, that I had no way to understand the terror and shame coming through my female friends' eyes and social media posts, that I had no #MeToo to add. But also feeling the terror, the shame, that yes, in some way, if not in this specific way—*Me Too.*

It was Lena who first told me that attention is not the same as kindness, but I have spent more lifetimes than I can count confusing the two, and hoping if they showed up together they would alchemize into love: that prized mirage sealed away for beautiful, thin girls who can pull off middle bangs and have never been so desperate as to consider writing poetry.

And though I knew sex was not synonymous with love, it was at least the same as attention. It was the same when, backstage at the high school play, an older boy I'd never spoken to cornered me alone by the dark stairwell and, so close I could smell the gum on his breath, forced his tongue across the expanse of my neck. It was the same when I offered to drive a college acquaintance forty-five minutes home when his car got towed at a party, and he insisted on reaching up my skirt and fingering me as I drove, despite my deflections, denials, and protests, as his way of "thanking" me. It was the same when I visited my former high school drill team "big sister" at her college apartment in Oklahoma, and her boyfriend of five years wordlessly slipped his hand under my clothes in the midnight dark while she slept beside me. It was the same when I was thirteen and my stepdad's friend, the rare adult who I felt treated me like a full human by listening intently to the story of my eighth-grade heartbreak, got too drunk one night and bent down in the kitchen to demand I let him kiss me, his sour breath all over my face. It was the same when, at twenty-five in the first year of my PhD program, standing on a dark Mississippi porch the eve of a hurricane, I handed my most reckless male friend a knife and drunkenly begged him to cut me.

What counts as a lifetime of violence?

And what if the violence is something we ask for, something we use others as a tool to inflict on ourselves? The last time John choked me during sex, it didn't disturb me because it felt violent, or felt like it could lead to violence, but because I realized I didn't want to have the same kind of default, destructive sex with him that I'd had with so many others. Those others, faceless blurs inching in a swarm toward my heart like ants toward a smashed cupcake, couldn't hurt me because I never hoped anything of them. But when you let someone into your life, when you allow yourself to hope they stay, the stakes become real. The trigger already cocked, even if no one's hand has reached for the gun yet.

***

As a writer and a person insatiable for the clean blade of narrative, I often wonder: what is our obligation—our compulsion—to make a record of the ever-shifting stories that compose our lives and the lives of those around us? Why keep tabs on the past at all?

In *The Art of Cruelty*, Maggie Nelson offers one possible answer when she reminds us: "…one of trauma's most troubling cruelties lies in its tendency to replicate itself."

Because I once spent Thanksgiving visiting a partner's family, and while watching a movie in their living room, when I realized that he and his mom and sister all had the same-shaped toes, and briefly wondered if one day my child would also have those toes, I thought about my mother telling me the story of her first Thanksgiving with my dad, and wondered if she thought some version of the same thing, and if in some way this simple act led to the windless river of grief flooding our lives. Because half of the moments I have loved any person have been curtained with a layer of dread that anyone I choose to solder my life to will end up vanished, another ghost in the machine of The Story. Because my parent was killed by a gun in the hand of a person he loved enough to marry. Because occasionally I woke in the night and listened to my partner breathe in the dark, and felt a swell of tenderness, and knew in my bones that the woman who killed my father must have once watched him sleep and felt the same.

Because for many years, I believed that to love is to hand your body over to be weaponized against you, or choose to become the weapon.

***

There is another picture of JJ and me, but he's not in it. He's standing just out of frame, and this time, the picture is in my kitchen, taken by my mom. It's my sixteenth birthday, and I'm blowing out the candles of my birthday cake, dressed in a brown babydoll top and white shorts, my eyes hollowing into dark circles barely hidden by self-tanner and too much makeup. My face too bony, limbs too long. The thinnest I have ever been, and despite my sword-sharp cheekbones and gaunt eyes, no one in my life would identify me as anorexic. I had been starving myself for four months, so when JJ saw me again, I would have become someone he wanted to be with.

My body was a constant, stressful conversation between us. For our anniversary, JJ stole and gifted me drug store diet pills because, "I love you but I don't know if I can be with you if you're going to look like this forever," and "it's easier for you to change yourself than for me to change how I feel." He promised me that as soon as I turned eighteen we'd get married, so he could monitor my diet and exercise, and make sure I was "healthy" before he got me pregnant.

Months before my birthday, I realized our relationship was unsustainable. JJ called me crying at least once a day, accusing me of inviting boys over to my house for gang-bangs if I took too long in the shower. He refused to let me spend time with anyone else, coming up with fervent arguments about why each of my friends were bad influences who were poisoning me against him, and once, threatening to break up with me if I took a twenty-minute trip to the grocery store with Mark. If I was with friends, I had to keep him in the room, on speakerphone, like Sara had years ago with me.

When he cheated on me with his co-worker from the American Eagle store in the mall, I started eating one meal a day, and only a fourth of what was on my plate, and instantly got compliments from teachers, my parents, my friends' parents; compliments that, for once, weren't backhanded in the vein of *It's a shame, because you do have a pretty face.* Dylan's dad came over to pick him up from my house and asked me if I was doing drugs; he meant it as praise about how fast I'd become acceptable-looking. The shadows under my eyes glowed like the diet pills in that bottle, blue and pretty yellow. I ate them one by one like candy. It did not solve me.

The night before my sixteenth birthday, with my mom's help, I lied to Mark about spending the night at a friend's house and stayed with JJ in a hotel instead. When we checked into the room and I removed my clothes, he said, approvingly, "Wow. I never imagined you'd do this good of a job. I'm so happy you're taking this weight loss thing seriously." We both ignored the unexplained black bruise spreading like an oil spill across my stark white stomach, over my liver. In the hotel bed, I tossed and turned all night, unaccustomed to sleeping naked, or with another person. I dreamt of shipwreck.

After birthday cake, I kissed JJ in the garage and watched as he got in his black sedan and pulled out of my driveway. There was a strange weight to the moment and I teared up, a premonition sweeping over me that this would be the last time I saw him. I told myself that wasn't likely, but as I watched him leave, I tried hard to take in every detail, tried to see him in the present moment as if in loving retrospect, as you might recall the last tender memory of someone tragically, unexpectedly lost.

Two weeks later, my dad would be dead. I would never see JJ again.

How To Talk About Dead Dads on Dates

1. You shouldn't.

2. You will.

3. Often, readily, inappropriately, and in thorough detail.

4. In biology class, when the mayor's son—your date to the sixth-grade dance, who you'd been simmering a low-grade crush for in the years since—asks if your parents are coming to Senior Night, follow his inquiry with an explanation: "My mom and stepdad. I mean, my dad is dead, so he won't be there." When his face goes startled, a new facet of yourself is revealed, a Lego block pressed into your heart with superglue and a satisfying click. Here, your Dead Dad Story grows an extra limb. "No, it's fine. Really." Smile, to reassure him. When the young boy asks: "Did he die, like, a long time ago?" "Three weeks ago," is your response. It will seem to you, already, like ancient history.

5. The Dead Dad is yours to keep, a shadow breathing loudly over your shoulder. The Dead Dad is your phantom bridge to every man you'll never reach.

6. When school lets out for winter break, start hooking up with your boss at the movie theatre. He'll probably know about your Dead Dad, even if you don't tell him. It won't matter—behind the wall of the box office where the cameras don't reach, in the backs of dark theatres, in the candy closet—there's no talking. On the loading dock, his cock in your mouth, there is only sweat and runny mascara. There's only "thanks" and a wink and a slap on the ass or kiss on the cheek. Your

boss will be kind of ugly, and engaged to someone else. Your boss will be twenty-four while you are sixteen, but most importantly, he will wear a suit, and people will call him "Mr.," and he will be fake-mean to you in public to throw the other managers off. He'll give you easy tasks, like a whole shift of sorting 3D glasses, where he can stop by to make out with you during his rounds. His power will taste like you'd once dreamed cum would. Don't wonder if he uses your Dead Dad's brand of shampoo. There's no room for talking with his fist in your mouth.

7. Quit your job at the movie theatre. Get a new job at the shoe store in the mall. Tell your new boss your Dead Dad Story on orientation day.

8. You'll be bright, fractured and holy. You'll be warped as stained glass, a light bulb patched with electrical tape. Your Dead Dad is the light. He flips switches in morose code. He flickers through the cracks in your smile.

9. Your best friend will tell you that talking about your Dead Dad on dates is a boner-killer. She will tell you the giggle trailing "murdered" makes people uncomfortable. You won't understand. At least not for a couple more years.

10. When you understand, even agree with her, it won't stop you from telling. Who would you even be, if not a daughter of The Story? How could they sign up to love you without knowing your dowry drips with blood?

11. You will inevitably meet people with Dead Dads and Dead Moms, with Stories of their own. At first, it will seem like the kind of thing soulmates could be made of. Like the magic of your collective grief could transform into a gingerbread house big enough to contain it all. But your Dead Dads won't get along. You won't understand why their Story leaves them staring out the window in tears, while yours has wings and a jester's face, its feet propped up on the coffee table.

12. When he tells you, smoking a cigarette after sex, how much he misses his Dead Dad, idolized him enough to take the nickname he'd bestowed on him as a kid (even though it sounds like something a belching trucker would be called), you'll lose respect for him. It'll make you feel like a monster, but so many things already do, and none of them are because your Dad is Dead.

13. When she tells you, eating pizza at the beach, her Dead Dad Story, it will be the first time yours didn't fall out first. When she says she was three and she doesn't remember very well, that the Story she carries doesn't amount to much more than an ambiguous ache, it is the closest you will have come to understanding.

14. There are more Stories living inside of people than just the Dead kind. You'll learn to recognize them by the silver bell lodged in their throats.

15. You'll realize, over a string of casual first dates during a transient summer, that holding your Dead Dad Story hostage is incredibly liberating. That if you're moving across the country in two months, there's no reason they need to know your real name, or where you're from, or that your Dad is Dead by murder.

16. So you gag your Dead Dad with a sock and stuff him in the closet before you leave the house. You meet strangers for drinks, kiss or fuck them sometimes, and you could be almost anyone.

17. You could even be two-parented, unblemished by the metallic smell of grief. Why be known and seen, when you could choose to be free?

18. You will meet someone who cracks you open bright and tender, like a tiny sun pried from a clam shell. On the anniversary of the Death, your Dead Dad Story will tumble out in front of him. You will have known him for three days, and already he will be the light of your world.

19. You will learn how to cry. For a while, everything will flood you. You will tell him all the ugly Stories you own, because you love him beyond logic or caution, because everything that comes out of you is raw and recklessly genuine, because there is no other way for you to be. You will offer him everything, and he will accept enough to know you. He will not be capable of loving you back, but he will be kind. It will feel like enough, until it doesn't.

20. At some point in life, you will find, by beautiful careless fate, a group of people who shine a flashlight into every slimy crevice, Dead Dad Story included, and choose you anyway. Who grow fond of your morbidly timed giggling. Whose Stories will begin to feel as comfortable and familiar as your own, like the well-worn pages of a favorite book.

21. At some point in life, you will stumble into intimate, healthy, healing friendships with men who know you and love you and do not try to fuck you.

22. At least once, each of these men will laugh, and their laughter will be the tender echo-song of your Dead Dad.

23. It will make you love them just a little bit more.

The Ditch

I'm nineteen, walking up the stairs to my apartment, when I hear a voice coming from the door across the hall from mine. There's a group of guys sitting outside my neighbor's front door in fold-out lawn chairs, beer bottles in hand. Above us, the yellow bulb buzzes as gnats ram their bodies against the light. I don't say anything, put my head down and fumble with my keys.

The voice starts in again: "I said hi to you, are you going to be rude?"

I don't look up.

Another guy says, "Dude, cut it out. Don't be a dick."

The first guy shouts out in my direction: "What are you, a dyke?" and that's when I finally unlock the door and quickly slip inside.

I drop my groceries on the counter, feeling strange, changed and unsafe. Once the passing minutes spread my adrenaline thinner, I'm angry at myself for not saying anything back. I'm shocked that word, *dyke*, stings as much as it does. I know, logically, there is nothing bad about someone being gay. Still, the syllable crosses my embarrassed face like the imprint of a slap.

I sit on the kitchen floor the rest of the night, imagining if I had met him in a dark alley, I would have stabbed him in the eye with my keys.

***

My and Stephanie's babysitter lived at the bottom of our street. Her name was Maegan, and though she was a high school freshman when I was in sixth grade, she quickly became more of a friend than a caretaker. She was an odd goose in her baggy, chained goth pants from Hot Topic, her obsession with T*he Lord of the Rings,* her short, stringy brown hair parted down the middle, barely covering the unexplained protruding bump at her left temple. Stephanie and I slept over at her house a few times a week during school breaks and summers, watching scary movies we pretended we were brave enough to handle, pulling all-nighters to request songs on the Top 40 radio station, or calling phone sex hotlines to giggle at the scandalous pre-recorded intros. I can vividly remember the way her bedroom carpet smelled: like rubbing alcohol and new pillow feathers.

When her dad and stepmom moved away, my mom and Mark offered to let her live with us, so she could finish her senior year of high school. She had become a close family friend by then, and though my parents could see she was a misfit, they were fond of her. She stayed in the spare bedroom upstairs, the one that was meant to be Trinity's but which Trinity never slept in, preferring my parents' bed or the living room couch.

The summer Maegan moved in with us, I went away to summer camp, and when I came back, she and Stephanie were constantly arguing. Having spent half a summer as siblings, they were passive-aggressively clawing at each other's throats.

Before that summer, Maegan told us she was bisexual. We didn't know of any boys she had dated—there was a weird boy she had a crush on for a while, who rode our bus and wore goth pants like hers, but it never seemed to amount to anything—but she told us she'd once had a fling with one of her female friends who lived an hour away. We'd even met the girl once or twice when she came to visit: a pretty, bubbly brunette named Sammi.

A week after I got back from summer camp, Stephanie told my parents Maegan's secret. They—as Stephanie knew they would—flipped their shit; they sent us down to the park with Trinity, and when we got back, Maegan was in the upstairs room, on the phone with Sammi, sobbing and packing up her things. They had kicked her out.

I asked Stephanie, "Why did you tell them? You knew they'd be mad!"

"I only told them knowing she was *that way* made me uncomfortable."

"You've never said that before."

She shrugged, "I was just tired of her. You haven't been here all summer. There's no way I could handle another year of her in our house.

She was soooo annoying."

I heard Maegan didn't go back to her parents, but moved in with friends somewhere down south. I heard she met some guy and had a baby. I never heard from her again.

***

Like many identity-based terms once slung as insults, the word *dyke* has been proudly reclaimed by queer people. The Wikipedia page on its etymology states this reclamation began in the 1960s, when lesbian activists repurposed the word as a label for "a woman committed to revolution." It's beautiful the way language can work: the literal revolution, the turning over, of an assembly of letters across time.

It's not a word I've ever felt comfortable saying—though now, I can see how lovely it looks on the page: the tall flourish of the *d* dipping into the low swoop of the *y* rising to meet the high swoop of the *k* and tying itself off with the delicate knot of the *e*. How it stretches across the limits of the line, a reservoir of mysterious beauty held within four simple letters. Like a bracketed lake I watch others disappear beneath the surface of, but whose waters I've never swum in, never let myself float suspended in its sparkling, dark-teal weightlessness.

The origin of the word is just as mysterious, it seems, but there are speculations: from *bulldyke*; "fake penis," named aggressively for its inhabitant's perceived lack. Or, from *ditch*—ancient slang for the vagina; an incidental hole, a piece of ground one falls into, dies in.

***

The landlocked place I come from harvested truck stops from the shells of torn-down diners; the open highway and the elsewhere it led were other people's luxuries; the only body of water I'd known was the path through the not-yet-razed woods behind our neighborhood, where we played pretend and cupped our palms to drink rancid microbes from a puddle; a stream that snaked through chasms in the forest floor, with a rusty pipe thick enough for us to walk across bridging the air above it; and when at twelve I came home to learn my mom and Mark rehomed my beagle pup while I was at school, it was where I fled, barefoot, through the winding concrete streets until my soles hit cool mud; and I ran as my family trailed behind me, shouts in the brush, until I was so far ahead they could not call out and make me hear them; and when I reached the roadside ditch by the truck stop and the highway that led out of town I lay down in the broken glass and fast food trash and beer cans and said to myself *this is my life now this is where I live I am free*; I was found, of course, minutes later when Mark drove past and dragged me by my arm from the pit into his truck; and tearfully I begged to be left alone, to be allowed to scrape a new existence from that pretty grave of shard and mud; some towns are like sirens, they drag a bright piece away and drown it; *sorrow* is not the right word and I am seasick of naming memories like this *forgiveness*.

***

In high school, my friend Dylan started dating a girl who lived in a nearby town. Her name was Morgan, her trademark features her bright blue eyes, dark hair straightened in choppy layers, and the fact that she was bisexual. No one we went to school with was openly queer, so her attraction to girls seemed mature, exotic. Because Dylan and I spent most days after school together, I'd gotten to know Morgan through his phone conversations with her, or the occasional visit, when she'd borrow her dad's car to drive down and hang out with us in Dylan's backyard: laying on the trampoline while Dylan and I set junk from the shed on fire in the yard for fun, a sliver of porcelain hipbone exposed between her band T-shirt and low-rise jeans.

Dylan often teased, good-naturedly, that I might be "like Morgan." I had never seriously considered that I might be attracted to girls, other than in the obvious way I'd always been hyper-aware of their bodies, envying flat stomachs and sharp hipbones and gravity-defying breasts I'd never attain. Same-sex dating was understood to be impossible in our town, deeply forbidden in the cultural Christianity of my family and the families of almost everyone we knew.

Dylan and Morgan's relationship lasted only a month or two, but they stayed friends, and she and I texted occasionally, too. More than once, our conversations turned flirtatious, and I'd participate hesitantly, all the while feeling with equal force dangerous excitement and uneasiness.

Sitting on Dylan's front porch one afternoon, copying each other's answers to math equations, I told him about my conversations with Morgan.

"See, I told you you're into girls," he joked.

"Honestly?" I said, "I think I might be."

"Really?"

"Yeah," I said. "I mean, I definitely like guys, like, a lot, but I might want to make out with a girl sometime, maybe."

"Cool."

That was the extent of our conversation. It hardly felt like a thing of importance.

But when Mark came over to pick me up a few hours later, Dylan's dad motioned for him to come inside, and for Dylan and me to stay in the yard. It was unusual, but so was Jackie, Dylan's dad—barely at home, in and out of jail for DUIs or bar fighting or minor possession charges, or away on long trucking jobs—so we didn't think much of it, just pulled down the tailgate of Mark's F150 and sat and talked until they were finished.

When the front door opened, Mark barreled out of it, keys in hand, and snapped, "Get in the truck." Dylan and I locked eyes, not knowing what had happened but that Mark was definitely angry, which meant I was definitely in trouble.

We sat in silence until we pulled out of Dylan's long gravel driveway, back onto the main road that ran through Anna, toward the schools and subdivisions of cheaply made houses.

"I bet you want to know what Jackie told me," he said, stone-faced. "I can't even believe what the hell I just heard. Can't believe it was my daughter he was talking about in there."

"What?" I pleaded, "What did I do?" I searched my memory for transgressions, past or present, trying to prepare, to anticipate, coming up empty. We'd just been doing our homework. Maybe Jackie found Dylan's cigarettes? But he never cared if we smoked, as long as it wasn't in the house…he'd even mixed me a shot of butterscotch schnapps once after school, weeks before. Maybe it was a test, and I shouldn't have accepted it?

"He overheard you and Dylan talking on the porch," Mark paused. "I think you know what I'm talking about."

"I really don't," I said. I really didn't.

"He heard you tell Dylan you want to date girls now. That you're *bisexual.*" He spat the word, and my heart dropped out of my body, crunched under the truck tires, smeared like roadkill on the asphalt under us.

"Why the hell would you say that shit?" He was screaming now. Red-faced rage I had never experienced, too untethered even for him, exploded and filled the truck cab.

"I didn't—I don't," I stammered. "I just said I was curious, that's all!"

"That's not okay!" he shouted. "That's not fucking okay, it's not something to joke about, and it's sure as hell not something I want to hear from fucking Jackie that my own daughter was talking about!" he screamed, and never stopped screaming.

When he parked in front of our house, he locked the car door so I couldn't leave, couldn't escape his anger, kept screaming, too much noise rattling the windows, too much night darkening the space outside into a closeness I wanted to run from and never stop running, too much of my face—the embarrassment and self-loathing disgust behind it too visible, too trapped, as he kept screaming about the things women do to each other during sex, the disgusting things they lick and the smells and each other's bodies, bodies that didn't belong together, repellent—and is that what I wanted? Is that the kind of disgusting act I wanted to do to another girl?—and women's bodies, beckoning hellfire and seeping damnation, the unforgivable choice of it all although there was never a choice, couldn't be a choice, I had already made my choice and it was the absolute wrong one, he screamed and he kept screaming and I wanted to take it back and I tried to take it back but it was too late, my words stung newborn raw in the world, what had I done who was I oh god, crawled down inside myself and burrowed though even inside my own flesh I was unsafe but what else was there, what safe place except howling regret, until the car door clicked unlocked and my mom was sitting in the garage smoking a cigarette, blissfully unaware and now she would know—I would ruin her too, ruin the daughter she thought she loved and here she was, my beautiful kind mother, she was about to find out what I had done what I had tried to be and even she couldn't save me now if she ever could, and he was screaming and still screaming and even all these years later a part of me still hears him screaming. Years later, I am in many ways healed and free and fully loved but even now I am trying to write down something about helplessness and failing, I am still fourteen and a breathing burning funeral pyre, he is still screaming and never stopping, I am still in that parked car.

***

In the garage, the night Mark found out I was possibly not-straight, my mom tried, graciously, to defend me.

"She didn't say she was gay, just curious. Everyone has been curious. Haven't you ever been curious?"

"Well no, Mary, 'cause I'm not a fucking queer."

"I'm just saying. It's normal to be curious. You only said you were curious, right, Erin?"

"Right. That's all. I didn't mean it."

I was so frightened, so spilling over with embarrassment and regret, there was no part of me that wanted to entertain the idea of being attracted, maybe, to girls anymore. And maybe, in the garage that night, I believed I could decide I wasn't, and that would be the end of it. I had always dated boys anyway, and wanted to. I was always, self-professedly, *boy-crazy.*

***

There are reasons the word dyke has never felt like mine to claim. *Dyke* is a woman who occupies a different realm of womanhood, who defines herself for herself. If you are a woman who grew up as I did, believing your primary purpose and obligation is to appeal to men, the idea of being relegated to a realm solely composed of women, solely *for* women, can be frightening.

Bisexual people exist at a difficult axis of queerness. They may have the privilege of "passing" as straight in a world where LGBT people are subject to discrimination and violence, but even people who are affirming of gay and lesbian relationships can have a harder time accepting sexualities that fall between heterosexual or homosexual. The internet is riddled with forums and advice columns where bisexual people ask if they're obligated to come out about their sexuality when they're in a monogamous marriage with someone of the opposite sex, or if they're even allowed to claim that label when they don't suffer the discrimination a more "visibly gay" person might. It's equally flooded with the laments of bisexual women who feel trapped between worlds: rejected from the lesbian community, where some lesbians accuse them of not being "queer enough," and rejected by straight people who read their bisexuality as a "phase" or an excuse to be sexually promiscuous.

The San Francisco Human Rights Commission reports that bisexuals are the largest single group within the LGBT population; in a 2010 survey (which one must imagine is a conservative estimate, compared to the results the study might garner as I write this in 2022) 3.1% of adults self-identified as bisexual, while only 2.5% identified as gay and lesbian. A 2007 study revealed that bisexual people have a greater likelihood of developing mood disorders, are less likely to receive medical treatment informed by their sexual orientation, and that bisexual women with heterosexual partners experience domestic violence at an increased rate—according to the CDC, 61% of bisexual women, compared to 44% of lesbians and 35% of heterosexual women, have been raped, stalked, or physically assaulted by an intimate partner.

Activist Robyn Ochs defines "bisexual" as someone who "has within [themselves] the potential to be attracted—romantically and/or sexually—to people of more than one sex and/or gender, not necessarily at the same time, not necessarily in the same way, and not necessarily to the same degree." This definition allows bisexuality to transcend the rigid binaries its prefix implies: bisexual people can be attracted to those that fall outside of "man" or "woman," including trans, non-binary, and genderqueer people. A person who is bisexual might be sexually attracted to both men and women, but only romantically attracted to men; or might be almost exclusively sexually and romantically attracted to women with only the occasional attraction, or flexibility for attraction, to a man; or might be sexually and romantically attracted to cis men and women, trans men and women, and non-binary people.

Living in a society that ingrains in women that their value relies on their ability to attract and retain the attentions of men makes it more difficult for bisexual women to discover where they fall along the spectrum of romantic and sexual attraction to people of other genders. I could desire to kiss and fuck and date women and not crave their validation, but with men, the prize of their validation was the thick layer of frosting that made all those things so intoxicatingly appealing in the first place.

***

From the few instances I remember, my dad was homophobic, too: once, when he picked Stephanie and me up from the airport, he ranted the whole drive home about two men we saw holding hands in the baggage claim.

"I just don't understand why they have to be like that in public, shove it in everyone's faces like that," I remember him saying, standing in his living room, blocking our view of the TV. "It's gross."

Death forces an end point, a point at which no more human progress can unfold. Just as I've wondered what my relationship with my dad would be like after he was sober, or once we could relate as adults, I've wondered if his social views would evolve. Though he grew up Catholic and attended Catholic boys' school, he wasn't religious in his adult life. I don't know where his prejudice came from, aside for the era he occupied. He's eternally frozen in 2009, before the rise in popularity of queer characters on TV and Pride Parade photos on Facebook, before the Supreme Court signed marriage equality into national law. Maybe he would have shifted over the years, if given the opportunity. I never would have expected that when I finally came out to Mark and my mom in adulthood, they would not only be accepting, but supportive. People change. Time and love changes them. I wonder if my dad would choose to accept me as I am now—all the versions of me he didn't know I was. At the moment of his death, I was only his teenage daughter, and to him, that's all I'll ever be. Maybe it's better that way.

***

I want to say *forgiveness*, I want to mean it, I want to make this easy on them. I want to say the years spent folding yourself into a secret no longer matter when the secret unfurls.

I was nineteen, weeks after the drunk man at my apartment door called me *dyke*, the first time I spoke up in my summer sociology class and called myself *bisexual*. Even though I said it—even though there was something pressing within me that compelled me to say it—once I said it, I didn't believe it was true. I told myself from some whispering hollow within me that I just wanted to be special, to have something to say, that I was putting the word in my mouth just to have something to gnaw on. There is a part that still whispers with that voice, that tells me I've made a secret of myself just to have something interesting to hate myself for.

When I came to believe the word was mine—was me—the word's only true meaning was *if my family really knew me, they wouldn't claim to love me*. I dug my finger into the bruise of that word as I sat folding underwear at my college retail job, as I drove through the bulbous Oregon mountains the morning after I first had sex with a woman, as Trinity jumped through the sprinkler in the yard, as my mother hugged me, as Mark said he was proud of me, every time my family cast their love upon me it curdled into bottomless shame, a shame that meant *this love is not deserved, this love is not safe, this love is not actually meant for you, they will learn this and it will be your fault and they will never let you see your little sister again.*

And once the secret was over, no longer a secret—once my family hugged me and said they loved me and they knew who I was as they said it—there is still this book; the abomination I must be to construct this story for you all to see. The bruise of the story whispering: *if they knew what I told, if they knew the words that have been sitting dormant on the page all these years, if they knew what was coming, they wouldn't claim to love me.*

***

She texts me to say she is waiting for me on a bench downtown. I text her to say I am on my way there, which is a lie; I'm standing in my closet, wondering what to wear for the first date I have ever been on with a girl. I have dated boys and known what to do, so I feel like this should be easier, come naturally, but it doesn't. Instead, it feels like waking up underwater and being expected to know how to breathe.

I decide on a dress, a blue one with birds, which compliments the yellow shirt she's wearing when I get there. We talk about our present and our prospective futures, about the way the park lights up at night during the winter months, and how the lights remind us both of snowflakes. We decide to go back to her house, and she drives. I am doing things that must mean I trust her very much for someone I barely know. I am allowing myself to be a passenger in her car, to let her take me somewhere I have never been before.

Her house is small and comfortable, and she pours sparkling water into a glass and hands it to me, while I sit in a wooden chair in the center of her kitchen petting her elderly Australian Shepherd. We laugh and talk all night, and when she drops me back off at my car, she hugs me and lets her body linger. On the way home I realize this is probably the best date I have ever been on.

I never call her again.

A Brief History of Cups and Bottles

I rarely remember that it was a date I almost didn't go on. Like everyone I knew, online dating was a standard part of my college experience. Reading profiles like they were homework, churning out responses to awkward icebreaker messages about what music you like, what your major is (and those are the ones that don't include a descriptive essay on the stranger's particular level of horniness) and every human being begins to seem lame, tedious, disposable.

Logan had fantastic hair. He used the forms of "your" and "you're" correctly. He liked pizza. He met all of my criteria.

He wasn't, perhaps, ideal on paper: he had an eight-year-old son, but assured me he was on good terms with the child's mother, so there was no lurking drama. He was an ex-Marine, which might have been a deal-breaker for me, if not for his "complex feelings about the nature of war and government at large." (Twenty-one-year-old me *swooned.*) Still, he was the most promising candidate I'd talked to in half a year or more. He asked me out for a drink, and I suggested one of the only two bars I had been to.

Logan was older: twenty-eight to my freshly acquired twenty-one. The only alcohol I'd legally bought was a twelve-pack of Lone Star—cheap, Texas-brewed beer that tasted like pennies, chosen because my favorite band mentioned it in a song. I'd gotten drunk for the first time at summer camp a month before my fourteenth birthday, and I regularly plowed through boxed wine with my college roommate, but legal drinking was a different game. I never knew what to order at bars, so I mostly defaulted to Jack and Coke (what Rachel always ordered), or cider that tasted like sparkling apple juice. The night I met Logan at Oak Street Drafthouse, I arrived thirty minutes early, ordered a pint of cider, and drank it in a locked bathroom stall.

***

A trip to the liquor store punctuated each drive when my sister and I visited our father. An unnamed brown bag, a question we wouldn't learn the answer to until we set our suitcases in our respective rooms and slid off our shoes: Vodka. Microwaved dinner. A rented DVD. Crawling on his hands and knees to the bedroom, shutting the door. By 8:30, my sister and I usually had free reign of the house. What we did with it was much of nothing: ice cream, maybe, and another movie, or the occasional forbidden online chatroom. We might have tried to sneak out and walk through the neighborhood if it had crossed our minds, but all the doors and windows were locked; even when he could barely stand, my dad never forgot to set the alarm.

I don't know if he liked vodka, or if it was the just easiest thing to hide in his orange juice before work—something I never considered until trying to pour sangria into a water bottle on the way to my afternoon literature class, two days after meeting Logan. My dad's tie was always knotted, his hair combed back and suit jacket crisp before his first drink. He was never late. Neither was I; if I reached the door more than three minutes after class started, I left and went home.

***

It was a date I almost didn't go on because I was on an upswing. I was entering my last semester of undergrad, and I'd recently moved into a new one-bedroom apartment that didn't stink of two years of chronic depression, dog piss, marijuana smoke, and molding dishes. I lost fifteen pounds that summer, thanks to the pills my gynecologist prescribed for my PCOS, which made me need to pee all the time and too nauseous to eat anything that wasn't cold and sweet—chocolate-flavored Adkins protein shakes, frosted flakes with almond milk, slices of Swiss cheese—coupled with Rachel crashing on my futon while she waited to move into her new apartment (which made it nearly impossible to binge eat) and the strange empowerment that came with turning twenty-one.

Two nights before my date with Logan, I had the epiphany that online dating could be used like food delivery, but for sex: while Rachel was working the night shift, I drank a bottle of wine on my living room floor, typed in the height and age I was craving, found someone who looked relatively harmless, and invited him over. He was a little nerdy, and a sloppy kisser. The sex was disappointing and didn't last very long, but we fucked three times and in-between we talked and it wasn't so bad. I was able to lay naked with him, un-self-conscious, because for once, I didn't care what he thought—and I was glowing with the success of not having eaten since my protein shake that morning. He commented on the rumbling emanating from my stomach. He seemed enamored with me. Afterwards, I kicked him out and ignored his text messages. I considered it a beautiful experience.

***

I finished my cider and ordered another before Logan showed up. When he walked up to the front porch of the bar and waved, I immediately felt I'd made the right choice to be there, with him, on that particular night. He was tall and sturdy in a green plaid button-up, sleeves rolled to reveal hints of a forearm tattoo. He had even better hair than in his pictures, gingery-brown and combed to the side. We hugged and I inhaled his cologne, warm pheromonic musk.

We opted out of the crowded vintage couches inside and headed for the backyard, populated with rows of wooden picnic tables. We talked about the books and authors we liked (neither of us had read each other's favorites), and I told him about the bands and movies I was embarrassed to admit I liked. He said he'd recently quit smoking, so he could be a better role model for his son. He talked about his time in the military, the guilt he felt for having killed, the PTSD and homelessness pervading the lives of many of his friends. He was handsome, funny, and considerate. "My Girl" played over the speakers under humid starlight. He finished his drink, and when I asked if he wanted a second, he said he usually limited himself to just one. I went inside and ordered myself another.

***

By the time I met Logan, I had five years' experience dating with a Dead Dad Story in my pocket. I used to take the Dead Dad Story out on first dates and wave it around before the other person even had a chance to ask, used to spread it wide over the table and force them to inspect every morbid fold. I saw the looks on their faces and laughed, made light of it, pulled it apart and stuck my tongue out at it so that they would understand how okay I was, how cool and casual, how Not-Broken. Later, I learned to keep it hidden until they asked, and when they did, I'd open my palm slowly, watch their eyes twitch with fear and wonder as they glimpsed the corners of it, before shoving The Story back into my pocket until I could projectile-word-vomit it across the table the way I really wanted to.

By the time I met Logan, I knew better than to prod at The Story at all, lest it ruin things. But after he confessed his guilt at having killed another person's child, even if they were behind enemy lines, I rationalized that it was only fair to empty myself out, too. I told him it was something "I almost never do." Then I told him.

He seemed surprised, but not scared, and soon after, we moved on to the topic of TV shows. He insisted that if I liked David Duchovny in *X-Files*, then I absolutely had to see *Californication*. I told him that I had a laptop, a couch, and an apartment with internet access.

Under fading streetlamps, he walked me to my car in the gravel lot. He asked if he could kiss me.

"Of course," I said.

He tilted my chin up with one finger, and gently wrapped a hand around the back of my head. Minutes after he walked to his car and I stumbled into mine, I was still lightheaded.

***

When I was twelve, I found my parents' divorce papers in a file folder on the floor of our "junk room," among outdated electronics and discarded boxes of pictures. According to one document, in the first years of my parents' marriage, my dad burned away his grandfather's inheritance on cocaine. (Then again, it was the eighties, and who didn't?)

I didn't hang onto the papers, so these facts can only be trusted as far as their consistency in my memory—which may not be very far. I couldn't have predicted how I'd end up trying to decipher my parents through archive-building their history, squirreling away scraps and untold stories like the ones in that document. I still don't know the total shape and depth of my father's addiction, or how it landed on the bottles and cups I remember, the shouting, semi-violence.

It would be easy to blame my father's alcoholism on the divorce, if it hadn't been such a large cause of the divorce. Still, it's safe to say that my mother leaving him and moving us from Alabama to Texas didn't make things better. With a house that was empty forty-eight weeks of the year, he needed something to fill the space, the silence.

When you live alone, there is so much silence to fill.

***

In the silver glow of fairy lights strung up in my living room, we kissed again, before moving to the bed. We attempted to watch an episode of the show, but by David Duchovny's second nude scene we were making out again, my body straddling him as his fingers floated gently over the back of my thighs, the hem of my dress. Everywhere our skin touched, I had chills.

"I have chills," he whispered.

He slipped my dress off, and moved to the edge of the bed to remove his shirt, smiling as he pulled it over his head. I looked up at him and grinned as I fingered the cool metal buckle of his leather belt.

And from there, it all fell apart.

***

From the time I saw it in second grade, I was captivated by the film *Titanic*. The lure of love, drama, death, and vintage decor snuck into my dreams nightly. I hid my mom's VHS box set in a special nightstand drawer reserved for it, along with white costume gloves from Claire's, a painted paper fan I received as a birthday party favor, and my prized possession: a heavy pearl tiara I bought with my own Christmas money from the discount jewelry store in the mall. Of course, Kate Winslet's beaded gowns were swoon-worthy, but my real obsession was Leo DiCaprio as Jack Dawson: selflessly kind, handsome and scrappy, his floppy blonde hair tragically perfect. Jack Dawson inhabited the mind of every lonely girl as a blueprint of the ideal man: he would free us from the prison of societal obligations, our judgmental families, and our insecurities. He would tremble in our arms after sex, overwhelmed by the terrifying depth of his love for us, and he would literally die in the cold sea out of politeness.

In college, I frequently fantasized about someone—anyone—walking into the store where I worked, locking eyes with me, then swooping in and plucking me from my uninspiring life, just as Jack did for Rose when he found her perched on the rails of the ship, minutes from jumping to her death. But it took me far too long to realize that doing so is not love's job; starry-eyed romantic gestures may seem like evidence of love, but romance is only the frame we organize the plot of our love inside. It is not the same as love itself.

The love Jack gave Rose was not a real love, either. Someone can tell you that you're smart and brave and capable, and it can mean everything for a while. It can instill you with the wobbly new belief that you are those things, and inspire you to begin walking through the world as if you deserve to be treated with dignity. That is valuable. But it's not the same as being loved. Being loved is validating, but it is also vulnerable, and true vulnerability is uncomfortable as fuck. Despite my starvation for love, I was not ready to be held in my truth; I was twitchy and feral, a wild fox lingering to leer at the light up close, then bolting for the safety of a burrow.

***

When Logan didn't text me the next day as he promised he would, I met Rachel at the park on her lunch break in an attempt to waste time. Later that night I texted him. Two days later, not having heard back, I texted again.

I couldn't believe the way it all shifted, that I would probably never hear from or see him again and not know why. When he left my apartment that night and kissed me in the doorway and said he wanted to see me again soon, I was so sure it must have all meant something.

I felt like the worst kind of person: I never bothered to cope with my father's death, but the second a man I'd met once ghosted me, I was armed to destroy myself, wearing the same sweaty flannel days in a row, suckling at a wine bottle in bed. Following one abnormally nice date, I became bitter, dismal; I became more negligent than I'd ever dared to be, going to school and work wallowing in some lame attempt at drunkenness. I wanted to implode, to really wreck something—my body being the only thing I owned.

But even in the height of my addiction, I wasn't brave enough to let myself appear as openly broken as I felt. I wanted to walk into work drunk, but was too scared of someone noticing to have more than two wine coolers. Though some nights after work I went out drinking and drove back to my apartment so obliterated I barely remembered how I got there—barely remembered puking up the leftovers my manager had kindly sent me home with, until I woke the next morning and saw chunks of my own vomit splattered *projectile* across the wall—I was too fearful and embarrassed to call in sick the next day.

In the periods of time that I finally allowed myself to spiral, my emotional upheaval was still neatly organized for others' convenience. No one knew I was secretly struggling, and part of me was desperate to fuck up badly enough for someone to notice—but even in the snare of various addictions, I have always been more afraid of being unlikeable, a failure.

***

For me, addiction was never only drinking, because food was never only food. There were the green beans and salad greens my mother bargained for after I was bullied for being fat, and the Weight Watchers meetings she dragged me to before I hit puberty. There was the spaghetti I slurped from my plate at the table when my dad took his portion to eat alone in the bedroom and my mom abandoned eating to do the dishes in distress. There was the leftover Lunchable another girl brought to the cafeteria table in third grade, too expensive and fattening for my own mother to allow; I offered to take the girl's trash and gorged myself on its remnants over the garbage can, so quickly I forgot to breathe, and when I sat back down, I choked it out over the same girl's sweater. There was the shame of getting caught with my hand sheathed in a bag of chocolate chips, the disappointment in my mother's voice when she said, "But you just ate." There was the refrigerator lock I fashioned at eleven out of bungee cords and a bike latch; I was desperate for change, for help, control against my own insatiable mouth, but it lasted only half a day. My mother grew bored of handing over the key.

There are so many stories I could tell you about hunger. About fantasizing liposuctions and gastric bypasses. Watching MTV shows where overweight teen girls sweat themselves brand-new over a single summer, while I ate a hunk of Kroger cheesecake and plotted my escape from my own flesh. What it's like to be trapped by the soft, asylum walls of a body, to rage inward and outward, the cycles of pulling in and expelling like a malevolent tide.

But there was a time when, in my absolute teenage loneliness, I found joy in cooking huge meals, like a tiny Christmas present I gave myself each evening. When I moved out of my parents' house just before turning seventeen, my friends all gone away to college or still in high school, food was all I had to kill the long hours between work and sleep, between waking and work. For the first time, I wasn't limited by my parents' budget or judgement. There was freedom in the family-pack of pizza rolls I bought with my own money during late-night Wal-Mart trips, cooked in my own oven while my roommate worked overnight at the airport. There was quiet at the kitchen table while I ate them all in pleasure. There were my own Lunchables, scarfed not over a trash can but a coffee table, cheese sticking in the carpet like blades of grass.

And the food was love until it was fear. And I chased the love and the fear with a bottle of sugary wine until the love and the fear became the wine, too.

***

In the following days, I tried to drown out flashes of our fingers interlaced as Logan slicked his tongue up my inner thigh, how gorgeous he was as he took off his shirt at the foot of the bed and stared down hungrily. The sex itself wasn't that great, maybe, but thinking of the tender moments in between—his arm draped over my chest, lying next to me and laughing into my ear—was unbearable. Lying drunk on my bedroom floor, I was terrified that no one would ever kiss me like that again.

In retrospect, of course the encounter didn't warrant any of these responses, or the reckless depression that came in its wake. It was, in reality, only an above-average date with a good kisser, but something about it cracked my long-practiced numbness.

I have often attempted to conjure soulmates into the bodies of strangers.

***

Around the time I started bingeing, I began to fantasize relationships with fictional characters. I'd cling to the idea of people on TV loving me so fierce their bones gave out, or they blew up a building, or climbed out of the underworld to save me from the troubles of the real and imagined world. I created detailed, tangling storylines of our ill-fated, drama-ridden love, which always culminated with me dying tragically in my lover's arms. I'd replay these stories in my head during class, standing at the register at work, on car trips with my family, while falling asleep. I could sit still for hours, staring blank-eyed at the wall of my apartment, dissociating completely from life to live in my head. In real life, I didn't date, barely had sex, and anything resembling the hope of a mutual crush felt unattainable. I was starving for connection, but restricted myself from reaching for it, afraid indulging in something that felt like love but was not love—was not safe and secure and certain—would ruin me.

The world I built from drugs and drinks and gluttony was built out of fear that I was not the kind of creature who was capable of being loved. I couldn't control whether other people cared for me, or what kind of story the universe spun my life into, but I could give myself the simplest substitute. I could gorge on delight until I split open and spilled forth the chewed remains of everything good; I could make sure I would never feel emptiness again.

***

All I know is that one day I'm scouring the aisles of a grocery store, fingernails digging red crescents into my palms. I'm standing in front of a display case for half an hour, unable to move or decide. Frozen. Panicked. Hating. Desperate. One day I've stuffed myself so full, I dread what I might have done, the organs that might burst, the infinite ruin of my body. I float from urge to urge in a self-created hellscape of lo mein and fried pickles and take-out baklava from a store my skin itches with anxiety just to walk into, knowing I have $30 worth of melting, unnecessary groceries waiting in the car, more than enough to feed some thin, pretty couple in a crumbling apartment for a week, yet I've just got to have that extra thing, that piece of sweetness to slot into the billowing hole at my center. Then the ecstasy of devouring the long-awaited spoils of war, and the guilt afterward, the thought that maybe I should throw it up before it roots itself there, feeling awful either way because (1) if I'm too lazy to vomit up the garbage I just glutted myself on, what does that make me? but (2) it's impossible to vomit enough to make an impact calorie-wise, and during the process I'll feel wrung out as a thrift-store Barbie, mascara dripping and spit flying from my chin, and seriously, that shit is so bad for your tooth enamel.

One day I wake up and food is as much drug as death, and I can no longer remember the glory of living like a normal person, choosing a meal without the panic and searing flames of self-hatred. One day I'm sitting in my car and a gulp of ginger ale burns my ulcerated insides like acid, so painful I scream. One day I come home, get drunk, get stoned, destroy full pizzas, destroy boxes of Swiss rolls, destroy pans of chicken nuggets shaped like dinosaurs. I fold destruction inside of me and fold myself inside of rooms. I am dying. I am safe.

One day I promise that the next day, I will do better, be better, be alive.

One day lasts for ten years.

***

In a 2015 interview with *Pitchfork*, musician Sufjan Stevens talks about the inspiration behind his album, *Carrie & Lowell,* written after his mother's death. He reveals that she was bipolar, an alcoholic, and often missing from his life. The interviewer asks Sufjan how his mother's addiction and distance affected his feelings about her death, and his reply stung as I read it:

"They always talk about the science of bereavement, how there is a measurable pattern and cycle of grief, but my experience was lacking in any kind of natural trajectory…I felt like abusing drugs and alcohol and fucking around a lot and becoming reckless and hazardous was my way of being intimate with her."

When *Carrie & Lowell* was released in March 2015, I was living near Seattle, and I was not thinking about grief. I was thinking about the ocean outside my bedroom window, the privilege of that after growing up landlocked, and the guilt I felt for not touching it every single day. I was hiding in my tiny seaside apartment, irrationally fearing the sliver of space above the windowpane that the drawn blinds didn't cover, listening anxiously for the muffled rustling of the woman who lived on the other side of the wall.

I was trying to get my eating disorder under control and failing. I sought out new rituals that didn't involve hiding inside portions of Pad Thai, or walking down to the candy store to stuff my purse with packs of malted milk balls to suck on in the dark of the movie theater, so I began to sit in bed and play *Tetris* instead, listening to *Carrie & Lowell* through earbuds on repeat until the evening was spent and I was too tired to search for food. I will forever associate the delicate pinging of the first track with moonlit tide and neon *Tetris* blocks.

Twenty-one, fresh out of college and Texas, I was unprepared for the wellness culture of the Pacific Northwest, and the embarrassment my relatively lower-class Southern background would spark there. A few weeks into my publishing internship, the coordinator invited us over to her house for a dinner party; I had no idea what to bring to what sounded, at the time, like a very *adult* gathering, and after I dressed with meticulous consideration and grabbed my keys to leave, I worked myself into a panic attack over whether the $12 "red wine blend" I'd bought at Safeway earlier that day would be good enough. Nervous about showing up with too little, I ran back into the store on my way there and bought a decorated chocolate cake roll. When I arrived at the dinner party, the host was exceedingly gracious, but I picked up on the distaste with which my coworkers looked at the store-bought dessert, how each of them bypassed it for a slice of homemade banana bread, exclaiming what an indulgence it was.

I gained greater insight into my faults when, a month later, I ran into the marketing director at the Safeway self-checkout—the same man who'd overheard me in the office mentioning my go-to mixed drink was Dr. Pepper and whiskey, and joked, "You may as well just drink a Snickers bar." I tried to distract him from noticing my cart full of binge loot: cheesecake slices, bags of cheese puffs, frozen burritos. He was hoisting a supersized bag of dog food over his shoulder, and told me he only ventured to Safeway for kibble, imparting his advice with a look of pity: "Everyone buys their groceries at the co-op."

I'd been inside the co-op only a few times before, on lunch break with a fellow intern who'd spent the previous year teaching creative writing in Berkeley. To me, it was a mysterious place that smelled of organic incense and oats; I hid the fact that I didn't actually know what a co-op was or how it worked, having never heard of one before, or lived in a town that had one.

The apartment I rented was composed of two small rooms connected by a tiny bathroom on the top floor of a large, yellow Victorian house. My landlady, the elderly woman who owned the house and lived downstairs with her three tabby cats, confronted me the first week about how my garbage bags took up all the space in the single can outside. She complained that she'd had to search through my trash to separate out the glass whiskey bottles, aluminum refried bean cans, and cardboard pizza boxes I didn't know I was supposed to recycle. I was so embarrassed of my excess that I began hoarding big black bags of trash in my apartment, sneaking them into my trunk to sling into the dumpster behind a brewery on my early-morning drive to work.

Despite the anxiety that kept me trapped inside my small apartment more often than I preferred, Washington was an unfamiliar, lushly magical landscape. It felt like escape and like a dreamland veil of home at the same time. I wasn't thinking about my dad's death, or his life, or what to make of all of it. I didn't write about him in the six months I lived in Seattle, except for one line: *There is only so much you can say about grief before it becomes something separate, something that lives on its own in the world and has little to do with you.*

***

In grad school, when I learned how to starve, it was like reaching the peak of a mountain after a lifetime of bloodying my feet to pulp on its rocks. I walked into the clinic near my house in Kentucky for a sinus infection, and the doctor took one look at me and offered prescription diet pills that made my heart race and my mouth ulcerous, but stuffed my brain and stomach full with blissful nothingness. I was delighted to wake in the morning weak and wobbly, knowing for certain that my body finally *needed* food, instead of the shameful, directionless craving my body had always tormented me with. When I learned how to starve, I felt for the first time in my existence not just desired, or desirable, but *deserving* of desire, like I was finally stepping through the doorway of a glorious world I'd only stared out at from the small window of a cell.

Because I had learned to starve, I finally deserved intimacy, and because I'd never known intimacy, I confused it with sex; the achievement of my emptiness in itself began to arouse me as I fantasized about all the opportunities for sex I could at last let myself claim. Soon, I could only get turned on if I was starving. I knew enough by then to know the anticipation of being filled was always more satisfying than the moments that came after.

When it came to attempts at actual human intimacy, I was also in a state of deprivation, but at least starvation was a familiar metaphor: the hunger that built like a high until I broke and stuffed anything in reach into my panicked, hollow center. Spend so long denying your needs, believing to *have* needs is a failure, and when someone finally offers you a crumb of affection, you can't simply accept the crumb—you confuse the crumb with the person who offers it and try to swallow them whole, until they are not a person at all, but another substance to plug up the great canyon inside. Until even their absence is nothing but another endless hunger.

***

If you're lucky, you may get to experience a handful of instances in life when a glinting moment swoons through you, something that feels like watching *Titanic* as a lonely, wishing child. A person may take your hand to drag you through the flooding hallways of your own life, and they might even help you fashion a raft that gets you to the other side of suffering. Maybe that devotion is something akin to love. I do not know what blood sacrifice is demanded for our happiness, what honest love ultimately gives or takes from us. But we cannot rely on it to save us. It will not save us from the world, and it cannot save us from what we most long to be rescued from: ourselves.

At the end of *Titanic*, all Rose has is a priceless, worthless necklace and the brief memory of a person she had to create the rest of her life without.

***

In college, I left work by 9:30 most nights and began my ritual of driving to the Target across the street and picking up a basket—one of the spritely, hand-held ones, not a metal pushcart, which was too clunky and obvious—and filling it with a liter of Diet Dr. Pepper, a bag of Lindt chocolate truffles, and a frozen pizza. By 10:30 I was in the bathtub, Joni Mitchell's *Blue* playing over laptop speakers, half-drunk on the poisonous sweet lifeblood of ¾ whiskey and ¼ D.D.P., hot water coaxing condensation to the surface of the plastic cup in my hand. When the water went lukewarm, I wrapped myself in the only towel that still fit around my body and poured another drink while the pizza cooked, then devoured every bit of food I owned and drank until I didn't feel bad about it, sitting cross-legged on the carpet.

I never felt as close to my father as those nights drunk in my apartment alone, crawling to my bedroom and laughing at nothing for no one to hear. For the first time, I understood his resolve to have three screwdrivers for breakfast and go about his day. I understood how much space five decades of emptiness made him hungry to fill.

But in the end, it was not the bottle that killed him.

ESCAPE

"I wanted to sparkle in the vast outline of the gone, because the gone took up the whole sky and air…Gone was a place where nobody could touch you."

–Sarah Elaine Smith, *Marilou is Everywhere*

"Nothing's gone, not really. Everything that's ever happened has left its little wound."

–Sarah Manguso, *Ongoingness: The End of a Diary*

Mountains

It is always *almost* raining. That's something they don't tell you about Seattle; they talk about the rain, but not the days the sky holds its breath, like someone on a diving board working up the nerve to jump. Over the phone, Grandma Irma asks if I can see Mount Rainier from my window. To me, the mountains are intimidating and holy. I haven't yet learned to live among them as domestic creatures, the way we forget that housecats are made of lions.

My grandma tells a story: "When we visited Tacoma, Steve was a toddler. We saw Mount Rainier off in the distance, and he'd never seen a mountain before, so I told him, 'Look, there's the mountain.' And he turned and said, 'Why's it floating?' I explained it was attached to the ground, there was just a cloud in the way, but he didn't believe me." It has been long enough that when she says, "Steve," I don't immediately think, "my father who is dead now," but can imagine the little boy, blonde and pantalooned, his conviction in the truth of floating mountains.

I can laugh at this, and do. I have long since domesticated grief and whatever grief turns into. Grief the cat, rarely resembling grief the lion.

When my boss mentions that his daughters call him "Papa," I smile and don't say, "I called my dad 'Papa,' too." Conjuring memories like these sometimes feels like beating ghosts with a wire hanger to keep them in the attic. There is only so much you can say about grief before it becomes something separate, something that lives on its own in the world and has little to do with you. Even the word *grief* sounds tedious, like trying to make conversation while walking uphill. There is only so much distance you can put between yourself and an event before the distance becomes nothing more than a map of everywhere you're not.

Above the streets of Beacon Hill, the sky exhales. I gulp down frozen air and hold my breath.

From the time I was eight when my parents divorced until the fall of my sixteenth birthday when my father died, I was in an airport twice a year, every year. As a result, I knew the drill of flying by heart. My father taught me: You get your ticket. You check your bags. You read the flights board, and go to your gate. My father complained about how he lived in the airport for good portions of the year as his shaking fingers struggled through his carry-on at the security gate. The skin of his hands was red and pudgy, and he had only stubs of fingernails from his ritual of nervous biting.

When I began travelling on my own, the ease with which I was able to find my flight number, check my baggage, get my ticket from the kiosk and move through security surprised me. The bustle of hurried bodies, the squeaking roll of suitcases across tile, and the stale taste of cabin air still feel stolen from a childhood memory.

I once read that there's a psychological link between early childhood experiences and those who travel; supposedly, kids who have a tumultuous family life, or the desire to leave their families at an early age, tend to travel farther and more often when they're older. Sitting in the airport, I looked around and thought of those people in suits or in sweats as sad little kids in big bodies with messed up parents. I thought about it then, and again after fighting on the phone with Mark four months later, sitting in the same airport; and again while driving 400 miles through the desert at night on a whim; and again and again to fill the quiet in the many small, empty hotel rooms I found myself in over the next few years. It came to define the part of adulthood I appreciated most: newfound, unconstrained freedom. My ability to run away and not to have anyone come searching with the intent to drag me back.

***

A town is a kind of grief. Not the pain of childhood, but the imprint of that helplessness. How it can sneak up again if you ever let yourself stop moving.

Anna, the small north Texas town where I grew up, a blip on the map an hour south of the Choctaw Nation, was built on the commerce of truckers passing through, their spots at the torn vinyl booths of Driver's Diner filled minutes later with others the same as them; everyone leaving and seemingly never going anywhere.

The sepia-tinted road that leads past truck stops, vacated ditches, subdivisions made of the same gray brick, the same cherry-stained plywood; the town's one stoplight near the train tracks and the convenience store costing teeth on teeth for a pack of Twizzlers, the nearest market another thirty miles; the rain-rusted drive-in malt shop owned by the family of a friend of a friend whose neighbor shot his wife in one of the crumbling houses out back; the equipment trailer repurposed as a catfish restaurant repurposed—I swear—as City Hall; the single elementary, middle, and high school of the city limits, jeweled with portable trailers where the football coach fumbles math equations; field pocked with the impact of boys' bones, where semi-yearly the circus stumbles through, elephants kicking up dried maggots from the barren soil and bringing police out to observe the decades-long burn ban; town named for the pale daughter of a rail-conductor, like the next town over, and the next town over.

The Anna I remember, the version only shown to people who found themselves trapped in its amber, was a townmind crazed with its own myth: the Quakers' cabin overtaken by KKK, then lost to wildbrush beneath the water tower; the Goat Man's Bridge, where a freed slave murdered by farmers returns costumed in hooves and horns to haunt white children; secret machinery hidden from the government, stirring below the abandoned baseball field. Each day the dust carries away someone's first and last and aching word, along with what remains of these stories.

I left my homeland quickly, my footprints marking the front yard with ashes on the way out, but Anna still lurks in my blood, breathing heavy as cornstalks. Being gone wasn't a choice for me. It was a lust for disappearing, a flame tangled into my DNA. My bedroom window had a view of the highway, a thin sinew stretched above a valley of gray shingles replicated across angled roofs. I'd sit awake and count the cars whose headlights flashed across the sky, roar of engines like faint lullabies in the distance. As soon as one appeared it was gone, and the bright call of another replaced it. My thoughts followed them to wherever they came from, wherever they would go. I longed to join the spectral fleet of anonymous travelers who left without realizing where they had been was Somewhere. That someone briefly saw their fractals of light and wished to know them, wished to be them.

***

Looking back, I've spent my life dreaming desperately of escape, without knowing why, or to where, or from what. These are the things I do know: the year I was twenty, I fantasized extensively about faking my own death, Sherlock Holmes-style, kept a brick of cash from my student loans taped to the inside of the electrical box in my closet, just in case I got up the courage to run. When I walk down the street with a friend, it's always a few strides ahead, as if my body itches to break away.

I know now what it's like to follow isolated winding roads through forsaken-looking small towns with names like Post and Tucumcari, a chorus of hollow historic buildings left in their wake, echoes of a time when the road sang out and the towns vibrated with life. I want to tell you how it felt, driving through the desert at ninety miles an hour, flat endless nothing to all sides; head blazing with the ghost of Jack Kerouac, utterly free and accountable to no one except the yellow divider leading onward, the pink sand from the mesas that sweeps over the asphalt. The sense that if there is a God, it most certainly resides in West Texas, in the winking of orange light through the trees as the sun saunters out of view like a celestial headlight, in the iron orchards of abandoned cars.

***

I want to tell you what it was like to be seventeen and alone in a strange country. Eight months out of high school, I booked a trip alone to Ireland, telling my parents after the fact. The trip was paid for with social security money I received after my father's death, and was perhaps a small act of rebellion against my mom and Mark, who'd forbidden me from moving to California with my then-boyfriend. At seventeen, I was enrolled in the community college fifteen minutes from the house I grew up in, and I felt I'd completely failed myself, my ambitions. To compensate, my new ambition became to travel as far and often as possible. This marked the beginning of my autonomy as a traveler, the transition between being shuttled east by my mother and dragged back west by my father, and actively running toward any direction of my own choosing. Perhaps I felt some small echo of my father there, in my first experience of international travel, in the airport rituals that became my inheritance.

On the flight to Dublin, eight hours long and my first overnight flight, I sat next to a retired couple from North Carolina. They talked to me like old family friends, asking about my college plans, my sisters, and my grandma's recent cruise to Alaska. After a microwave dinner of lukewarm Salisbury steak, the captain extinguished the cabin lights, and in unison the people in my section leaned back in their seats, put the hospital-quality pillows behind their heads and thin felt blankets over their faces. I couldn't sleep, imagining they could all be dead under those blankets, if not for their raspy breathing. I hovered over the Atlantic in that airborne morgue with restless leg syndrome for the next four hours, until a glimpse of sunlight and grass came peeking through the oval window.

Ireland.

Before going through customs I stopped in the bathroom, and at the sight of the oddly-shaped European toilets I understood I was truly in a different place. I took out my cell phone. It had no signal, and the wrong time; the device was completely useless. I had never felt so free.

The Dublin airport was tinted chrome and green, a geometric wonderland. I heard the singsong accent of the young customs officer with sapphire eyes, and it seemed as though anything could happen. I still had to call my parents, however. I slipped the coins in the pay phone slot, felt the cold receiver against my face, listened for the dog-whistle dial tone.

"Hello?" My mom, her words slurred by sleep. It was about three in the morning for her.

"Yeah, I'm here. I just got through customs and I'm about to leave the airport."

"Okay. I was getting worried. I'm glad you made it there safe, honey."

There was warmth in her voice. I could imagine her in bed, her thin blond hair messy against the pillow, the pores on her face bare and visible without makeup.

"I'm fine. I haven't been kidnapped and killed yet." I glanced around the bustling dome.

"Okay, you're going to call me when you get to your hotel? How are you getting there?"

"I'm taking the bus, Mom. It's in the itinerary I left for you on the fridge."

"You're going to call me when you get there, right?"

"I don't know, it depends on if I can get to a payphone. I'm calling you now."

"No, you need to try to call me when you get there so I know you're safe."

"Okay, I'll try. I've got to go, love you."

"I love you too. Be safe, baby."

Finding the right bus was easier than I expected it to be. Staring out the window as we passed through Dublin, I could hardly believe I was witnessing one of the greatest cities on earth in action. Giant clocks, masses of pedestrians, painted pub doors, squash-yellow taxis and fancy iron bridges; everything seemed like a landmark. The towers of carved marble and droves of people were exciting, but it was nothing compared to what I saw when we pulled onto the motorway heading north out of the city. First were patches of grass, and then strips of furry swaying land, trees draped in ivy, until as far as I could see, everything was enveloped in the ten-thousand most brilliant shades of green that ever existed. I felt the breath leave my body all at once like it had been knocked out of me.

***

The following summer, Rachel and I traveled to Montreal. Our first night in the city, we were walking back from dinner at a Mexican restaurant (who knows why, after flying six hours from Texas, we sprung for a mediocre version of what we could easily get at home) when she twisted her ankle on the hostel steps. The next morning when I got up and dressed for the day, she was still lounging in the bottom bunk. Her laptop was propped on her chest, her ankle wrapped in an Ace bandage.

"I don't feel like I'll be able to walk a lot today," she said, "You should go do things, though, and when you come back later we'll get lunch."

I was excited for the chance to explore by myself. Unlike Rachel, who was afraid to walk down the street unaccompanied in the unfamiliar city, I was itching to set off alone amidst the pedestrian hordes and howling train stations. I walked past dark stone cathedrals with grassy lawns, papier-mâché string lights in rainbow colors hanging overhead, left from the recent Pride Parade. Rachel texted around lunchtime, asking me to bring her food, and I ignored the text for an hour before reluctantly heading back up the concrete hill to our hostel.

Rachel's mother had organized the trip for us, taking care of each detail, reading reviews of hostels and choosing ones in safe neighborhoods. She even made us flashcards of common French-Canadian phrases, although we only learned *fromage*, the word for cheese, and *Parlez-vous Anglais?* to which the Quebecois replied with confused looks; despite our exotic imaginings of Canada, everyone spoke perfect English in Montreal. The fact of her mother's influence over the trip didn't feel smothering, as it would have if it were my own parents. In fact, it was nice to relinquish control, to let myself be taken care of for the first time in as long as I could remember.

The next morning, I left the hostel while Rachel was still asleep. Gray mist hung in the air as I took the Metro to the Mount Royal Station across town. Mount Royal crowned the skyline, creating a concrete amphitheater of the city below it. I climbed the path up the mountain, passing wildflowers and dogs with their owners, elderly couples in posturepedic shoes. By the time I reached the top, sunlight burned through the trees, dissolving the fog. The electric cross at the peak towered over the city at the altitude of my own fascinated gaze.

By the next day, Rachel was fully recovered, and we had a whole catalogue of interesting experiences together, but in some small way the two remaining weeks in Montreal were spoiled for me. I began to wake up just past dawn to sneak off to breakfasts alone at the café down the street, to wait for Rachel to settle into her bunk for a nap so I could steal an hour aimlessly wandering the cobblestone path by the river. I remember walking between a row of skyscrapers, just another body moving in rhythm among strangers, and thinking, ecstatically, *I could be anyone. I could be no one at all.*

***

Traveling alone, observing this planet fresh and foreign, is one of the only ways we might connect with who we are, what we think, and how we move through the world when we are context-less. But of course, no one truly moves through the world without context, or without a daisy-chain of ghosts trailing behind them. First, the context through which you have the option to travel depends on, among other factors, the body you are born into and the cultural system that defines how you are freed or limited to move through the world inside of it.

When I visited my family between trips or moves, my mother would tell friends and neighbors where I'd gone or was planning to go, and the women in the room would inevitably reply with some cocktail of fear and amazement, "Oh, wow, I could never do that alone."

And I'd tell them yeah, they could, if they had a bit of money and a car and childcare, they could take a weekend trip for themselves. There were websites to find places, things to see along the way, plan it all out. I recognize the privileges of childcare and money to spend are not accessible to everyone, but for these women, they were. Still, they insisted: they couldn't go alone, they wouldn't know how, they wouldn't enjoy the silence, it wasn't safe, they just hadn't ever done that sort of thing, *women* just didn't do that sort of thing.

Reflecting on these conversations, I'm reminded of an oft-quoted passage from Sylvia Plath's diary: "My consuming desire to mingle with road crews, sailors and soldiers, bar room regulars—to be part of a scene, anonymous, listening, recording—all is spoiled by the fact that I am a girl, a female always in danger of assault and battery." Though I was not able to escape so many of the burdens and scrutinies imposed during girlhood, somehow I didn't internalize its limits of mobility. Or perhaps I was so motivated to leave Anna and live some kind of elsewhere-life that I blindly burned past them.

Yes, there was the drunk man who harassed me in a coffee shop and followed me outside to the parking lot on a transient night in Pocatello, Idaho; and there was the tow truck driver who found me out of gas at two a.m. twenty miles outside of Roswell, New Mexico, who could've easily knifed me out of existence in his truck cab; yes, girls and women disappeared, in body or in mind, after what was done to them on the road. But when I began traveling alone I was either too young to understand what there was to protect myself from, or to understand I was something worth protecting. In a sense, I was looking to disappear, anyway—to lose myself in order to become myself, to escape the body and life I was told must be mine, but could not be fully mine.

In ancient Greece, *hysterical* was the word for how the uterus was believed to wander around the body, aimless. All women's rage, sorrow, fear, mania, was said to be caused by this wandering. If only she'd stay put. If only there were a way to chain her to her body.

***

There's an instinct that pushes further, compels me to bolt for some place that does not know me, does not expect anything of me; I don't only want to be adventurous, I want to be anonymous. I want to drown in a hurtling sea of strangers, to consume the city with ravenous eyes while remaining unobserved and unobligated. This is not something I chose. It just is.

Which brings me back to that magazine quote, the airports, the empty hotel rooms. If childhood has something to do with it, you'd think all children of divorce would have a secret hoard of frequent flyer miles, a folded map in their back pocket at all times. My childhood reeks of embarrassment, longing, and frustration, but so does almost everyone's.

Memory tends to cloak the dead in ambiguity, grief to relieve them of accountability, so it's hard to be accurate. In the same breath as I remember my father's drunken outbursts, I also remember the golden leaves on the Harvard Yard when he took us to Boston.

***

I have seen snow piled on cows' backs like lumps of sugar. I have seen smoke rise up from pastures under a ghostly lavender sky. I have seen the ground beneath me crack like unloved taxidermy. I have seen gutted neon motels, and a snakebird perched on the nose of an alligator under a crumbling bayou bridge. I have seen phosphorescents skitter across the Puget Sound, and slept in a driftwood fort by the water's edge. I have touched castle walls in Ireland and felt the echo of pasts reaching back. I have traced shorelines from the front bow of a ferry, as if in a dream. I have seen delirious sunsets over four coastlines and understood them to be eternal, have watched the landscape bleed from desert to mountain to bright green, mossy grave. I have reached through a broken shop window in Memphis and pulled out a lipstick-kissed card with a disconnected number for the Greyhound. I have foraged for a skeleton key by the Barren River in Kentucky and thrown it into Wisconsin's Fox River three years later, fireworks blurring the sky to gunpowder. Summer rain filling the Hudson Valley as I paced half-naked in the hallways of a wooden mansion. The bleached bone of the Mojave at 110 miles an hour, January cracking my windshield. We move through the world as the imprint of everyone and everywhere that has entered us. We set down grief for the last time, only years later to pull it from between our teeth.

***

At twenty-five, staring out from a rooftop pool at a sherbet-orange sunset spreading across the Tampa Bay, I realize every mile behind me, every box of clothes I've hoisted across the country, every city I ran from or burned through or tried to love until it broke me, has been an attempt to honor and destroy the ten-year-old child I was—following the headlights across the sky, dreaming of someday when I could be anywhere, anyone, else. The lie and the ecstasy of the gone that whispers: *Orphan yourself.*

I'm trying to say, I think, that the women I know write with fire under their skin because there is a fire under their skin. Maybe their words were ignited by some man—father or lover—who made them feel the lightness of grief, or tried to drown them in remembering. Or maybe women are born of fire and spend their lives clawing their way back from burning, creating meaning from the ash and rubble to make up for the shame in singeing everything they touch.

Here, I am writing myself out of the record, and perhaps I have always been. This is just another kind of leaving.

***

The first time I stayed with my parents again after moving away, I stood in the bedroom I grew up in, my former fortress, where the air brimmed with sleepovers, tears, laughter, friends, fears, first loves—now vacant.

The lime green walls bare, scarred with staple marks. The exciting and unsettling aura of a life condensed neatly into cardboard boxes. It was the realization that home is not a place, but a feeling, the ember inside you that must be nurtured. The house still survives, but home no longer exists, except in faded memories.

Perhaps that's what I've been struggling to escape to: home. I've searched for it in bleached hotel sheets, in foreign countries and foreign bodies, in the pounding of wheels on pavement. I've caught a flicker of it from time to time: in a sandwich shop in the bone-cold rain, a galaxy of milk poured into hot tea, the line in that glorious song when Paul Simon sings, *"Losing love is like a window in your heart..."*

Escape, like home, has rarely been about running toward something, and more often about running from it. I would like to believe it's a craving for new experiences alone that keeps me constantly moving, unsatisfied with limitations of place and time. For some, that's enough to keep a bag packed in the trunk, a flight schedule open. For me, it isn't about escaping from a place; it's escape from my small, choked voice, the responsibility of *being*, from my very skin.

Every family is a concoction of good and bad, scarrers and menders, perpetuators of fears that drive each other away and comforts that call them back. Families are made of people, after all, and people are that way: Messy. Complicated. Life moves, eroding everything in its path, until a child is grown and sitting in an airport, wondering what made her want to leave so badly in the first place. Knowing she will not return unchanged.

***

I want to tell you about ascending the narrow stone steps, so steep it required clinging to a frayed rope as I shoved my body toward the sliver of sky above. At the top of the thirteenth-century castle is The Blarney Stone, often called the "The Stone of Eloquence," and like many things Irish, its origin is winding and legend-filled: it was bestowed to Cormac MacCarthy by a witch he saved from drowning, or was used as an "oracular throne" to decide royal rulers, or was the deathbed pillow of a saint. For as long as The Stone has been in residence at Blarney Castle, the story has been this: press your lips to it, and receive the gift of otherworldly speech.

When it was my turn, I lay on my back on a rubber tarp. A slight Irish man wearing a windbreaker and a patchy goatee struggled to fit his arms around my torso. He told me to grip the metal rails on either side of my head; all there is to do is lean backwards, and slot your upper half into a hole that could tumble you head-first onto the green, green, faraway ground.

I couldn't do it. My fear of heights overwhelmed me, and I couldn't trust that gap of blank space not to suck me under. I wished for the courage, tried for a number of minutes to force it while the man encouraged me: *Reach back, lift your head, kiss, you won't fall.* But just as when I climbed to the top of the high-dive at thirteen, and the space between myself and the blanket of chlorinated blue expelled me like the wrong side of a magnet, I was frozen in place. The man, growing exasperated as a line began to form, suggested: *Maybe just reach back with your hand, if you can do that. Just touch it. That's good enough.*

I wanted to make this into a myth about my right hand imbued with that superstitious magic, to let you believe that pressing my fingers to the stone, instead, brought the gift of eloquence to my writing. But you should know: it was only because I was too afraid to lean over the edge, to trust the arms that held me, to stretch my mouth out to history and receive its mystic kiss, that I had to build this story. That I had to learn how to claim a different kind of voice.

FLORIDA

"I love it more than anywhere in the world.
As if it were a person. More than a person."
–Jean Rhys, *Wide Sargasso Sea*

I did not want to have to tell you about Florida.

***

2018

I moved across the country, for the third time in five years, in August 2018, the month of my 25th birthday. By sheer luck I was offered an escape hatch from my bleak customer service job in Nashville: acceptance to a prestigious PhD program in Tallahassee, the jeweled armpit of the Florida panhandle. I did not think it ominous when, in the frenzy of summer's endtail, that two-weeks-long gin-and-tonic-blur of department meet-and-greets and pre-semester parties ricocheting through the damp floral night, my left earlobe swelled to twice its size from wearing cheap earrings for days on end. At night, after I stumbled home from the local tiki bar, I tended it with swabs of hydrogen peroxide, and come daytime, pierced the scab with a larger earring to cover the swelling; a trickle of blood my souvenir for pulling off the illusion of beauty.

***

2020

It is February and I make a quick trip to Publix to buy eggs and butter, and end up curled on the dirty, speck-tiled floor, my back to the half-wall dividing the florescent aisles from the bathrooms. I'm listening for the smallest acceleration in the rain or the hint of metal beams beginning to capsize, the way I once lay on my teenage bedroom floor beside the stereo to listen for the singer's faint, human inhale. Above my eyeline, carts with boxes of produce rattle into and out of the back, and I glimpse an employee walk out to smoke under a sky gray with tornado threat. When it's over, I wait ten minutes, stand up, and drive home.

It is March and April and May and June, and I've never been afraid of storms but suddenly, quarantined alone in the height of Florida storm season, I'm terrified of the slightest thunder. I cower in my little corner by the cat food and the washing machine, wincing as powerlines pop outside my window. On the weather radar I religiously check, the worst of the storms usually leave Tallahassee relatively unscathed. In order to survive this panic that leaves me insomniatic or heaving bile for days at a time, I tell myself: the universe is keeping my city protected, or maybe, this land has learned how to protect itself without maiming itself to do it.

When the sky cracks furiously and the walls rattle around me, forcing my fear to outweigh my embarrassment, I dial John (who is, at this point, my partner of over a year) on speakerphone so I can leave the weather radar open in my lap.

"So, it's storming, and I'm feeling a little freaked out."

"Really? It's barely raining on my side of town," he says.

"Get ready. It's...loud." I manage a strangled laugh to beat back the tears behind it.

"Well, I don't know what to tell you. That's Florida," he replies, a shrug in his voice. He was born and raised in this violent state, and assures me in the six years he's lived in Tallahassee, "nothing bad has ever happened here," but I know from anxiety-fueled research there have been tornados, hurricanes, trees that fell on houses and killed people in their sleep, debris that impaled unsuspecting people on their couches, or narrowly missed doing so. Earlier this year, a man who was homeless and camping on the side of a rural road was struck dead when a telephone pole fell on him. But I am guilty, too: when we're far divorced from the fear of what could happen to us, we pay little attention to what has happened, is happening, to others.

"I'm sorry to bother you," I say, my voice breaking, "but I'm really scared. I know it's stupid. I know nothing will happen. I just don't want to die in this shitty house alone."

He laughs. At first, I think I'm hearing wrong, that it's static on the line. But I hear him laugh, and the sharp, bottomless pain I've fought from cresting to the surface so often in our year together sucks me down into its vortex. I begin to sob, quietly, holding the phone away from my body so he can't hear.

"Sorry, I didn't mean to upset you," he says when he realizes, though his tone is still light. "It's just that I'm used to it, I guess. Your fear is kind of hard for me to relate to."

He tries to comfort me over the phone, but my voice goes limp, and my mind sinks down into the familiar dark tunnel of myself. I am assured, before I hang up and the storm passes, in the great emptiness of what I have always known to be true: there is nothing that, in the end, a person does not have to face alone.

It's not just tornado alarms or severe thunderstorm warnings that bowl me over into apocalyptic levels of fear, but the slightest rumblings of rain. In Florida summer, the rain is daily; there is nowhere to escape.

***

2018

Tallahassee began with meeting Hunter in the basement of the university English building. I was sipping acidic orange juice from a paper cup, battling between my hunger for free donuts and my embarrassment of eating in public, when I overheard the deep-voiced man behind me say, "Lately, I've been writing lots of poems about my dog's asshole."

I turned around. "You're a poet, too?"

"Yeah," he said. "You?"

"Same. I mean, I write a little of everything, but I applied in poetry."

Hunter introduced himself and told me, "I want to write poems that taste in somebody's mind the way the ground beneath an uprooted tree smells."

"I completely get what you mean," I said.

We turned our chairs to face one another and talked for the better part of an hour, until a woman announced the campus tour was leaving. "Are you going to that?" Hunter asked.

"I think I'm probably going to sit in on one of the classes instead," I said. "There's a 'women in travel literature' seminar that looked kind of cool."

He smiled charmingly. "No, you're not. You're going on this tour with me."

His directness was surprising, a little exciting, made me a little wary. I considered.

"Okay. Sure."

We walked with the group through paved paths and under brick arches, pointing out our favorite trees and locking eyes occasionally with some wordless understanding. "I really can't fall in love with this place," I told him. "I'm already planning to go to this PhD program in Illinois I visited a couple weeks ago. They offered me a special publishing assistantship...so yeah, I probably won't come here, unfortunately. It is crazy beautiful, though."

Hunter looked down at me, the Florida sky its bluest blue. "That's bullshit. You're gonna end up here," he grinned. "You're gonna move here and we're gonna be friends."

That night, we walked with fellow writers through the humid darkness, drunk and jovial. Back at the swanky downtown hotel the university had paid to put us up in, we all parted ways in the crowded elevator with hugs and gushing hopes for shared futures. When I woke hungover an hour or two later, I quietly slipped out of my room into the empty hallway. I was waiting for the elevator when a set of automatic doors to my right wooshed open, like something from a sci-fi movie. Like an invitation from the universe. I walked through them, and found myself on the glowing deck of the rooftop pool.

I looked over the balcony at the city and swooned, a smile spreading: below, a patch of live oaks dripping with Spanish moss twinkled with warm lights. I'd later learn *Tallahassee* is a Muskogee word for "abandoned fields," but to me, even the city's name sounded like incantation, like a spell to lull a child to sleep. I did not know then if I would return, but considering the possible futures where I didn't, my heart snagged with a twinge of longing.

Hunter and I spent our first months in Tallahassee bouncing from class to bar to bar, then debriefing with the stark honesty we saved exclusively for each other, sipping PBRs and smoking American Spirits on the porch of his townhouse. As a man, Hunter was a factory of billowing red flags, but as a friend, he was intoxicating to spend time with. He called me *powerful*, and because he seemed to believe everything he said with a deathless fervor, I began to believe it, too. Our personal moralities and views of the world were often in disagreement, but I was in awe of Hunter's fearlessness; to know he thought I was Someone felt like being coronated by a mountain.

Early September, humidity drenching our skin, we met up with a group of friends outside a bar, including Sam, a nonbinary poet Hunter had befriended over the summer. It was the night of the Swamp Party, a department cocktail party held at the eerie former-plantation home of a Pulitzer Prize-winning novelist. Because I have no talent for graceful endings, when everyone else was ready to retire for the night, I usually wanted to keep flooding my throat with cheap hazy booze and wandering the sidewalks. But that night, I felt an unpredictable and inexplicable sadness beginning to take form, and decided to leave before it revealed itself. I said a quick goodbye to Hunter, Sam, and the others, and walked to the parking lot a few blocks away.

A secret wistfulness always pricked me in moments like those—the wish that someone would chase after me, the way every fateful scene in every movie promised. Stories had ruined my expectation of reality; my knee-jerk reaction to the smallest hint of sadness creeping in was expectant hope for someone to follow me into the depths of it. It never happened.

The gravel lot was in view when I heard a voice call out behind me. I turned around and saw Sam, jogging to catch up.

"Hey," they said. "I hope this isn't weird, but can I catch a ride with you?"

***

2020

It is March, and friends and lovers are buying stamps, sending letters through the mail, but *Jane Eyre* has become my only kinship. How Jane and I bite and bolt for control like "a wild frantic bird rending its own plumage in desperation." A handful of times a day I leave my blind-drawn hovel and step outside onto the screened porch to confirm the world's still there: all that lovely sunlit green staring back at me like a glory, like an existential joke. I dread nightfall, begging the daylight to stay.

I take long walks around my neighborhood, open my face to the abundant sunlight and hope for photosynthesis, wondering if this horror can be a gift—maybe the imposed isolation will force me to reacquaint with the quiet, to rise from the numb hole I'd crawled into, and heal.

Then it's July, and I am all survival mode.

It's April, and I'm a bad animal seeking any hole to burrow in.

***

2018

Sam's apartment was less than half a mile from mine, and they didn't own a car, so I'd offer to drive them home after classes, department meetings, literary readings, and the bars that always followed. We'd sit in my parked car watching raccoons climb down from trees to scavenge for garbage, and releasing secrets about ourselves into the dark interior. We quickly forged a rare, genuine connection in a place that felt to both of us thrilling but corrupt: a comet's blaze that brought wild nights with interesting people who stoked our creativity, but also the slimy, elitist politics of the university, the expectation that no one could be fully trusted.

In October, Hurricane Michael swirled toward the Gulf. Hurricanes were the most exotic of natural events to me, and for half a day I imagined staying to ride out the storm in my apartment with crazed glimmering eyes and messy hair, cackling as the rain poured, reading by candlelight when the power went out. To weather a hurricane was the most Floridian thing imaginable; it would prove I truly knew my chosen home, that I loved it to the point of danger. I believed, then, that you must weather such destruction to prove the extent of your love.

When the university cancelled classes, Sam, Hunter and I slid into a grimy booth at Leon Pub, a beer-only dive where you could smoke indoors and old men watched game shows on the crackling TV above the bar. Hunter's aunt owned an empty house in Gulfport, and we could drive out the next morning and stay until the storm passed.

Four days later, our last night in that gorgeous, strange house lined with gator pelts, we drank on the sprawling back porch and wrote down our truest words and spoke them at one another. Hunter left a cemetery of PBR cans trailing in his wake, and he was happy, he said he was *feelin' breaky*, he was coming unhinged, hurling potted plants into the yard and laughing gleefully at the destruction.

I half-drunkenly scrawled in my notebook: *I am a moth to the light of broken men,* and Hunter, shitfaced, tried to kick a metal cannister and sliced his foot open. Sam and I coerced him into bed, all six-foot-four of him stretched across the mattress like a felled pine, and I bandaged his ankle and wiped the blood from his skin, and afterward cried standing alone at the kitchen window because I reminded myself inescapably of my mother.

That night, Sam and I stayed up talking on the porch, and talking turned to flirting, and then they asked me to kiss them, and I did. They rubbed the cold from my unshaven thighs, both of us shaky and light-headed. We walked to the beach and made out for three hours in the endless sand under the endless stars, nothing but the purple light of the casino in the distance, clawing ravenously at each other's bodies.

I told them, "If we don't ever go back, I'd be okay with that. I'd be totally okay with doing this until we both dissolve to bones."

They told me, "We have to promise not to tell anyone about this." They said, "You know you can't write about this. For obvious reasons."

The reasons were obvious: they were in a long-distance relationship. It was just the "hurricane energy," we rationalized. It was just a crush, mutually discovered and adventurously fulfilled, but it wouldn't follow us back to real life. It couldn't happen again.

"I know," I said. "You can trust me. I promise."

***

2020

April 2020 was one of the most active storm months on record in north Florida, with less than five days between April 8 and April 29 that were not marked by some form of severe weather. Less than five days that panic did not clench in my chest, wring me out, make me crawl and cry and vomit. The Atlantic hurricane season surpassed every known record, producing thirty named storms, eight of which struck the Gulf Coast. The concerns of the internet hivemind briefly shifted to consider at what point regions become unoccupiable—when people must abandon their beloved places in order to survive them.

Wildfires blazed uncontrollably across the western United States, pictures circulating of dark-red midday skies, people trapped in their homes breathing the soot of a burning world, and can't help but posit through the clarity of fear that it's karma; when toxic harm is done and silently buried, it's only a matter of time before a reckoning roars to the surface.

***

2018

My affair with Sam was all-consuming, my daily motions and minutes incinerated by the question of desire and whether it would be reciprocated the next time we were alone together. The secret of the cycle, the longing and the crash of bliss and swell of longing again, was an exciting one, but it was a secret I essentially carried alone; at any moment, Sam could—and probably would—deny everything that had happened between us in order to save their relationship. Sometimes I felt delusional, wondering if I remembered any of it accurately when it seemed I was the only one remembering. My heart went as animal as the landscape, each pang of want like the restless stirring of small, clawed beasts.

I was finally forced, in Florida, to interrogate my serial attraction to unavailable people. I'd spent my life yearning for something as simple as a mutual crush, but if the rare person pursued me outright, I grew suspicious. Some part of me believed anyone who claimed to like me must be either wrong or lying.

Which is why, after returning from Gulfport, when Sam and I kissed again, all animalheat in our midnight office, and in the back and front seats of my car, and after the golden high of the house party, and after swaying to local indie bands, after climbing to the roof of an abandoned warehouse, after stumbling through the moon-splattered gates of Old City Cemetery, after it began to pour and the rain soaked our clothes, and I pushed Sam against the side of a mausoleum and pressed my wet body to theirs—when it happened again and again and stopped happening and kept happening—I knew I'd be less interested if there wasn't suffering involved.

***

2020

It is August and Lena tells me she's learning to meditate, that a purple buzzing is healing her from within. I tell her I'm afraid to find out what color is inside me, but on my 27th birthday, a quarter-machine fortune tells me to wear amethyst, so I buy an estate ring at an antique shop in St. Augustine, the band jammed onto my heat-swelled finger, the purple jewel shiny like a Ring Pop. I buy yellow sandals too narrow for my feet, I buy underwear that kills the planet as everything kills the planet, I buy clay earrings from a girl I went to college with who I once helped move out of her apartment while her boyfriend was in Argentina. I buy things no one sees me in, purchasing pieces of a life to make me feel like someone I was or someone I want to be so I don't have to feel anything about the person I am.

It is May and I walk the neighborhood learning new names for native flowers: azaleas are the pink harbingers of spring that wilt when jasmine stars the shrubs, replaced by sky-blue mums blooming at the bottoms of mailboxes. It feels good and natural to know these things, to put one's hands in a bed of herbs, to touch and report nothing of the land's secrets, or my own.

***

2018

When I remember that first fall in Florida, I remember drinking—three or four weeknights and every weekend in a combination of the same bars with the same people. Otherwise, shame about how I'd hardened myself to navigate my new life snuck up on me. Plus, I knew Sam would only be physically affectionate if we had the excuse of being drunk.

We decided to let whatever was between us play out for the final weeks of the semester. Sam would be visiting their partner over the winter break; they said they'd likely break up, but had already bought the plane ticket, so they felt an obligation to go. The night they told me this, we had sex for the first time, after months of steamy, half-clothed encounters. The final line of my journal entry from that night: *The intimacy will not destroy me (yet).*

Less than a week later, in a random text conversation, it ended: Sam casually mentioned all their relationship problems had suddenly been fixed, offering some indirect, lame apology. I spent Christmas failing to avoid the internet. Every time I flipped through my feed, Sam was posting pictures with their partner, declaring how in love they were, and each post was another quick, sharp wound.

Lena visited me in Florida for New Year's, and as is our tradition, we read tarot cards to set our intentions for the coming year. The final card in my spread pictured a dark-haired woman in a field of colorful birds, but my future was not as hopeful as the card's landscape.

"War and bloodshed," Lena translated from the paper guidebook. "Destruction, struggle, strife, untrustworthiness," she rattled off. "But! Eventual triumph, at least."

"That doesn't sound ideal."

"Erin, I don't want to scare you, but this is saying there's going to be a big conflict before anything good happens, so you might want to prepare yourself."

In January, as the new semester loomed closer, my ache began to ease. At least the constant, searing uncertainty was over; regardless of what I'd felt for Sam, or how closely it had inched toward the tender bruise of love, it was always going to end eventually.

I thought, as I stripped off my clothes and stepped into the shower, a peaceful calm washing over me, *At least my body will be only my own for a while.*

***

2019

By which I mean that in February, the ugly cling of winter, there was a dental assistant who took me to plant nurseries and taquerias and fucked me on his living room floor, and a wealthy Bostonian who fucked me atop a beer-stained Patriots blanket, and a handful of others, blips in the haze of my indignant thirst, binge of bodies I commissioned to fill and heal and hurt me. It was not yet spring or any season of release, and I was swelling like a tick with want and pizza, growing increasingly manic; when I say *manic* I mean I lived as a stripped engine on the fumes of any man's glance, grubbing any man's heat from proximity; I mean I had nothing else no other way to survive; I mean I didn't shower for days, the salt of three men compiled on my skin, and imagined myself a cackling empress, hair tangled in the tree-shadow looming from a near-stranger's bedroom window; I mean I was fevered with flu and a back spasm, but sunk into the pain and bent over his couch so he could fuck me before the party, so we could drive separately, and not speak all night, his semen leaking like so many secrets under my floral dress.

Sam and I attempted to resume our friendship, but history hung like a carcass between us. Feeling guilty that my hurt had obviously outlasted what they were willing to entertain as an appropriate mourning period, I began trying to repair the bridge with Sam via a strategy I came to think of as "bagel penance." Every Wednesday in the university writing center, we were given fancy bagels for the staff meeting: I wrapped mine in napkins, tucked it in my purse, and when I saw Sam in class later that afternoon, I gave my bagel to them. It seemed to help smooth things over, a little—and of course, the tickle of starvation that flowered in my core felt like a bonus.

***

2020

It is June, and worn ragged by constant anxiety at weather warnings, the startle of the AC kicking on, planes flying overhead that I'm sure are bound to drop bombs or crush my house, I start seeing a therapist. At our first virtual meeting, when she asks me about myself, I realize I'm not describing this new, fearfully feral self, but the previous one—the one who enjoyed talking to any person in a room, the one who was striving, curious, hopeful. A self that now feels completely out of my grasp.

She recites Maslow's hierarchy: a person grappling for safety can't levitate to the "being our best self" level of the pyramid. She says if sprinting only manages to keep us in place, we have to let go of the desire to progress, the hope of being better. I tell her with a bittersweet laugh that crushing my hope before something else has the chance to is my specialty.

I wonder why I identified the person I was during my first years in Florida as my "best self," when I have so many memories of waking hungover and leaking tears onto my thrift store couch, lying comatose all day, smoldering with self-consciousness and regret. But inside the skin of that self—always the last one at the bar, always the only woman in a group of men, plastered with the façade of the sexy, heartless, *cool girl* like those I'd admired from a distance but never imagined having the literal or figurative stomach to be—I felt in control. Or, I felt completely out of control in a way I chose. Or, I felt wanted, even though I suffered for it. Or, it was a suffering I chose, and at least the pain was interesting.

Who are any of these selves for?

***

2003

Early childhood in Alabama, eating lunch in the sunlit kitchen with my mom and sister; the sky darkens, my mom shepherds us into the closet, and an hour later, we return to our half-eaten ham sandwiches as if nothing happened. In Texas, when a tornado leveled a middle school classmate's house, dads all over town claimed to have seen it from their backyards—a note of pride in their voices that meant they belonged to a long lineage of invincible men, and had gained another article of proof that it would continue to be so.

I watch videos of tornadoes, surprisingly awed in a way that borders on affection: heavenly masses darkening as they stretch toward the earth; massive ghostly white columns gracefully splicing the land from itself; the spindly ones that snake to the ground like a witch's sharp fingernail and stir the world asunder. Almost beautiful, how it leaves us no choice but to look up and surrender. In one of the videos, the man recording calls the storm "marvelous." We call this chaos a marvel when we are privileged enough to remain only its observers. The beauty in the sublime is that you get to walk away from it; you should have died to have witnessed it, but somehow, you survive, a piece of its terrible wonder replicated in your head.

***

2019

It was in the midst of this manic era that I met John. He was sweet, shy and funny, and after he struck up an innocent conversation one day when our shifts in the writing center overlapped, it became my mission to make him obsessed with me.

Though he was only two years younger, a master's student, it was obvious he'd never had a girl sparkle so intently at him before, the way he smiled bashfully every time I inched toward flirtation. Summoning that smile to the surface was a nice distraction for me, and he rewarded it with attention, which was, at the time, the only currency I was interested in.

And then, of course—because insatiability—I rode the wave of his admiration until it felt something like a crush. Then we were at a dive bar, talking while he ate pizza and I sipped from my plastic cup of gin and tonic, and I was fidgeting in my cardigan like a first date, though neither of us had given it that name, and then I was bringing him to the graveyard like muscle memory. I teased him out of his shell enough that he kissed me, sitting on a stone ledge beside the mausoleum I'd rutted against with Sam four months before. He was flushed and trembling, and I didn't think it meant anything except that I was a Bad Person, a person who would take in this lovely eager bird knowing I was bound to crush it in my careless fist.

On a Thursday afternoon, I stockpiled booze from the liquor store. I invited him over and we got shitfaced on my couch, and—as if I thought anything else could happen—any remaining boundaries between us evaporated in my bed. I woke on his chest the next morning and it was spring, quiet but for the finches babbling through the wall. And my mind was still.

He told me he listened to my heartbeat as I slept and was struck by how wonderful it was to hear another creature's heart. I recalled the night before when I realized, mid-sex, that he was maybe the first person I'd slept with who might genuinely care about me.

He left and I showered, and then drove eight hours to Memphis to give a poetry reading. In Memphis, I chose to read poems about joy—which for me are poems about loss, too, that worthy underbelly of joy—and on the radio Paul Simon sang:

I may be obliged to defend
Every love, every ending
Or maybe there's no obligations now

The night before I drove back to Tallahassee, I fell asleep nearly giggling, realizing that for once, I could have the whole glorious world if I only chose to give myself over to it.

***

2021

In April, storm season begins anew, and though I'm armed with a year of therapy, a bottle of CBD oil, and a prescription for anti-anxiety pills, when John and I are sitting on the couch in the apartment we share and the tornado warning flashes across our phones, I am plummeted back into survival mode.

I wrap myself in a blanket and sink down into the corner while John stands in the living room, peeking through the blinds and reporting on the sky. Despite spending a third of my measly graduate teaching stipend on therapy each month, I still can't stop bracing for impact—in every movie I watch, every story I hear, every calm moment, I am searching for the turn, the tumble down the stairs, the inevitable fault line where the big bad arrives and any illusion of the good or safe vanishes.

John walks over and wraps his arms over my blanketed shoulders in a hug. "I'd sit with you down there, but the floor is kind of gross." He adds, "I don't want you to be lonely, though."

"But I am alone," I respond reflexively. He looks surprised and a little hurt, and because the words felt so gut-level true, I am a little surprised, too.

"But I'm here," he says. "I could protect you."

"You can't protect me from the weather," I say. "I appreciate you trying to help, I just mean, like, we're all alone when we die, ultimately. No one can save us, even if they want to."

A person might try to hold you in your pain, but can they sit with you in it?

***

2019

Florida summer creeping in like sludge, John and I drove to Wisconsin to work as counselors at a summer camp. We'd made our relationship official two months before, but as soon as we did—as soon as it occurred to us there was something at stake—navigating it became painfully difficult. He was nervous from his lack of experience, unpracticed in showing physical or verbal affection, or knowing how to respond to mine. I was terrified of overwhelming him and being rejected by the first person I'd called 'my boyfriend' in seven years, so although I was unsure some days if he even liked me, starved for any morsel of reassurance, I worked strenuously to hide it.

Admittedly, in large part I'd chosen John precisely because of his lack of experience, his shyness—because he seemed safe. After the wreckage of my affair with Sam, there was no part of me that was willing to risk exposure to another emotional upheaval. But the assumption that any person, any relationship, could be incapable of causing hurt only made the constant anxiety and disappointment I felt with John that much more paralyzing. If I told him how rejection sliced through me like a physical strike every time he made a thoughtless comment, every time I spoke with excitement and he looked at me blankly or changed the subject, every time I tried to move close to him in a crowded bar and he pulled away, I didn't see any way he wouldn't leave, exhausted by my always needing more. So I forced myself to need less; I quieted, and contorted, and romanticized the crumbs of the good into a feast.

I wanted to shut away all feelings, to stop the words in my mind from coming. In the numb bliss of boredom in the camp office, or afterhours at the dive bar where I sat and read alone, I believed myself happy because, for the first time in years, I did not feel compelled to write. I had no need to record who I was or what happened to me or what I felt about it, my brain blank as a linen-crested hill.

There were also nice moments John and I shared that summer, quiet vines of our growing together. We got drunk and kissed in alleyways, coordinated our weekends off and rented cheap motel rooms in town to have sex and watch *Law & Order* on cable. The day I left Wisconsin and kissed him goodbye—he was contracted to stay at camp another two weeks—I walked through the farmer's market, bright with flower stands and trumpet music, silently thanking the universe for that summer. I would leave that place fondly.

Within seconds, it seemed, a dark cloud barreled in and covered the sky. Rain began to pour, and tornado sirens wailed out. Families ran with jackets over their heads, and vendors hurried to pull their goods under tents that were already crumpling and floating down the street. I hurried to my car and drove, blinded by an endless white sheet of rain. I didn't know where to go, didn't have anywhere *to* go, and couldn't have driven there if I did. I parked beside a row of brownstone houses, across the street from a library, and noticed a small doorway under a metal stairwell, just below ground level. I remembered hearing you should lie in a low place if a tornado catches you on the road, so I ran into the rain, across the street, and climbed into the doorway, but realized when I got there that it wasn't any safer, since I was uncovered to the elements, where the stairs could fall directly onto me. I ran back to the shelter of my car.

I sat in the front seat, dripping wet as tree branches ripped loose and piled on my windshield. Panic clenched me in its fist, fear ringing through every capillary. It seemed increasingly likely with each roar of the storm that I might die there and then, alone in my car.

I called John, who was herding his campers into the cafeteria basement. I told him what was happening, how frightened I was. He said he was sorry, but couldn't talk long. Before I hung up, I told him I loved him—and though he'd said it many times that summer, when I happened to need it most, in that moment he was surrounded by other people, too embarrassed to say it back.

The rain would pass, and our relationship would eventually morph into something better, but part of me remained stuck: trapped in the panicked prism of a moment. Unloved. Alone.

***

2011

At Baylor, there was a large tree stump in the yard that I could see from my dorm room window. Steeped in college angst and fantasies of leaving my bland world for the magical ones on TV, I often stared out at the tree stump and imagined the blue police box from *Doctor Who* landing with its alien whine, where I would, without a second thought or a glance back, enter it and shut the door behind me: abandon that hot, depressing place to travel all of time and space.

One afternoon after my roommate and I arrived home from class, it began to storm. I fearlessly ran out into the rain, climbed onto that tree stump, and stood proud, laughing, dancing, drenched, as my roommate watched amused from the doorway. I lifted my face to the sky greening with strange weather above, closed my eyes, and sent a telepathic message to whoever, whatever, was out there:

Come and get me. I am brave. Please, let me be brave elsewhere.

***

2021

When I began at sixteen on my mission to flee to a place no one, not even grief, could come snarling down the road to drag me back, I believed to be a woman alone is to have agency, and to be loved is to be captive. Then, I fell for a man from this land who is leaving it—who will soon trade this lush, vined swamp for an empire of sand. He knows Florida better than I ever will, and that is why he can't love it. Home is the thing you can't love until it's behind you.

At the lake, we sit together on the *Since I Found You / Looking Through the Eyes of Love* bench, adjacent to the *Women Whose Lives Have Been Taken by Domestic Violence* tree. I have learned a relationship is not a panic room you can barricade yourself inside of; the truth of love, of living, is an open window, the gift of its breeze lingering on your skin after you walk away.

When I devoted myself to a place but held my heart at a distance from the people in it, I could pick up and leave whenever I began to feel too much of myself spilling out. I could walk away and it would be an ending I chose. But what does it mean to let someone else move forward into an era that may not include you, to leave the story ongoing, relinquish control over which direction your roots might grow—to be the one who chooses to stay?

bell hooks writes that love is a choice, but I would argue there are two kinds of love: a love that is made up from choices, and a love that drives our choices.

Tallahassee, my last love letter to choosing.

***

2020

The night before I boarded a plane to San Antonio in early March—not knowing the world as we knew it would be swallowed like a tidal wave when I returned—I was eating sushi with John when he received a phone call. I watched his face twist with concern, then ecstasy: he'd been accepted to a graduate program in Las Vegas. In the restaurant parking lot, we sat silently in the car as he read the offer email. I watched the rain drizzle green streaks on the windshield, and feigned enthusiasm. It was what he wanted, and I was happy he'd gotten it. But it was also confirmation that our lives would change irrevocably.

As I packed my bags for San Antonio, he sat on the bed and asked me to follow him to the desert. I told him I'd think about it, but I knew in my gut as soon as the call arrived: I did not want him to leave, but I would not leave with him.

***

2021

After five days covering two-thousand miles, and hours of nothing but rock caging us in from all sides, the mountains parted to reveal the pale orange valley of Las Vegas, and John's eyes began to burn.

"It must be allergies or something, but holy shit," he rubbed tears from his vision.

"Are you okay? Do you need me to drive?" I asked.

"Maybe. I'm not sure. It really hurts. Fuck."

"If you can pull over, I can drive, it's not a problem." I opened the glove box and began to sift through. "Here, let me find a napkin or something, maybe that'll help—"

"Just be quiet!" he snapped. "Leave me alone. Please." He rarely raised his voice, and the strike of it lingered in the cab of the car, static that itched on my skin. I pulled my sunglasses down over my face and stared rigidly forward, the glow of the landscape and my excitement sapped from the moment. A few seconds passed and he said, calmer now, "I really just need you to be completely quiet so I can concentrate."

We rode in the heavy silence of the engine and his pained sighs, surrounded by the ruined sunset. Minutes later, he managed to pull into a gas station.

When he got out of the car to pump gas, I silently began to cry, blotting tears beneath the oversized lenses of my sunglasses, careful not to smudge my makeup. We'd spent the past year home-bound in my one-bedroom apartment, and I'd gotten good at crying inconspicuously—or crying openly with slightly less shame, if there was no way to hide it. I was surprised to learn how easy it is to hide things from a partner in close proximity, and how hard.

After a cross-country road trip from Florida with his belongings packed to the ceiling of his 90s Toyota, we arrived in Las Vegas: the place he was moving, which also happened to be the place I was born. Although the trip was about his future, as I sat in the car alone swiping tears from my face, I couldn't help but envision scenes from my inherited past; my mother and father living here together, my mother my exact age when I was a newborn. My parents' marriage was never easy, as I understood it—my dad had been a little like John, actually: quieter and more reserved, less comfortable acknowledging emotions, easily overwhelmed, lashing out when annoyed. More cold than violent, but quiet violences linger. I could easily imagine my mother spending moments like this, crying in secret, then forgiving quickly to erase the discomfort and reroute them toward happiness.

John got back in the car and pulled the mirror down from the visor to inspect his face.

"How are your eyes feeling now?" I asked.

"A little better, but still not good. I don't know what happened. It just came suddenly."

"The dust," I suggested.

"I'm sorry I snapped at you," he said. "I feel bad about it. I just got overwhelmed."

I believed he meant it. But over the past four days—and truthfully, the past two years—we'd played out similar scenes, recited similar lines. In Albuquerque when I was driving and he got frustrated because I missed a turn he never told me to take, or in Flagstaff when I relayed directions from the GPS, and he missed an exit and blamed me for not directing him in exactly the words he would've used. And afterward, he'd apologize, and we'd talk through it, and he'd tell me he didn't have bad intentions, he was just reacting in the moment and couldn't control it. And I'd tell him he wasn't a bad person, but he needed to learn to react differently, and he'd look at me solemnly and promise to do better.

By then, a year of therapy and the gradual easing of the pandemic had allowed me time to thaw from my hibernation of panicked survival mode, and I'd slowly become more comfortable speaking up to John about the problems in our relationship. During the year we'd lived together, I knew was not exactly easy to live with, either; I was not mentally well, and I was constantly apologizing for that fact. I was stuffing down my feelings in every direction, trying to bury whatever I had to in order to make our relationship—this one morsel of stability in my life—last.

In the moments when I broke my silence, it was because I was physically incapable of walling away the pain any longer. He wouldn't know how to respond, but he would patiently listen, and that was more than anyone else I'd dated had done. Ultimately, we had a good friendship, even if the romantic partnership fell short for reasons that had more to do with a profound incompatibility than any one person's faults. When I began to reawake from depression and regain my confidence moving through the world, I began to wonder if it wasn't that I needed too much from him, but that what I needed was more than he was capable of.

"Listen," I said this time, "I understand you didn't mean it, but we've talked about this. We've talked about this same issue at least three times this week."

"I know," he said, "It wasn't even really about you, I was just frustrated."

"I get that, but…no matter what your intentions are, the result is that I'm spending a lot of time with a person who makes me feel bad when I'm with them."

He paused and looked down. "I really am trying to do better."

"And I see that. I know it's not easy for you. But I don't deserve to be yelled at. I'm sorry to have to say it this way, but I'm serious. Something has to change, or we're going to break up," I said. "I am not going to be a woman who spends her life crying in secret."

"Okay," his face looked red and miserable with regret. "You're right. I'm sorry." Partly, I felt guilty for speaking to him so bluntly, despite his apology. But the larger part of me felt a foreign and exhilarating empowerment. I was done suppressing my pain. I was beginning the long road to reclaiming a self.

We pulled out of the lot toward the highway, toward what was left of our trip, and our time together. "Oh, look," I mentioned mostly to myself, pointing at the building on the other side of the gas station. "That's the hospital where I was born."

The remainder of our time in Vegas passed in a smooth blur of glittering casino smoke, the majesty of the Bellagio's botanical gardens and painted skies in Caesar's Palace, walking through long carpeted hallways pumped with sanitized air. And my resolve to reclaim the life I felt so lucky, after the past year, to have left to live, came to another culmination: in the corner booth of an Italian restaurant, in the warmth of free-flowing red wine, it was there, in the city where I was born, on the night before my twenty-eighth birthday, that I took my last drink.

***

2022

As I write this, I've been sober almost a year: it's new enough that I haven't yet found the right language for it, but long enough to believe it's going to stick.

The choice to quit drinking snuck up on me, which is why it can feel strange to talk about: it was not, at the time I decided it, difficult to accomplish. I didn't make the choice from rock-bottom; I'd clawed my way up the cliff and stepped away from the ledge years before. It's been four or five years since my habits were those of an obvious alcoholic, and two or three since social drunkenness was a regular part of my life. As I passed further into my twenties, my self-destructive impulse grew rarer—or more exhausting. Or more complicated, heeding to more complex coping mechanisms. Like fantasy. Like silence.

In July 2021, still deeply unwell after a year of seeing two therapists weekly to manage my mental health, I began taking antidepressants. It is too simplistic to say they solved me. But the veil of despair and self-annihilation lifted almost immediately. A new voice floated into my body, wise and calm—the voice of an unfamiliar, more compassionate self who wanted good things for me. The pills did not throw a blanket over my feelings, as I'd worried they would; instead, it opened up more space inside me for the feelings to spread out, so I could see them for what they were, not the tangled mass I'd experienced them as before. The panicked, guilty, writhing voice I've lived with all my life did not go away, but when it spoke, this new voice answered louder.

I'd heard you're not supposed to drink on antidepressants, so I figured I'd play it safe at first. That's what I told my friends at the bar that weekend: "I'm probably not going to drink for a while, until I adjust to the meds." So, I suppose it wasn't the choice of sobriety that snuck up, but the choice to continue it, and the realization that making the choice mattered to me.

Flashes of story orbited my mind like deep-space debris: my grandmother's mother abandoning her, the abuse she endured from alcoholics, the marriage that alcohol exploded, the son it nearly killed. My dad, the struggle of his life that I understood only when he was gone and the struggle became my own. Coors bottles piling around my mom in the garage, or Mark's angry glass of amber. The shame of remembering unkind or selfish things I'd said and done when I was drunk; the living burial I pantomimed privately night after night; the sobbing mess I used alcohol and drugs as an excuse to construct publicly so others would try to clean it up, to save me from myself; self-blame and self-hate corroding me from the inside when I couldn't stop. My dad overcoming his "hereditary defect," only to die before he got the chance to begin a life free of it. My sobriety means breaking the curse, for him, for them, as much as for myself.

That August in Vegas, as I prepared to return to Florida, an ominous feeling loomed. I hallucinated the machine of fate stirring; only days before, I'd stopped drinking, and when my dad chose to get sober, he died less than two weeks later. In the superstitious logic of The Story, the potential for my untimely death seemed especially timely. But days after my birthday, my plane landed safely in Tallahassee, a smooth descent bordered by ruddy pines.

My sobriety is the first promise I made to myself that I have actually kept. And that promise lead me to new ways of thinking about self-worth, about who I am and hope to become, what I choose to spend the remainder of my life on.

In March 2022, I boarded a plane back from the AWP conference in Philadelphia. John and I had been living apart and dating long-distance for almost a year, and our third anniversary was two weeks away, but whenever I tried to envision it, I felt only a pit of dread heavy within me. On the plane—the conditions so similar to those two years before, before the world collapsed and rearranged—it felt like the universe was offering me a do-over. This time, I did what I knew I should: I landed, called John, and broke up with him in the kindest way I could, which I knew would not be enough to dampen his hurt. I told him I was grateful, and I genuinely hoped, when time softened these memories until they seemed as if they had been lived by caricatures of past selves, that he would feel the same.

The previous October, John and I drove through Las Vegas, down flat sandy highways, beneath stucco overpasses, through neighborhoods of Dutch cottages built from adobe. When I was there, a passenger to the city, I thought of my parents; these roads they traveled together, these places that were backdrop to the early years of their marriage. Young and looking out over the horizon of their lives, so much was unclear except being together there and then. Though I was the same age they were in this place, my life looked very different from theirs. In some way, I think that's the point: our stories help those who come after us to have different choices.

In the place of my origin, a spectacle of electricity drowns the night sky, severing the city from any view of the stars. But when I look up, I know they are still there. And there is so much to see here on land, in this monument to glamour built in the isolation of a desert valley, such saturated beauty it can only exist self-contained. When I am there, I am one dark cell swimming in a body of light that can be seen by even those who have left Earth's atmosphere. I do not miss the stars; they'll be there when I return to them.

On the sunrise flight back to Tallahassee, I leaned back and closed my eyes, began my ritual of fearful prayer as the plane's wheels left the ground. But this time, I watched as we ascended, and saw the glint of the Strip fade into misty mountain dawn, the snaking river of the reservoir electrified by the waking sun. If that plane went down, I'd keep one eye on the dazzle as I fell, for to witness the beauty of this world we were given is to have been given so much already. There is so much wonder in where we are right now.

***

2023

One final time, during my last year in Florida, I found myself leading a man through the moss-draped darkness to the gates of Old City Cemetery.

As an ending to our date night of fancy mocktails nearby, I showed him the witch grave, where people often left coins and seashells as offerings (the "witch" was actually just a wealthy woman who died young, at 23, and whose grave happened to face west). In the first weeks of 2020, three friends and I visited the witch grave to perform an amateur esoteric ritual for luck in the new year, and joked afterwards that we'd accidentally conjured the pandemic.

He observed the historical graves while I narrated, until I noticed he'd fallen quieter than usual. "Are you okay?" I asked. "We can leave, if this creeps you out too much."

He shook his head. "It just feels weird, to be near all these buried people, and I haven't touched any of them."

I pulled him into a hug. He slid his hands around my waist and I kissed the pale crook of his neck, my mouth automatically seeking contact with any stretch of his skin in reach.

On our first date, six or seven months before, we'd sat in a booth at an ice cream shop and talked until the store closed. We discovered with mutual astonishment that the summer camp in Wisconsin where I'd worked years ago was on the same campus where he'd gone to college, and that the dorm room I'd lived in was directly across the hall from the room that had been his more than a decade before. He was an emergency room nurse, and told me that when his patients die, he makes sure he is the last person to lay a hand on their bodies before they are wheeled away, so they can rest knowing the last person who touched them cared deeply about trying to keep them alive.

I cried, of course. On all the best first dates I've been on, I've cried. His blue eyes held a still, relentless gentleness. He looked at me like he could see through my skin.

Now, I led this rare and beautiful man to the stone ledge behind the mausoleum, cradled in spring humidity. We sat together in the dark, talking, sometimes laughing, sometimes kissing, leaning softly against each other in a world gone quiet but for the gentle buzz of orange streetlamps at the border of the cemetery, who knows for how long. Time had a way of slipping through us.

And who knows how the topic came up, in our winding conversation about what parts of us are surrendered to death and what of our souls and stories survive, but there in the graveyard he confessed that shortly after we met, he researched my father's murder.

"Oh, really? What did you find?" I was at once surprised, curious, and flattered. "That one long essay?" Years ago, I'd published an essay that I knew came up as one of the first results when someone googled my name, a compilation of vignettes about the murder, a trip I took to my dad's birthplace of Chicago, and musings on the strangeness of grief's aftermath. When John and I started dating, and I met his mother, her having found and read this essay was the first thing she wanted to talk to me about. That had felt a little uncomfortable, almost invasive, though of course I was the one who'd chosen to publish the piece, and by then, I was a practiced professional in casually discussing the murder.

"No," he said. "Well, yes, I read that, too. But I found the court documents, some newspaper articles. I read what you had written for the trial."

"The impact statement?" I ask. "I had to read that the sentencing. Wow, I was only a teenager when I wrote that."

"I know," he said. "You could break hearts and build worlds in your writing, even then."

It is hard to explain why this meant so much to me, why knowing he had sought out and read the words I'd written at eighteen—the first time I'd written about my dad's death in any capacity—healed something within me.

"What made you put the effort into finding all that stuff?" I asked.

He paused thoughtfully. "It seemed like the thing to do," then he added, his voice sincere, "if I wanted to understand you."

The morning I finally leave Tallahassee for good, it is his text message that reaches me with wishes of safe travels as I exit the live oaks downtown, the dawn still dim enough to make out a faint glow strung through the branches. Now, when I remember walks around Lake Ella, or wandering in the graveyard, or Railroad Square, or the rooftop pool where I stood alone overlooking the twinkling, misty wonder of Tallahassee, considering whether I could call this place my own; and half a decade later found myself there again, tucked against his warm chest on the penultimate night of a new year, telling him the story of how I almost missed out on all of this—when I remember the places that defined those years, memories and lost selves dancing over the city like phantoms, I think, first and fondly, of him. He taught me what Florida truly meant, in the end: learning how to recognize the first, if not the final, place that feels like home.

***

2019

I was riding to the airport, flying to Fargo, North Dakota for the release of my first book, and my Uber driver, a tattooed butch lesbian from the swamps of Wakulla, told me how she ate too many moonshine cherries the day of Hurricane Michael and held tight to her truck bed in the storm, cackling with excitement as the world swirled around and her mouth filled with rainwater.

Years later, when the breaker sparks on a wet Florida night and a live oak branch splits loose over the street, and I, animal-eyed and alive, inch onto the screened porch—when the sky growls luminous red and I stand to face the fury of the storm alone—I will think of her.

In the Heart of the Heart of The Heart Of

The spring of my first year in Florida, I was invited to give a reading at a bookstore in Dallas. It had been five years since I last crossed the state line into Texas—since the summer I returned from Seattle to help my mom box up the house for their move to Tennessee, where Mark had already begun work; sleeping on the concrete floor of Rachel's apartment or in my sparse teenage bedroom, before I moved to Kentucky for grad school. Since I'd left, my college roommates got married and had babies, and Stephanie had given birth to a second child, my nephew—a child I hadn't met and don't know if I ever will. Rachel still lived in Denton, with a college friend and two middle-aged chihuahuas, and offered me a place to stay for the weekend.

I drove fourteen hours through the night from Tallahassee, and early the morning of the reading, merged onto I-75 toward Anna. That day happened to be the Vernal Equinox, the radio informed me between over-produced country songs: the one day of the year when an equal amount of sunlight spreads over every place on Earth. A day, perhaps, when all places shine more brightly, even the ones that formed us.

The thin gray road in my memory was now beige and widened to five lanes, and filtered by my lack of sleep and the strange morning light, driving it felt absolutely alien. I never thought I'd live to see the day when Anna gained a Wal-Mart, but there it was, next to the lot where they tore down Driver's Diner to build a Whataburger. A sandstone wall now stretched across the back of my old neighborhood, blocking the backyards and their flimsy brown fences. But as I drove toward what was once the town's single stoplight, deepbright spots of memory called out to me, pockets that shone as if from déjà vu, hidden among the ugly growth of strip malls and fresh concrete: the Texas Star Bank, whose lobby we rented out for Trinity's baby shower and my thirteenth birthday party. The Coyote Den convenience store where Stephanie and I stopped along the drive to school to buy expired bottles of Snapple. The brick building with "Beech Nut Bacon" painted in yellow on the side, empty as ever beside a new baseball field. Even the cornfield I lost myself within at twelve, my first attempt at escape that left me grounded a whole summer, was razed of its vast mystery, the field shorn.

I stopped to buy a butterscotch shake at The Malt Shop, the rusted ice cream sign one brilliantly unchanged thing. Standing in the gravel lot was like touching past lives—like retracing, as if I'd just remembered it existed, the *realest* life, sunk deep at the bottom of me, barnacled and fading, now excavated clear and true. Like a heartbeat, my mind reverberated: *I am of this place.* I wanted to reach down where I stood and fill my mouth with a fistful of the dry dirt.

That night, at the reading in Dallas, Dylan came with Phoebe, his partner of ten years—whom he spoke to for the first time via Myspace messenger, sitting at the computer desk in my parents' room after school while I lounged on the sagging bed beside him. We tramped through Deep Ellum streets and bar patios and taco stands, the moon like a wildflower bulb grieving brightly in the sky. When Dylan and I recalled how my mom kissed him on the beard when she was drunk, how his dad held garage sales at our house as an excuse to flirt with my mom, how we skipped school and sat on the back of Dartanian smoking soggy cigarettes in the rain when his Nana died, I realized: you can tell your stories to anyone, but there are so few people who know the shape and smell of them, whose precious broken years are intertwined with your own.

We reached the gate of Dylan and Phoebe's apartment, and my heartstrings snagged on the dwindling minutes. I think I felt then what I've heard other people describe feeling with their families—normal people, whose family relationships aren't bloated with layers of shame and guilt. To be among people who've known the many iterations it took you to arrive at this spot, who see those pasts in the face of the person you are now. People with whom, after however many dislocated years, that love and knowing resumes effortlessly.

Earlier that day, as I left Anna, I turned into the side-entrance of my old neighborhood. I parked across the street, in the driveway of the now-vacant house where Mark lived before meeting my mother. The door to our house was painted turquoise blue, a ceramic frog in the entryway, my mother's birdbath plucked from the yard. I wondered how it would feel to go inside, to see those small pockets of *mine* swallowed by the overwhelming *not-mine,* like I'd seen all over town. I knew by the next time I returned, those few glimmers of the dreadful, magical town I was raised in would be snuffed out, and so I knew that I would not return.

As I stepped out of the car, my flip-flop broke—same as it had some years before, when I lied to a realtor so I could walk inside my dad's former house. I bent over to fix my shoe when a car pulled into the driveway and a dark-haired woman got out, walked up the path, turned the knob of the door, and disappeared inside. I got back in my car and drove away.

When I moved out of that house at sixteen, as I was packing up my room, I found a picture of my father and I at the beach: me wearing his oversized sweater, his hand on my back, us blending into the waves as we walked shore-bound. Since then, I have moved thirteen times, reducing my entire life to series after series of cardboard boxes, and I can't find the picture. I don't know where it's gone, and I miss it more every day.

RENDERING

"I am happy every time to see real personhood resist our tricks. I am happy to see bodies insist that they are not shut up in this book, they are elsewhere. The tomb is empty, rejoice, he is not here."

–Patricia Lockwood, *Priestdaddy*

After my father died, I began to follow men around the grocery store. Middle aged men, men with dark hair and bald spots, glasses-wearing men in white sneakers and too-tall socks, in tucked polo shirts, in dark suits. Men with thin hair combed back, a slight tan. Men who looked like him. I began to see my father in strangers, began to watch strangers for a glimpse of my father. I watched men who look the way he might have looked were he still alive; a more pronounced bald spot, the jowls and papery skin that come with age. I didn't follow them through stores and streets, but I let my gaze linger. With these strangers, I staged an exhibition of how he moved through the world.

My father was a computer engineer. In the months surrounding my birth in Nevada, he drove an hour to a government facility in the desert, and boarded a jet plane with blacked-out windows. Even he didn't know exactly where he went, just that he couldn't talk about it to my mom—not to anyone.

These are only pieces I've heard, from him when my sister and I visited, from my mom and grandma, but as I was growing up, I didn't know exactly what he did for a job. Aside from his drunken rambling about aliens and Area 51 at a Ramada Inn when I was twelve, I still don't. There is no reason to believe that he worked for the CIA, or the FBI, or any government agency that would feasibly require someone to fake their death, leave their life, disappear. But a year after he died, I began to have dreams.

In the dreams, my father faked his death because he was undercover for the CIA. He's back now, alive. He's glad to see me. He pulls up a chair to a desktop computer and I catch him up on everything he's missed: pictures from my high school graduation, trips to Europe, grad school, my many moves and pets and partners. There are variations: In one dream, he didn't work for the CIA at all; I go to grab a bottle of wine from my grandmother's basement on Thanksgiving, and find him hiding behind the shelves, among the ancient moonshine and pickled okra.

In one, he's lying on the hardwood floor of my apartment, completely bald, completely naked except for his glasses. I try to show him the pictures, but he won't move. I tell him I've been writing about him. I try to push him into my office so he can see, ask him if it's okay to write about him, if he's mad, if he likes the words, what he thinks, but he won't talk to me, he won't tell me, won't say anything.

I woke smelling his aftershave, haunted.

I play these games, look for him in crowds, dream about the CIA. But it wasn't until I was sitting on the elevated train in Chicago headed to Sears Tower that I realized:

I actually believed he would show up there.

***

Hello I am calling from Washington D.C. wondering if you've ever seen this city & how sad that I can't tell your footprints from my own anymore, in a coffee shop outside the metro your funeral song played & I wondered if your hair would be graying or gone, whether you were trying to answer a question I don't know how to ask yet.

Hello I am calling from Seattle & sometimes I see a car glimmering charcoal smell new leather think of you sometimes I think of you not for weeks or months at all until Grandma calls & says are you thinking of him? & I lie sweetly tell myself the fact that I am writing this makes me not guilty of not loving makes me not unlovable, tell myself I have just moved on I am living my own life whatever that means.

Hello I am calling from Kentucky where I live yes Kentucky I swear the people here have teeth but here is the place I unfurled into impossible painful lightness here is the place I exorcised myself from myself, I heard on a podcast trauma makes you tourniquet your soul from your body & it's true that I once thought of my legs as dead tree limbs but I have never thought of this as trauma, only a necessary becoming. & maybe that's part of the problem.

Were podcasts around when you were? You would be so excited about Google glasses Apple watches & all those dumb weird beautiful tunnels of data that make our lives so cloudlike now, I think of you sometimes.

***

My dad began his life in Harvey, a suburb on the south side of Chicago. Now, a Google search auto-fills the space after Harvey, IL with "crime rate," and reveals images of derelict buildings burnt and boarded, grotesquely peeling billboards, taquerias with steel-barred windows. My Grandma Irma describes an idyllic American boyhood where my father played baseball under cool skies, paying no bother to grass stains. My grandparents brought pop-out chairs and sat near the bleachers, hauling a cooler of ice-water for the boys on the team.

They moved to Palatine, on the north side, when he was ten or eleven; he took his south side accent with him then, and into adulthood. Even after living all over the country, the hard whine of an "a" punctuated his voice, especially when he said "Chicago." It's the only word I can still hear him through clearly, the only way I can remember how his voice sounded.

***

These are things I was told in adulthood, only because I asked. Because I only thought to ask after he was dead seven years, when I realized I didn't know him. I'm still not sure I do. With each discovery, more questions sprout from me like twigs and branches than there are answers to flower them.

What I have for sure is this: a black and white polaroid photo, labeled *Stevie, April 1962.* A small boy stands on the concrete steps of a brick house. He is wearing suspenders and a bow-tie, his head almost too big for his body. He smiles for the camera.

***

I have never felt overcome with grief, but rather, overcoming, like I forget I am climbing a steep hill. More than suffering, his death merged into my life has been a kind of smothering.

It was not until five years after his death that I missed him, craved him the way I occasionally crave spirituality or an imagined lover. Guilt has always been my default: I feel guilty that my first thoughts after learning of his death were selfish ones. I feel guilty that I never cried in front of my family—that even over a decade later, I wall myself off in animal instinct, crawl beneath the bed like an ailing pet rather than be seen *feeling* about the one thing I probably deserve to feel something about. I feel guilty that the relationship between my father and I was a strained one, exacerbated by his drinking and my resentment. I was a shitty teenager to him. Most teenagers are shitty to their parents, but most of their parents aren't suddenly murdered.

Grief as I know it has been more like a doorway, constructed as I descended the stairs and saw my mother's face, heard her voice as she told The Story for the first time; the story my family would tell a million times over until it was learned by heart, the lines practiced, the intonation of each word memorized. I descended the stairs a teenage girl and walked back up them not a woman, exactly, but some kind of newly born, unfamiliar creature. I closed my bedroom door behind me and my life officially began.

Of course, there's no way to know if any of the stories we tell are the truth.

This is the story I tell to others—to myself—about my father's life and death, about the tiring complexity of how I handled (or didn't handle, or am still handling) the puzzle of it all.

Once the story solidifies, everything before the moment of impact becomes myth along with it. There is only life as we see it in retrospect. There is only after.

***

Hello I am calling from slightly-embarrassed penance where yes I remember the way I resented branding your death onto my life said I wouldn't carry your picture at graduation wouldn't build you like a canopy over my one-day-distant wedding ceremony wouldn't ballroom dance with a ghost, yet here you are inhabiting my writing a space more true than life & that means something, right? Hello are you listening am I also dissolved to radio static? I am writing from the groping dark of the future believing that when this is finished I will belong to myself again, though these words you made in me have made me. These pages used to gouge you have sewn you into the hem of me. Or exposed the oozing seams I was born with.

***

Here's another story: I visited Chicago for the first time the summer before I turned fourteen. I remember walking with my dad and sister through streets that sprouted into skyscrapers. Beside an ivory bridge and a body of water, a Black man in loose jeans and a white tank top walked beside us, and I remember my dad being visibly frightened of the man, placing his arms around my sister and myself as a barrier. I remember trailing behind, embarrassed by his neuroses and how easily it had ballooned into racism. The man walked past, and when he was far ahead, my dad whispered something about gangs.

He took us to Sears Tower. The guide on the ground floor told us that the building was built to sway with the wind. As the numbers on the screen rose and we approached the 100th floor, I was terrified the elevator cables would snap. I didn't look over and see my dad shaking, or wringing his hands, but he must have been. He was too nervous to ride escalators at the mall.

At the top, he looked briefly over the city, pointing out Wrigley Field, then receded back from the windows. I inched toward the glass, woozy with height, and imagined the sensation of a plane toppling the building, or the floor underneath us capsizing. I could have sworn I saw the bridge where we had walked earlier. I could have sworn I felt the building sway. My dad stood somewhere behind me, unseen, watching me watch the city swirl alive beneath us.

***

The first words I wrote about my father after his death were: *There are some things you never knew about me.* Since then, every sentence has been a revelation that there is so much I don't know about him, may never know. My writing has become a search not only for the cosmic meaning in life and death and sudden rippings from one to the other, but for what it means to live with a death in the blood.

There's something about the shape a man leaves when he's gone—work unfinished, days untangle-able. I remember the funeral of my maternal grandfather and how my grandmother shriveled without his elephant largeness, how she became a trembling bird in a dress as pale blue as a drowned child's cheeks. Whether heart attack at the kitchen table or blood spilt on a living room carpet, there is a need to exorcise the story, to relay cause and effect so that we can be done with grief, or at least, tell ourselves we are.

The motive behind this book has been to know my father in retrospect, to render him on the record in order to understand the part of myself that carries whatever remains of his death-fractured, daughter-told story. But can the ghost of a story ever truly be laid to rest, when its host moves through the world, carrying it in their DNA?

***

Epigenetics, the study of molecules that control inherited genes, says that frightened fathers of mice pass along impulsive stress responses to their offspring; that if a woman's grandmother was born during a famine, that woman's heart will more easily grow diseased; that children of war prisoners are ten percent more likely to die an untimely death than their peers. *The New York Times* reports that experiences of suffering—grief, trauma, poverty, post-traumatic stress—can trigger physical changes, literally alter a person on a cellular level. Then, these trauma genes can be passed along to descendants.

Before a woman is born, then, her family's trauma is written in her body, carved into her ovaries and eggs, ready to pass its ghosts through her, back into the world. If I were to take on the role of parent after having a dead one, I might stain my child's life with the ghost of an untended grief, emotional weeds that flesh out the garden of a troubled family past like delicious cancer. And who would that child see themselves to be, one-fourth phantom of lover's violence?

There are worse problems, though, more difficult and pressing ones. There have always been, and those clusters of human sorrow ripple out to graze us all. When Dr. Pauline Boss speaks of the Holocaust and Civil War, Salem Witch Trials and slavery, she explains, "We are a nation founded on unresolved grief."

Was there something in my father's smile that was born ready to curl up and become a fossil? Something in me that was created to decipher its grooves?

***

This story my inheritance has forged me & become me: record of days the dead leave behind fragments half-truths little aches & wonders. So it turns out I am the story or the body your story passes through a breathing narrative of doorways that carries the burden of your whole purposeful living, leafing through a semi-stranger's moments finding them redacted in places heat-sharp in others. Searching through your failings to build myself into something better I owe you at least this, every ghost is owed a story whether or not it's the shape of anything they recognize as theirs.

***

I have been telling the story of my father's death for twelve years, and it wasn't until recently that I've begun to wonder whether this story is the truth, or if it hinders me from truth.

So much about The Story doesn't add up, even as it feels true. I know for a fact it wasn't until days later that we learned the circumstances of the shooting—that he was writing her a check, that she shot him in the back of the head—but I'm almost sure I remember my mom telling us those details that night. I can clearly remember her telling us his eyes would be donated, but I don't think I actually knew his eyes were given away until I read a quote from the impact statement my grandmother gave at Pam's sentencing, printed in the newspaper over two years later.

Because a mind can repress, shatter, and dissociate memories after a stressful event, the relationship of trauma victims to the truth can be especially complicated. Grief has no pattern, no reliable narrator. As Laura Gray-Rosendale writes in her memoir *College Girl*, "Our stories are necessarily always about slippages, about what we know as much as what we don't know."

***

I wonder if my father would condemn these words if he could read them. I wonder if he would see that there is love in my brutal honesty, that even in recalling his offenses I am trying to know the person he was, not the airbrushed icon death reduces the dead to.

I have always been adamant that if nothing else, I would not saint him simply for the fact of having died, the way my aunt and grandmother seemed to. I promised I would remember him realistically. But is that really what I'm doing? Is it even possible? The reality of who I thought he was has changed with each year he's been lost and I've lived.

And though he disapproved of my becoming a writer, I use these words to preserve him and everything that came after he was killed. I am a writer, and the last thing he did in his life was put pen to paper. At the moment he died, he was writing.

***

Sometimes you seem a detail of my past no longer relevant, reduced to a song in a coffee shop a good sharp ache to loosen up convenient tears & other times for weeks I am preoccupied with fantasies of you posthumously scrolling through my selfies finding that I bloomed beautiful & sighing finally with rest. I am calling from my kitchen my office my sweet realm of delusion where you are in hiding with the CIA or flying roundtrip the circumference of the Earth just for good old abandonment's sake, where you are capable of using the internet or knowing that two months ago a woman who bled her waterlogged world with fire words said I owe you this & I was crying ugly. & later on a drunken park bench I sat with someone I saw then as pure luminescence & he swaddled my stories of you in sweet-smelling forgiveness blankets wrapped my wrists in understanding & I will not marry him but probably I will marry someone & you won't know what they look like, won't shuffle through the awkwardness of begrudging your blessing on some beautiful vagabond who wants to tie our lives together until our bones break.

I am calling from Nashville where I dared to ask a psychic where your phantom lingers during that collection of months I unraveled in love & became briefly fearless. I paid her way too much it was all a hoax except I wanted to believe so I did, she recorded the session but at the very instant I said your human name the tape died, & she told me you were disappointed with these words. She said bummed she said you were a little bummed by what I'd written exactly the word you would use, even now your minty stubble comes crawling fierce after it & I have to trust that words mean something because elsewise there is truly nothing left.

***

The words we have at our disposal shape how we think about the aspects of life they represent. There are some words, like the French *dépaysement* (the feeling of displacement in a foreign country) that can't be translated precisely to English. Language shapes our cultural consciousness, limits the ideas we can explore.

As a child, I called him only *Papa*. *Papa* is the name of running through the kitchen and jumping into his arms when he had been gone on a business trip. *Papa* is the name of being small enough to sit shirtless in his lap. After the divorce, I began to call him *Dad* or *Daddy,* and now that he's dead, he is *My Father.*

My father was not a writer, but in the weeks before he died, he kept a diary. My mother says he wanted my sister and me to see it, allegedly, "so they don't make the same mistakes I did." My grandmother has possession of it, but I've never been allowed to read it, though I've asked multiple times. She only said, "There's stuff in there you don't need to know about him."

There's another French word, *aplaventrisme,* which means, "to submit to authority without a fight."

***

I see a man at the gym who looks like my father, and I wonder if he will recognize me. I'm not wearing makeup, and am often worried people won't recognize me without makeup. His hair is white and he struggles to keep his pace on the elliptical, firm bones and sinew stretched strong beneath sagging skin. Was he here to spy on my life from a close distance, or had he accidentally ended up in my town, through no intention of his own? If he caught a glimpse of the deep red my face is after sweating, maybe he, like so many instincts of animals, would recognize that as kinship, as his own, as daughter.

After a few minutes, I realize this white-haired person is too pale, marble mannequin of a man, all the color washed out of him. He is not my father.

***

[EXHIBIT VIII]

Oct. 8, 1959 - Aug. 23, 2009 Steven Charles Slaughter, 49, of Madison passed away Sunday. Survivors include his children, Erin Slaughter and Stephanie Slaughter...

Online, the rest of the obituary has been archived. It wasn't easy to find hidden under the many news articles about the murder, most of them badly written and featuring a weary mugshot of Pam in prison stripes. But here, the murder isn't mentioned; he *passed away*, the way leaves pass into autumn.

There was no deathbed, no goodbyes under white sterile lights. He was my dad, and then he was my dead dad, with no space in-between to make sense or amends.

Survivors include his children…

That the word "survivor" is used to describe the family of the deceased strikes me as strange. What have we survived? Not grief, which by the time the obituary is printed in the daily newspaper hasn't even begun to settle in a person. As if death had come for us, too, and we only nearly stepped back from the blade unscathed. We are all eventually the victims, leaving behind a trail of our own survivors.

The graveside adage reminds us: *"In the midst of life we are in death."*

***

In my Grief Archive I collect articles and newspaper clippings like those, and late one night I found myself walking around my apartment in the dark, imagining my life could be a whisper that doesn't truly move anything.

I pulled out the manila file folder from the desk drawer and sifted through its contents: a pile of legal paperwork, handwritten notes and phone numbers with the words Victim Services, and printed online articles with typos I hate almost more than the fact that I'm still reading them. Last summer, I added three pictures to the folder: the black and white polaroid of my father as a toddler, a picture of my parents on their wedding day (they looked like they loved each other, which was startling to me in a way I hadn't expected), and a picture of my grandpa walking my mother down the aisle, the veil draped over her face, her blue eyes doe-like, almost frightened.

In a local newspaper article recounting the details of the sentencing, something stuck out to me, something I don't remember having heard before:

"She testified that one of the last things he said to her was, 'You and I

have lived alone for many years.'"

***

It might seem strange, but when I think about my father's death, I often forget someone was the direct cause of it. This is the story I tell myself: that it was fated to happen this way, inevitable, planned by the cosmos, sewn into the fabric of the universe. From my father's ashes, I was born into flames. In the midst of tragedy, my life as I know it began.

But Pam killed him. Perhaps it's also strange that although I know this to be the truth, I don't feel the burning need for justice or revenge that the rest of my family does, that any normal person in this circumstance might. I feel mostly indifference about the woman who killed my father, my stepmother of only one short summer.

It causes me to reflect, again, on the terms "survivor" and "survived by," the contextual space between them. It comes down to the question: who is the recipient of the trauma?

Though my father's death was significant enough, as only a few events throughout the course of a life are, to cleave my understanding of self into "before" and "after," I don't know that I will ever feel honest identifying myself as a victim. Many of the people I know, who have survived what seem to me to be jarring and horrendous traumas, also express not feeling comfortable identifying themselves as "victims" or "survivors." These are the words we've been given to describe ourselves, those of us who have been pressed through the needle's eye of suffering and emerged to go on living, but they sound like movie archetypes. Language, especially when it has been created not *by* a group of people, but *for* them, comes up inadequate.

***

I saw a video online in which a doctor found a family of cockroaches living in someone's ear canal, netted into black wax. I wondered if the patient knew before they were told, if they felt a phantom togetherness inhabiting the cavity of their head—like the lingering aura in the next room of someone who has already left the house party.

Grief is like that: when it comes, however suddenly, there is some ancient part of you that knew it would. That was already carrying it, dormant, waiting to be felt.

***

[EXHIBIT IX]

After finding that line in the news article, I realized Pam had answers I didn't. For a few weeks, I considered going to Alabama to visit her in prison and interview her. Everyone I mentioned it to thought it was either a horrible idea or a great one. Either way, I was wary; I didn't want her to try to explain herself to me, to apologize. I wanted one thing: to know what my father's last moments were like. What his last words were. What shape the light was as it left his eyes. As if by knowing that, I could come to know the truest version of him.

After some research on Wetumpka's visitation process, I discovered that it was going to be nearly impossible for me talk to Pam face-to-face at the prison. So instead, on a whim, I wrote her a letter:

December 14, 2015

Pam,

It may seem strange that I'm writing you a letter after all these years, and even now as I begin to write it, I'm not sure what I want to say. When I think about my dad's death, The Story of it is always there, like a broken record, but I sometimes forget that you were the person who caused it. And I wonder about you, about your daughter and what happened to her after you went to jail. I wonder about the story you tell yourself about the day my dad died, just like the story I tell myself, or what it's morphed into over time. By force, you became a part of my story, the catalyst for the defining event of my life.

I remember being excited to have a stepmother. I remember staying at your house and liking it there, feeling glad that my dad was part of a new family. I remember after that trip (and maybe you had already separated and he was in rehab) when you called me and said you hoped the two of you could work things out. I don't remember much about that conversation, but I do remember feeling good about it afterwards. The thing is, I was so young when he died, and because of the divorce and his drinking we didn't always have the best relationship anyway. I wish I had gotten to know him as an adult, as he'd be now.

There is only one thing I need from you: I want to know what my dad was like as a person, what it was like to know him. More than anything, I really want to know what his last moments were like. What were his last words? Do you ever think about him, or dream about him? I know you don't owe me anything, but I hope you can please just do this one thing for me.

My return address is on the envelope.

I dropped the letter in the mail and drove to Texas for New Year's. I didn't tell anyone about it, and didn't plan to. But I was staying at Rachel's apartment when I drunkenly ended up mentioning the letter.

"That was a really bad idea," Rachel said.

"Why?"

"I don't think it's genuine," she said. "I don't think you actually want to hear from her. I think you just want to be able to write about hearing from her."

"I said in the letter I didn't want to hear her apologies. I just wanted her to tell me about my dad's last moments."

"Yeah, but she's not going to! She's only going to try to clear herself of guilt. She's *a literal murderer.* She's not going to be rational."

"Yeah, but—"

"Look, I'm just saying, you're not going to get what you want from her. It's going to cause more harm than good."

"I don't know," I sighed. "Maybe you're right. Who knows if she'll write back, anyway."

When I arrived back from Texas, the letter was in my mailbox, marked with a red stamp that read *Return to Sender—Refused.* I put it in my desk drawer, in the folder, where it still sits unopened.

***

So now I understand: you had a life full of many things interrupted by the bright messy shock of my birth & suddenly you find this creature clawing wailing bleating out its hungers—encoded with the worst of you. & gloriously ignorant to its own nature. How do you look something like that in the eye without breaking open spilling out on the floor? How do you survive long enough to escape the things that claim to love you & I realize now it was Love that slaughtered you, either loving my mother so endlessly you walked into the mouth of someone else hoping to be swallowed or worse—actually brimming with pure ridiculous light for the same eyes & smile & hands that held a gun to your head & said destroy. In which case I would like to say forgiveness, to tell you that I too have glimpsed an unbearable shining from the corner of my eye & been full-ready to sign my body away.

***

Rendering: from the Old French, Middle English, and Latin; to recite, to dare, to give back; to hand over, to represent, to cause; to perform; to melt down.

Rendering as noun is a work of art; a translation of life to canvas; a plastering of holes; a relinquishing.

Render as verb is to deliver a judgement; to pull a conclusion from the ethereal realm of what is known; to depict artistically; to strip apart the carcass of an animal, slice away what obscures. To make from the remains of the dead something useful.

***

When I took my first trip alone to Chicago in the spring of 2016, I made time to meet my grandmother at the mall in Schaumberg, a thirty-minute drive from the city. She gathered me into her arms for a hug, and touched my cheek, her eyes sparkling with genuine delight.

She squealed, "Oh, you look as beautiful as ever!"

"So do you," I said.

She linked her arm in mine and we walked into the mall together.

***

A year before my trip to Chicago, I drove to Alabama. I didn't tell anyone I was going.

Driving through Madison was like journeying into the belly of a toothless shark. I passed the old Blockbuster where we rented DVDs each time we visited (now a DIY pottery shop), and the thrift store Stephanie and I stole scented candles from the week of his funeral. Once I found Wall-Triana Highway, I didn't even need the GPS; it was like navigating in a dream—I suddenly knew where to go, and then the house was lying ahead of me, at the end of the road.

It looked the same as I remembered it, the same gray garage door and tri-color brick, except that the front door seemed a slightly different shade of brown. I planned to knock and ask the people who lived there if I could look around inside, even began to plan what I would say, until I noticed the FOR SALE sign stuck in the grass.

I called the number on the sign. A man with a gravel-thick accent answered.

"Hi, um, I saw your sign at the house at 101 Dawn Drive? I'm just in town for the day, so I was wondering if there was any way I could see it?"

"I can be there in thirty minutes," he said.

As I sat in my hot car and waited for the realtor to arrive, I wondered what the actual hell I was doing there. I felt crazy. I felt brave. I couldn't help but think, *this is going to be an incredible story later,* and hated myself for it, for the running typewriter in my head that kept me from staying present in this significant moment. A fly buzzed around the passengers' seat.

The realtor pulled up in a white truck, and when I stepped out of my car to meet him, my flip-flop broke. He watched me struggle to slide it back on my foot as I hobbled up the driveway.

He shook my hand and unlocked the front door.

The house was exactly as I remembered it, but shrunken. The man told me the number of rooms and bathrooms, and that the last owners had refurbished some things.

"How many owners has the house had?" I asked, walking through kitchen, now painted pink, orb-lights hanging over the bar.

"Just two," he said. "The current owners bought it in 2009."

Through the hallway was the room I'd slept in, where I'd watched my dad remove his glasses and set them next to the computer each night. "What about the first owner?" I asked.

"I don't know much about them, it'd be back in the records, I suppose."

I was surprised to realize I had forgotten the existence of whole rooms: the laundry room that led to the garage, and the bathroom by my old bedroom. The linoleum on the kitchen floor, where he'd lain that winter as he seized and called out for my sister, kept the same blue-bordered squares. The crown molding had been painted black in the dining room, which we called "the dancing room," because our dad kept it empty so we could slide our socks over the wood floors and twirl like ice skaters.

The man said, "Through here is the master bed and bath."

My dad's room was much smaller than I remembered, too, the ceiling more sharply angled over where his bed used to be. In the bathroom, the new owners had hung a cloud-shaped light fixture over the jacuzzi, but I could still remember the mint smell that lingered there as I watched him take a wet comb to his hair. Looking into the mirror felt a bit eerie, like a private joke between my dad and I that the realtor wasn't in on.

Dad, I'm here again. Look who I am now.

I wished the realtor would stop talking about the amenities and price points, or that I could have more time to explore the house alone, but I knew I was fortunate to have been inside at all. I blurted out some excuse and thanked him, and he gave me his business card.

I intended to go to the house where my dad was killed. I always assumed I would want to see the room he died in. But after seeing the place where he lived—the house he bought after the divorce and lived alone, where we visited him and knew him—I decided not to. In the end, remembering the place he lived felt more important than investigating the place he died.

***

This is a story I never tell: When I was in third grade, my father tried to explain that he tested things at work, using words I couldn't spell. I liked experiments, or the idea of them. I asked what kind of experiment I could help him do, and at the kitchen table after dinner, he told me about air-sealed rooms in laboratories, and how scientists inject mice to see if what they're testing is safe to try on monkeys, or humans. He asked what I wanted to test. This was after 9/11, the planes and flames and the word "terror" still echoing on TV a year later, and I didn't know what anthrax was at age eight but I knew it was a white powder that killed people and it could show up anywhere, in the mail or on teacher's desks or even at the White House. It was a problem I hypothesized to solve with the things I knew and had handy: a purple gel pen, a shiny silver nickel, and the albuterol capsule from my inhaler. My dad sat at the kitchen table with me and helped me formulate a plan, how I would draw on the nickel with the gel pen and then melt the metal down, stir in the albuterol; how once the vaccine was finished we could go to a lab and test it on mice. I wrote it out on a piece of paper with the same gel pen I imagined could save the world.

The next morning before I left for school, on the kitchen table was a typed and stapled document, printed on fax paper with perforated sides. It was my experiment, typed from my notes after I had gone to bed.

Sometimes I think my father didn't do much for me. But he did that.

***

Sometimes meeting a stranger I make up stories tell them my dad is alive & working in Huntsville or Boston, costume myself in an undamaging that grazes my skin like freedom. Sometimes my friend tells a story & there's a hazel sparkling in his eyes that looks like you & glitters more like safety than I have ever known any man to be. & this is no one's fault, sometimes I forget if you were resurrected you wouldn't love me maybe, hello did you know I sleep with girls did you know I eat myself into ruin I vandalize my body with strangers & with ink did you know I am a slave to useless language & all things incapable of wanting me back? Do you realize dead is only different than dad by one measly scribble, that dad is just dead without the e. But here I can trap you in your own story make you all mine though I refused your ashes because why would I want to drag around some herb-pinch of your corpse unpacking & repacking you into cardboard boxes every year, another dirty secret that guilts me from the junk closet like your watches CDs baseball cap the T-shirt I sometimes wear to yoga.

***

We got a table for two at the PF Chang's inside the mall. Grandma Irma ordered a water with lemon and unfolded the cloth napkin in her lap. She asked how my studies had been going, and we talked about her knee surgery. I was enjoying spending time with her. I didn't plan to bring up the diary, but it happened anyway.

"I wanted to talk to you again…to ask you about the diary Dad wrote when he was in rehab?" I started.

"Yes?"

"Well…so, I know we've talked about it before, and you said there are things in there you don't feel like I should know about him..."

"Which one?"

"What do you mean?"

"Well, there are two diaries," she said. "One he kept during the time he and Mary were getting divorced, and the other is some stuff he wrote while he was in Bradford."

"I didn't know there were two," I said.

"When we found it while we were going through his belongings, I said, 'I'm not going to read it.' But then Deb said, 'You have to read it, what's there to lose now?' So Deb and I read it and we were stunned. We had no idea how bad it really was between them. No clue."

"Did he talk about me and Stephanie?" I asked.

"Yes, some—how he didn't think it was fair, how you girls didn't get a chance to be kids, because of all of it."

"I can understand why you wouldn't want me to read that—but I'm interested in the one from Bradford."

"Oh, there's nothing in there that would be useful to you. It's just things they had him write there, as part of the program."

"I just…I'm trying to figure out who he is. Who he was. There were things I didn't understand when I was younger, like the drinking. Things I resented him for. And now—okay, I haven't really told anyone this—but the last couple years, I had troubles of my own with alcohol. In going through that I think I finally understood a lot of what he was going through. He was lonely."

"He never got over your mother, after the divorce," she said.

"I get that now," I said. "It was hard for me to understand then, when I was a kid, and all the things he did…but I'm writing about him now, and I've been thinking how valuable it would be to have something he wrote. In his own handwriting. To look at it and be able to think about the place he was when he wrote it, what he was feeling…and if he wrote that diary in Bradford, it must have been only two or three weeks before he died. That would be so important to have. For my writing, but also for my life."

She said, "I'll have to look at it again. I don't know what all is in there. I'll have to take a look, but I'll think about it."

"Yeah, don't worry about answering me right now, just think about it."

"I'll think about it."

***

To render is to sacrifice a memory at the altar of the story it is translated into; to discard the tender parts of living to what writer Patricia Lockwood calls the "arrowness": that forward-hurdling machine a writer becomes when they lock eyes with a story, like a predator glimpsing a whisp of fur across a field's expanse. Nothing sharpens the arrow like the mad clarity of grief, but those who come to understand their grief only through its telling—as I did, and am doing, here—are in danger of only experiencing grief itself as a story, something separate from them, something they create, begin, and end at will. And worse, coming to believe the purpose of suffering is to mine from it a bright, pulsing narrative they can surgically remove from their chest and then walk away from.

On writing through grief, author Maryanne O'Hara says: "Every writer I know has two selves—one who records what is happening as the other experiences what it knows it will one day write about." I can't help but recall Claude Monet's admission that while watching someone he loved die, he spent up those precious last minutes staring at her—memorizing the pigments in her eyelids, deciding how he would paint her once she was gone.

***

After lunch with my grandmother that day, I drove back into the city. Over Wicker Park, the sky was unraveling into deep blue. I bundled up in a scarf for the chilly night.

I was walking to the train station when I was distracted by a sign on the sidewalk advertising a psychic: *$10 special.* I rang the doorbell, and a teenage boy invited me in.

He said, "She'll be with you in a moment."

I sat on the white linen couch, embellished with Mediterranean beaded pillows and a white faux fur blanket tossed over the side. Through a crack in the double doors behind me, I glimpsed a kitchen with an open laptop resting on the table.

The woman descended the stairs slowly, clunking down one step at a time. I stood up. She had teased black hair and a New Jersey accent, and after I handed her my ten-dollar bill she led me to a rounded wall with a door in the center. The outside of the wall was adorned with turquoise mosaic tiles, and when she opened the door, we stepped into a dimly lit circular room, draped in candlelight and burgundy velvet. She sat on one side of a small, round table, and I sat on the other.

"This is how it works," she said. "You have three questions you can ask. First, to get a sense of your energy alignment, I need to know your star sign."

"Leo."

"What time of day were you born, and where?"

"8:49 p.m., in Nevada."

"And your name?"

"Erin."

"Good," she smiled. "What is your first question?"

"I want to know when I'll meet the person I'm going to marry."

"I see it happening twelve to eighteen months from now," she said. "You will meet your soulmate, the person who will be the greatest love of your life."

"Really? That's so soon," I giggled.

"Yes, and when you meet them, it will be sudden, and it will move fast, but just let it happen. Don't hold back, because it will be very good for both of you. Based on the energy I'm feeling from you now, that's what I see happening."

"Okay," I said, the top of my head beginning to tingle. "Thanks."

"What is your second question?"

"What publisher will I publish my first book with?"

"Well, I don't know about things like that—I don't know the names of those things. But I see it happening in around three to five years, and it will be very successful. I can see people coming from all over to see you."

"That's good to know," I said. I was feeling like maybe I had made a mistake coming there, that it was probably all bullshit, and I should've spent my ten dollars on pizza instead.

"What is your last question?" she asked.

"Oh...I don't know, sorry. I only thought of two."

"It's okay. You can take a moment."

I thought of asking something ridiculous. Just to see what would happen. A test to prove her real or fake, at least so that I would know for myself.

I hesitated before saying, "Is my dad still alive?"

"What do you mean?" she asked.

"I mean, like, I haven't seen him in a really long time, a bunch of years," I fumbled, "and people in my family say he's dead. But sometimes, I suspect otherwise. And I wanted to know…if he's really dead."

"Well," she said, "based on what I see right now, he will be gone for a very long time. You will be unable to reach him. But you will see him again."

"When?" I asked.

"It will be quite a while from now, but he will reveal himself to you. When he does, it will be because of your writing."

***

On Christmas Eve the year that I am 23, Mark asks me to come stand with him on the front porch while he smokes a cigarette. This house is not the house I grew up in, but the place my parents and Trin have moved to in rural Tennessee. The wooden porch looks over a small, unkempt yard, an antique iron bell hanging from a pole in the center, and acres of as-of-yet unexplored forest surrounding the house from all sides. Ivy coils up the side of the wooden railing. I eye the green vines as Mark speaks his concerns.

His concerns are about my future. He'd overheard me talking to my mother, telling her my fallback plan when my master's program ended was to move to Ohio with Lena, who had just been accepted to a PhD program in Bowling Green. I'd brought Lena to their house for Thanksgiving a month before, and they'd enjoyed her.

"I just don't want to see you settling, following anybody around," he said. "You've never been a follower. You've always gone off and had your own adventures."

"It's not a for-sure thing," I said, "just something we've been talking about. Because I don't know what I'll be doing after all this is over. It's just nice to have an option."

He sighed, shifting over the wood boards, igniting a faint creak. "But what about if y'all break up?"

"Wait, what?" I asked.

"Come on, you don't have to play dumb. Your mom and I knew when you brought her. Why do you think we set y'all up out in the camper? So you'd have privacy."

This shocked me only a little. Lena and I often joked about our "romantic friendship," though it had never gone farther than that. But what shocked me more was that my parents had been so considerate. That Mark had set up the pop-out camper in the yard and made up the two beds, only one of which he expected to be slept in. The porch ivy tangled in the wind.

"Lena and I aren't dating," I said, not looking quite at him. My nerves felt metallic, collapsible. My throat opened fire-worn. "But, you know, um, I think you should know. I do date girls. And boys. Both."

"I mean, I assumed that," he said. "Your mom and I assumed that, at a certain point."

Did the world go quiet then? The porch the sky the trees the wind the inanimate misplaced ivy greening behind my eyes?

"Nothing about that could make me love you any less, though," he said. "I don't care who you date or who you end up with, as long as they're good to you."

"Thank you," I said, lump-throated. "I mean, that's just a little surprising, based on things you've said in the past." I didn't mention the yelling in the car, that night when I was fourteen. I doubted he'd have remembered.

His dark eyes began to water. "You're my daughter. The incredible person you are, and the joy you bring to my life is too important for anything else to affect that."

That same Christmas, Mark took me to his bedroom closet and showed me his old journals, jammed with loose papers scribbled with poems, written during his twenties when he was briefly homeless, and in his roaming years afterward. He asked me if I would edit and re-collect them as a favor to him. It is very likely that when he is gone, these pages will be all I have left of him: another dead dad's diary.

***

I didn't want to go to Sears Tower, but I had already purchased the ticket. It felt like an obligation to the memory I had there with my dad, to the person I was then. A person who didn't know what I know now.

And then, sometime between boarding the train at Division and getting off at Quincy, I realized a subconscious part of me believed my dad was alive, and that if I went to the top floor of Sears Tower, he would be there. As soon as I thought it, I knew how irrational it was. Somehow, years of looking for him in passing cars and airports turned into an underlying presumption that if I were to just look hard enough, go to the right place at the right time, he would come out of hiding.

I have always understood that my father is dead, but dead is different than gone. Dead is a veil that separates you from communicating, but gone is deeper. Gone is ruin, a deletion that can never be undone. And the thought I'd never truly confronted—that there will be no reconciliation, no closure—felt like falling through air. Dead is easy to grasp, but gone is the bottom dropping out from underneath.

***

Sometimes I forget I am a living grave marked daughter sometimes I wait for your ghost to split the wall.

***

It was full-blown night when I stood in the elevator and climbed past the fiftieth floor, then the ninetieth. I didn't want to be there, chasing him up into the sky. I was terrified the elevator cables would snap.

Sears Tower, I learned, was renamed Willis Tower in 2009, the year my father died. The Skydeck was cold, with gray carpet underfoot as tourists walked the circumference of the floor, snapping pictures inside glass boxes that suspended them over the city. A group of Mennonite women in long dresses and bonnets passed through the gift shop. I didn't remember there being a gift shop. Did we buy something there? I have a memory of seeing the bridge where we walked by the water, but that was impossible from every angle. What did we do in Chicago all those years ago? What did I think coming back here would solve?

I pressed my nose to the window and stared past the glare of ceiling lights into the blackness, conglomerations of stacked buildings lit up in orange. I wanted to cry, but couldn't force the tears to come. I wanted this to be a defining moment in the story of my grief, but what if there was no story, no narrative to make sense of?

There is an Inuit word, *iktsuarpok*, which roughly translates to "the anticipatory frustration of waiting for someone to show up," and there is a Korean word, *won*, which means, "the reluctance to let go of an illusion." But what came to me in those moments were Joan Didion's words:

"Why did I remain so unable to accept the fact that he had died? Was it because I was failing to understand it as something that happened to him? Was it because I was still understanding it as something that happened to me?"

***

Three years later, a small urn of his ashes displayed in the sunroom of her new home, my grandmother tells me of my dead dad's garden and how he'd once forced her to come over to prune the tree in his yard. I've got a childhood colored by the story that my father never wanted children: he blamed the melting skies, quails gassed limp in their hutches, the veins of trains carrying bombs across the mountains and through their tunneled centers. But now I learn he was afraid that if he touched it, he would kill the Chinese maple. And his graveless ash drifting over us then was like the hole left in the ground after a fist of roots gives up, and lies soft beneath the halo of a storm.

***

This is a story I never tell: When my parents were getting divorced, the night before we left Alabama, we went out to one final dinner as a family, and afterwards my dad took us to the toy store, where he told us we could buy whatever we wanted. I picked a Barbie doll dressed as Hermione from the Harry Potter movies. When we got back to the hotel room where my mom, sister and I would stay before our migration to Texas the next morning, my dad sunk down onto his knees to hug us. He was crying. He told us he loved us, wanted us to know this was an important moment, not to forget. My sister cried and clung to him. I held my doll and smoothed down her wild hair, the corners of her plaid skirt. I wanted him to leave. I wanted it to be over.

***

There are hundreds of ways to tell this story. One is: how to take this grief and transform it into love? What is the archeology of sorrow?

I never took your ashes I took your story though I didn't ask for it & now I am constructing the gravestone I don't have, shaping it from granite & moonlight.

***

A month after Chicago, I arrive home on a Wednesday night to see a package propped against my door. I cut it open with the sharpest key on my keychain and pull out a block of bubble-wrap, yellow envelopes, and crate paper. In a series of sticky notes, my grandmother's pristine handwriting guides me through:

[EXHIBITS X - XIV]

On a black folder, she's written, *Student at North Texas State—Mom's request for Christmas present.* Opening it reveals a picture of my dad in the mid-eighties, almost comical with feathered hair, a chunky Casio watch, and a wispy moustache. In a larger folder, she's written *1973* in pen, directly on the bottom left corner of the photograph, etching it into the grass where a boy kneels in a baseball uniform, wearing nothing of my father I recognize except for his eyes.

I reach for a mass of bubble wrap with a taped note: Steve's supervisor said *'What a loss—we will never know what this enormous talent would have done in the future.'* I peel the tape off carefully and unfold from the bubble wrap a wood-framed shadowbox. In the shadowbox, six medals are embedded in navy velvet, engraved with the logos for SAIC, iRobot, Boeing, with some variation of an American flag and "Supporting the Armed Forces." Three of them have come unglued, broken out of their sockets, and are wading around the bottom of the frame. I look to see if there's a latch, a way to open it up and fix it, but there's no way in or out from behind the glass. I shake the frame and try to shimmy the medals back into place, like pinball. One sticks. I wrap it back up, but can't get the bubble wrap to fold the same way.

On crate paper, Grandma Irma's handwriting says, *One of my favorites.* I brush back the packaging and find a gold-framed portrait of our family—dated 1999, it's a picture I remember taking. We are color-coordinated in gold and black; my mom has short hair and a leaf broach pinned over her heart, my sister is soft-faced, and my father stands in the back wearing a red tie, the width of his shoulders spanning our bodies like a mountain range.

I stare at myself, garnished with an enormous gold bow, a small golden cross hanging from my neck. I try to catch my reflection in the glass and make it match up with the younger girl's, but nothing about our faces are the same. Even the shape of my mouth when it smiles has changed.

Underneath the packaging, I spot an envelope labeled *Bradford*. I drop the picture and reach for it.

***

[EXHIBIT XV]

I carefully pull out a thin stack of papers, my fingertips in tremor. On top of the stack is a sheet of yellow, lined paper from the legal pads my grandmother keeps all over her house, covered in her cursive. An introduction. Her own story:

Bradford family sessions were 3x wk for 2 wks. Pam refused to go—too busy! The enclosed sheets are his worksheets he brought home with him…

The one session he had with Pam towards the end of his therapy was a disaster. She kept yelling that he lied to her about the drinking. The next day he was released and I went to pick him up. His roommates told me after the session with Pam he returned to their room crying and they were glad I was there to take him home and not her. That night he told me he knew he would not go back to her house or he'd end up drinking again…

I enclosed a copy of a letter sent to me from Pam. I know you have seen it before—but thought you would like to have as proof of her "crazy" behavior. I guess the difficult weeks she mentioned were the Bradford weeks…

I hope this doesn't make you sad. It doesn't cheer me up any!

***

[EXHIBIT XVI]

A photocopy of faded, round handwriting on white computer paper. She was right, I had seen this before. It came to my grandmother's house in the mail the week of the funeral.

Dear Irma,

Words cannot adequately express the sorrow and regret I feel. I loved Steve. I still do. And I miss him so much!

I'm sorry I took your son—no mother should suffer such a gut-wrenching loss. I'm sorry I took the girls' father. Poor Steve will never see his grandchildren...

You were my friend and confidant during those difficult weeks. I've wanted to come to your home, fall on my knees and beg your forgiveness. I would expect you to scream at me, even strike me. That would be alright, completely understandable. And I would cry with you...

I wish I could do more to ease your pain, Irma.

Sincerely, Pam

***

[EXHIBIT XVII]

When I spot my father's handwriting, I immediately begin to sob. His block letters are scribbled in blue pen on a simple piece of creased notebook paper, words marked out and underlined, and suddenly I am transported; the veil is lifted and I am there with him before The Story was ever told or imagined. He is sitting at a desk in a beige room somewhere, his skin warm, his heart beating, organizing his pain into bullet points; and I am somewhere miles away, sixteen again, at dance team practice or theatre rehearsal or lounging in a lime green bedroom with my friends' names drawn in bubble letters and posters of punk bands stapled to the walls.

Before, all I had of his handwriting was the last birthday card he sent me, two weeks before he died, where he had written *Sweet Sixteen!* on the pink envelope and signed, *Love, Dad.* Now, I can see the spaces where the pen ran out of ink and dragged his E's into N's. I can touch that window to the past.

It's a pros and cons list. In the header, he wrote and underlined *OF USING.* He printed his full name in the top right corner, like a school assignment.

PRO	*CON*
-AN ESCAPE MECHANISM	*-HABIT FORMING*
-CAN TURN OFF / SHUT DOWN WHENEVER I WANTED	*-SHUTS OUT FAMILY MEMBERS*
-ANGER MANAGEMENT	*-SOMETIMES GOT EVEN ANGRIER*
-MAKE LIFE'S PROBLEMS GO AWAY	*-MUST DEAL WITH EVERYDAY PROBLEMS*
-DEAL WITH DISAPPOINTMENT	*-MAKE IT WORK*
-FIXES BOREDOM	*-FIND SOMETHING TO DO*

***

[EXHIBIT XVIII]

Underneath is a packet of what must be the worksheets. A note is stapled to the top: *1st meeting with him since he entered Bradford. I attended "family therapy for the victim" since Pam said she couldn't. On his release day he told me how thankful he was for my love and support. –Grandma*

The worksheet is typed in Comic Sans; when I notice, I can't help but laugh at the choice to use such a ridiculous typeface to prompt deep questions about addiction. My grandmother's letters are looped and faint, floating in white space. My father filled the boxes with the same blue block letters.

Bradford Family Services—Communication Exercise

Please complete the following sentences as if you were speaking directly to the person you are with in the Family Program. You will share this exercise during group session on Wednesday.

Name: *Irma Heimberger (Slaughter)*

Right now I feel... *Very proud that you personally accepted your need for professional help to control your addiction.*

Something I regret having done is... *Allowing you to drive with my grandchildren in your car.*

I was most angry when you... *Spoiled two of our Christmas celebrations with your daughters and letting your girls see their father at his worst.*

Some important things we've lost because of drinking/drugging are... *Mutual respect and trust we always had for each other.*

What I really need from you now is... *To continue at Bradford until you finish their program; to go to AA meetings and stay clean.*

Bradford Family Services—Communication Exercise

Please complete the following sentences as if you were speaking directly to the person you are with in the Family Program. You will share this exercise during group session on Wednesday.

Name: *STEVEN SLAUGHTER*

Right now I feel...*CALM, COMPLACENT, CONFIDENT THAT I HAVE "TURNED THE CORNER," SUPPORTED, LOVED*

Something I regret having done is...*CAUSING ANXIETY DUE TO MY DISEASE TO YOU AND OUR FAMILY*

I was most angry with you when you...*HELD ME UNDER THE PROVERBIAL "MICROSCOPE" GROWING UP, AND CONTINUE TO DO SO AT TIMES*

Some of the important things we've lost because of drinking/drugging are...*QUALITY TIME TOGETHER, ESPECIALLY WHEN MY GIRLS ARE IN TOWN*

What I really need from you now is...*UNDERSTANDING—THE "OLD STEVE" IS GONE, AND IT'S ALL ABOUT MOVING FORWARD NOW—FORGET WHAT THE "OLD STEVE" DID AND SAID—HE'S DEAD NOW*

***

He's dead now.

He's dead now.

He's dead now.

A plea surfacing from beyond the grave, shot straight into my nervous system:

Forget what the "Old Steve" did and said—absent Steve, brown-bagged vodka in the trunk Steve, seizing on the floor Steve, my red-faced daddy who was gone, or mean.

Forget. He's dead now.

It's all about moving forward.

***

[EXHIBIT XIX]

The back of the worksheet prompts a list of the ways they planned to celebrate together for each month of my father's sobriety. In the blank next to "1 month," he wrote in *HAVE DINNER AT IRMA'S.* At "3 months": *DINNER AT 'FANCY PLACE.'*

Below, each of their signatures, and the date: *8/5/09.* They would never get to have that first dinner. A month later, he would already be dead thirteen days.

***

Five years after the night I received the box, almost down to the day: I'm on the phone with my mom, calling to confirm a few details for a piece I'm planning to write. She's just finished re-wiring the chicken coop to fortress it against a raccoon who keeps sneaking in to binge on birdfeed.

"Did Dad ever talk to you about his drinking, or connect it to his family history of addiction?" I ask.

"Yeah, he always felt like something was wrong with him. He called it…oh, what was it. Hold on," she pauses, but I can hear her pinging buttons on her cellphone. She gets back on.

"He called it his 'hereditary defect,'" she says. "Sorry, I had to check to make sure I got the phrase right. He said it in that voicemail I've kept all these years, from when he was checking into rehab."

I'm stunned. I've never heard of this voicemail's existence. She tells me she's transferred it across three phones, over twelve years, to preserve the last recorded message he ever sent her.

She says, "Don't call me weird, but every once in a while I just want to hear his voice."

This is the kind of vulnerable moment I would have instinctively shuttered myself against just a handful of years ago, but instead, I soften and respond, "That seems completely normal. I mean, you were married to him for almost half your life."

I ask her to send the voicemail and when I hang up the phone, an audio file and three screenshots of the transcript blip into my messages. As I'm about to look, my partner comes out of the shower, and I quickly close out of the message, saving it for when I'm alone.

***

[EXHIBIT XX]

I notice that he always used blue pen on the worksheets and I wonder if this was by choice. Maybe it's calming for addicts in withdrawal because when the pen bursts from nervous chewing, blue ink splatters the tongue as a Rorschach of waves collapsing onto shore, not the void-black tentacles of fever dreams.

I'd steadied my breathing, but when I arrive at the final paper I choke out sobs again, and sit in a ball clutching the page in silent wreckage before I can begin to read it. After the first line, a wild laugh slips out, remembering how nerdy and dramatic he could be. I reread it five times, tracing the slant of his pen, breaking down over one line again and again.

The page is filled up by his blue words. The header says: *GOODBYE.*

DEAR ALCOHOL (AKA DISEASE),

SO, HERE WE ARE AGAIN, YOU RAVENOUS BASTARD.

YOU HAVE BEEN ALIVE INSIDE ME SINCE MY CREATION, MANIFESTING YOURSELF IN MY TEEN EFFORTS STEALING LIQUOR FROM NEIGHBOR'S GARAGES…AND THAT DUI BACK IN '91, HUH? YOUR FINEST HOUR. HOWEVER, I WON SINCE I DID NOT LOSE MY GOVERNMENT SECURITY CLEARANCE…

YOU AWAKEN AND DESTROY MY FIRST MARRIAGE…

NOW I HAVE TO CONTINUALLY WORRY THAT YOU MIGHT HAVE SEWN YOUR EVIL SEED WITHIN MY DAUGHTERS…

IN THE PRESENT DAY, YOU THREATEN TO DESTROY MY MARRIAGE TO THE MOST WONDERFUL WOMAN I HAVE EVER MET…

ENOUGH! I HAVE DISCOVERED THE ONLY WAY TO DRIVE YOU OUT.

***

When I look back at the earliest bits of my writing about my father's murder, the word "forgiveness" shows up repetitively. *Forgiveness* was a prayer of sorts, an ambiguous deity I softly suffered in alienation from, a spiritual ache. It rarely showed up unaccompanied by the generalized guilt that pervaded every aspect of my life for many years. Although I've healed, or am beginning finally to, the echo of that directionless guilt still shadows me like the dark glimmer of a halo. I'm not sure who the craving for forgiveness was directed toward—my father, or myself. Yet I continued to write it, aimless and aflame.

Lidia Yuknavitch writes: "Maybe forgiveness is just that. The ability to admit someone else's story. To give it to them."

***

[EXHIBIT XXI]

When I finally listen to the voicemail, I'm sitting in bed, the phone speaker turned down low and pressed to my ear, the door locked so this moment—and whatever may rise within it—stays safely barricaded from my partner, who sits unknowing in the next room. Even after years upon years of creaking open the metal latches of my psyche in therapy—of writing and rewriting this story, rooting around inside my father's murder—I still instinctively bolt, hide, resist, isolate in the face of grief; the thought of being comforted in this moment makes me feel ill and frightened.

I anxiously press play.

The first thing that strikes me is that I do not, after all the retracings of the memory, accurately remember how his voice sounded. It's an octave higher than I remember—or maybe just tinny through the speakers, warped by the file's transfer across a handful of phones in the last decade. But what remains of my father as I knew him, always, is his Chicago accent, jammed up in the fog of him holding back tears. He sounds sincere as he talks about seeking help. He calls my mom *honey*, though they'd been divorced so long.

When a person dies, they become someone else's story. They cannot correct details or pave over bumps in the record, so all we're left to construct them out of is a trail of myths and memories, the fragments we piece together and call a person.

In the voicemail, he is so much more a person to me than in my memory, more than in my writing, more than when he was alive. He is a person, just some person who was trying hard to carve a path through his damage and come out clean, a person who didn't deserve to die. A person who wanted to live.

I want to be around for my kids, he said—says again now from within the machine that preserves this final piece of him. *I want to be around for the rest of my life.*

***

I'm not sure what I believe happens when we die. Most often I assume there must be some "after" to consciousness, a place like climbing through a forest canopied by trees. A place where my dad is and where I'll see him when I am also dead, but I have never felt his ghost in this world. In the days after his murder, my aunt claimed to see him rounding the corner of my grandmother's house, and my mom claimed to hear his voice, but I have never felt him there. Not at his funeral, or at my sister's wedding, or my graduations; not at Sears Tower, and not now that I am calling out for him with everything in me. And if the air is empty of him in this moment, more than any of the others, he must be nowhere. He must be gone.

***

[EXHIBIT XXII]

iPhone Voicemail Transcript Beta
0:52 seconds
7:46 a.m. on --/--/2009

"Hi__need Good morning how you ____ um I don't want to scare you or anything like that um finally come to the conclusion that um I need to do something here_____I have substance abuse problems as um you know ha I mean through out our marriage it________ I'm checking in the Bradford mental health festivity in Madison at 10 o'clock it will be in patience_____another words I'm gonna go away for a few days probably about three weeks in all I got to do this for myself I'm almost 50 years old it's about time to do something about this hereditary defect that I have and____at this point I am in no way shape or form ______ to hurt myself or in my cell or anything like that I've just come to the conclusion that I'm not ______ and I'm go___ take care of it but like I said it's going to be an impatient situation if you need to um get status or contact me or anything just _________________I have the love in the care and the support from everybody's close to me and that include you and our children and I greatly appreciate that I'm just going to go away for a little bit and have some professionals help me out with____________ bottom line I'm trying to save my life I want to be there for my kids I want to be _________the rest of my life end of story

OK all is good will be better and I'll just take care of this and then I'll be in______________________________

OK bye..."

***

[EXHIBIT XXIII]

When I am finished with tears and wild noises, there is still another yellow envelope, labeled *photos.*

I watch my father grow from black and white baby portraits to his fourth birthday, to his eleventh, to bell bottoms and blackheads on his nose, to the marshmallow-pink suit of his senior prom. Finally, he stands left of frame, a blurry wisp in red cap and gown.

I shuffle through the Polaroids, watching his body morph and build around his brown eyes. My chest expands. I feel my limbs burn and see the sad freckles on my arms and know I cannot come away from this unchanged, knowing if I ever have a son all I will do is think of these pictures, that in every small and large boy I see out in the world I will be reminded of what they lose as they sprout thin like sunflowers and their Halloween costumes fade into suits. How the space around them will billow in their absence. The sudden emptiness left when they are lost.

I understand now why my grandmother grieves so deeply, why she clings to the fact of his death so tightly, why she texted me just weeks ago: *u know my grief is still the lion.*

Imagine the sweetest thing you have ever given yourself to. Imagine a closet full of Polaroids and the remainder of a life spent grasping at what you split your own bones to give breath to and loved with more than words and can never touch again.

Acknowledgements

Thank you to the many friends, fellow writers, teachers, mentors, editors, agents, and others who have in various ways shaped and shepherded this book through a decade of writing, revising, and searching for its place in the world.

A special thanks to Dale Rigby, who first believed in this manuscript when it was a young, hopeful germ of an idea; Natalie Edwards and Cassie Mannes Murray, who gave it direction and advocated for it; and Sarah Munroe, whose feedback inspired a major and necessary revision.

Thank you to Michael Wheaton and Amy Wheaton of Autofocus Books, a dream team in publishing, and some of my favorite people on earth. That this book ended up in your hands in the end means everything to me.

Thank you to my grandmother, Irma, for sharing her story with me, and helping me to keep my father's story alive.

Thank you to my family, for your forgiveness.

***

Grateful acknowledgement is given to the following publications where excerpts of this book, in various forms, first appeared:

Alyss; Another Chicago Magazine; Autofocus; The Boiler; Birds Piled Loosely; Blue Earth Review; Cosmonauts Avenue; Free State Review; GTK Creative Journal; The Grief Diaries; Memoryhouse Magazine; North Texas Review; The Offbeat; River Teeth; The Tishman Review

"In the Heart of the Heart of the Heart of" was included in the anthology *Unbound: Stories of Home* (New Rivers Press, 2022).

An abridged version of the "Rendering" section of this book (titled "On Grief") received a Special Mention in *Pushcart Prize XLIII: Best of the Small Presses* (2019).

References

The citations listed below encompass any sources that were referenced or quoted in the work, as well as select sources that the author found to be significantly influential on the style, form, theme, and/or content of the work.

"2020 Atlantic Hurricane Season." *Center for Disaster Philanthropy,* 1 December 2020. Web.

"23 Enigma." *Wikipedia.* Web.

Abbott, Karen. "What (or Who) Caused the Great Chicago Fire?" *Smithsonian Institution,* 4 October 2012. Web.

Barker, J.C. "Premonitions of the Aberfan Disaster." *Journal of the Society for Psychical Research,* December 1967. Web.

Carey, Benedict. "Can We Really Inherit Trauma?" *The New York Times,* 10 December 2018. Web.

Callaway, Ewen. "Superstitions evolved to help us survive." *New Scientist,* 10 September 2008. Web.

Cixous, Helene and Catherine Clement. *The Newly-Born Woman.* University of Minnesota Press, 1986. Print.

Cole, Jean. "Woman gets 30 years in killing." *The News Courier,* 20 September 2011. Print.

Crum, Maddie. "23 Fascinating Words with No Direct English Translations." *The Huffington Post,* 20 February 2014. Web.

Dagnall, Neil, et.al. "Paranormal belief and well-being: The moderating roles of transliminality and psychopathology-related facets." *Frontier Psychology,* Vol. 13, 2022.

Didion, Joan. *The Year of Magical Thinking.* Vintage, 2007. Print.

Dombal, Ryan. "True Myth: A Conversation with Sufjan Stevens." *Pitchfork,* 16 February 2015. Web.

"Facts + Statistics: Hurricanes." *Insurance Information Institute.* Web.

Gani, Aisha. "How Common Are Plane Crashes?" *The Guardian*, 24 July 2014. Web.

Gray-Rosendale, Laura. *College Girl.* SUNY Press, 2014. Print.

Greenberg, Julia. "Friday the 13th: History, Origins, Myths and Superstitions of the Unlucky Day." *International Business Times,* 13 May 2016. Web.

Haskins, Shelly. "Ardmore Woman Gets 30 Years in Prison for Killing Husband of Two Months." *AL.com,* 19 September 2011. Web.

Keats, John. "Ode to a Nightingale." *Poetry Foundation.* Web.

"Kübler-Ross Model." *Wikipedia.* Web.

Lockwood, Patricia. *Priestdaddy: A Memoir.* Riverhead Books, 2017. Print.

Manguso, Sarah. *Ongoingness: The End of a Diary.* Graywolf Press, 2015. Print.

Mann, Jen. "8 Signs You Have 'Daddy Issues' — And What That Actually Means." *Instyle.com,* 13 January 2022. Web.

Markson, David. *This is Not a Novel and Other Novels.* Counterpoint Press, 2016. Print.

McNamara, Patrick. "Precognitive Dreams." *Psychology Today,* 30 July 2011. Web.

Nelson, Maggie. *The Art of Cruelty: A Reckoning.* W. W. Norton & Co., 2012. Print.

------. *The Red Parts.* Graywolf Press, 2007. Print.

------. *Jane: A Murder.* Soft Skull Press, 2016. Print.

"NISVS: An Overview of 2010 Findings on Victimization by Sexual Orientation." *The National Intimate Partner and Sexual Violence Survey.* The Department of Public Health. Web.

O'Hara, Maryanne. "The Salvific Power of Writing Through Terrible Grief." *LitHub,* 21 April 2021. Web.

O'Hogain, Daithi. *Irish Superstitions: Irish Spells, Old Wives' Tales and Folk Beliefs.* Gill & Macmillan, Ltd., 2002. Ebook.

Orr, Gregory. *Poetry as Survival.* University of Georgia Press, 2002. Print.

Plath, Sylvia. *The Unabridged Journals of Sylvia Plath.* Ed. Karen V. Kukil. Anchor, 2000. Print.

Rabins, Alicia Jo. *Divinity School.* American Poetry Review, 2015. Print.

Risen, Jane L. "Believing What We Do Not Believe: Acquiescence to Superstitious Beliefs and Other Powerful Intuitions." *Psychological Review,* Vol, 123, No. 2, 182-207, 2016.

Rhys, Jean. *Wide Sargasso Sea.* W. W. Norton & Co., 2016. Print.

Savage, Dan. "How do I come out as bisexual without misleading people or having to reveal too much?" *Savage Love; Chicago Reader,* 12 July 2018. Web.

Simon, Paul. "Graceland." *Graceland.* Legacy Recordings, 2012. CD.

Smith, Sarah Elaine. *Marilou is Everywhere.* Riverhead Books, 2019. Print.

Stefanescu, Alina. "My Favorite Untranslatable Words." Typepad post, September 2015.

Stephey, M.J. "The Science Behind Psychic Phenomena." *Time Magazine,* 24 December 2008. Web.

Stowell, M.S. "Precognitive Dreams: A Phenomenological Study; Methodology and Sample Cases." *American Society for Psychical Research,* 91-163, 1997.

"TAE Significant Weather Events." *National Weather Service.* Web.

Tippet, Krista and Pauline Boss. "The Myth of Closure." Audio blog post. *On Being.* NPR, 23 June, 2016. Web.

Tippet, Krista and Bessel Van Der Kolk. "How Trauma Lodges in the Body." Audio blog post. *On Being.* NPR, 9 March, 2017. Web.

Ulrich, Lindasusan. "Bisexuality: Impacts and Recommendations." *San Francisco Human Rights Commission: LGBT Advisory Committee,* March 2011. Web.

Ward, Sarah and Laura King. "Examining the roles of intuition and gender in magical beliefs." *Journal of Research in Personality,* Vol. 86, 2020.

Washuta, Elissa. *My Body is a Book of Rules.* Red Hen Press, 2014. Print

"What Are Archives?" *Society of American Archivists,* 12 September 2016. Web.

Woolf, Virginia. *Moments of Being.* Mariner Books, 1985. Print.

Young, Heather. *The Lost Girls.* HarperCollins, 2017. Print.

Yuknavitch, Lidia. *The Chronology of Water.* Hawthorne Books, 2011. Print

Zimmer, Carl. "Can a Parent's Life Experience Change the Genes a Child Inherits?" *The Atlantic,* 21 June 2018. Web.

About the Author

Erin Slaughter is the author of the short story collection *A Manual for How to Love Us* (Harper Perennial, 2023), and two books of poetry: *The Sorrow Festival* (CLASH Books, 2022) and *I Will Tell This Story to the Sun Until You Remember That You Are the Sun* (New Rivers Press, 2019). Her writing has appeared in *Lit Hub, Electric Literature, CRAFT, The Georgia Review, Prairie Schooner,* and elsewhere. Originally from Texas, she holds an MFA from Western Kentucky University and a PhD from Florida State University. She is currently Assistant Professor of Creative Writing at Coastal Carolina University.

— also from Autofocus Books —

Duplex — Mike Nagel

XO — Sara Rauch

Until It Feels Right — Emily Costa

Cleave — Holly Pelesky

Nextdoor in Colonialtown — Ryan Rivas

Too Much Tongue — Adrienne Marie Barrios & Leigh Chadwick

Picture Window — Danny Caine

the nature machine! — Tyler Gillespie

A Kind of In-Between — Aaron Burch

How to Write a Novel: An Anthology of 20 Craft Essays About Writing, None of Which Ever Mention Writing — ed. Aaron Burch

Hiraeth — Mistie Watkins

That Spell — Tate N. Oquendo

My Modest Blindness — Russell Brakefield

A Calendar Is A Snakeskin — Kristine Langley Mahler

Culdesac — Mike Nagel

Razed by TV Sets — Jason McCall

In the Away Time — Kristen E. Nelson

The Body Is A Temporary Gathering Place — Andrew Bertaina

Daughterhood — Emily Adrian

A Healthy Interest in the Lives of Others — Teresa Carmody

Leave: A Postpartum Account — Shayne Terry

Yes I Am Human I Know You Were Wondering — Erin Dorney

Organic Matter — E.N. Couturier

Out There in the Dark — Katharine Coldiron

If I Can Be Honest: Selected Prose from the Four Years of Autofocis Lit (2020-2024) — ed. Michael Wheaton

Marginalia — Naomi Washer

A Revisionist History of Loving Men — Lena Ziegler

www.ingramcontent.com/pod-product-compliance
Lightning Source LLC
LaVergne TN
LVHW091118080826
845145LV00008B/1971

* 9 7 8 1 9 5 7 3 9 2 4 0 0 *